I0024691

Eastern Africa Series

THE CRISIS OF DEMOCRATIZATION IN THE GREATER HORN OF AFRICA

Eastern Africa Series

The Crisis of Democratization in the Greater Horn of Africa

Towards Building Institutional Foundations

EDITED BY KIDANE MENGISTEAB

JC JAMES CURREY

James Currey
is an imprint of Boydell & Brewer Ltd
www.jamescurrey.com
and of
Boydell & Brewer Inc.
www.boydellandbrewer.com

Our Authorized Representative for product safety in the EU is
Easy Access System Europe – Mustamäe tee 50, 10621 Tallinn, Estonia,
gpsr.requests@easproject.com

© Contributors 2020
First published 2020

All Rights Reserved. Except as permitted under current legislation
no part of this work may be photocopied, stored in a retrieval system,
published, performed in public, adapted, broadcast, transmitted,
recorded or reproduced in any form or by any means, without the
prior permission of the copyright owner

The publisher has no responsibility for the continued existence or accuracy of URLs
for external or third-party internet websites referred to in this book, and does not
guarantee that any content on such websites is, or will remain, accurate or appropriate

A catalogue record for this book is available from the British Library

ISBN 978-1-84701-247-0 (hardback)
ISBN 978-1-84701-248-7 (paperback)

Typeset in 10 on 12pt Cordale with Gill Sans MT display
by Avocet Typeset, Bideford, Devon, EX39 2BP

Contents

List of Illustrations

TABLES

FIGURE

Notes on Contributors

Asma Hussein M. Adam is Associate Professor at University of Bahri, Sudan. She held several administrative tasks, chiefly, the positions of head of political science department and Deputy Dean at the College of Social and Economic Studies, University of Bahri. She has several published articles and book chapters, most of which are written in Arabic. Most of her research focuses on peace, political conflicts, patronage system and inequality, corruption, education and peace, and gender.

Meheret Ayenew served as the Executive Director of the Forum for Social Studies in Addis Ababa, 2002–2010. He is the co-editor of *Challenges and Opportunities for Inclusive Development in Ethiopia* (2017). His other works include, 'Decentralization in Ethiopia: Two case studies on devolution of power and responsibilities to local authorities' in Bahru Zewde and Siegfried Pausewang (eds), *Ethiopia: The Challenge of Democracy from Below* (2002) and 'A Rapid Assessment of Woreda Decentralization in Ethiopia', in Taye Assefa & Tegegne Gebre-Egziabher (eds), *Decentralization in Ethiopia* (2007). He is also the co-author of 'Democracy Assistance to Post-Conflict Ethiopia: Building Local Institutions?' in Jeroen de Zeeuw and Krishna Kumar (eds), *Promoting Democracy in Post-Conflict Societies* (2006).

Kassahun Berhanu is Professor of Political Science at Addis Ababa University and since 2012 has been Guest Researcher, African Studies Centre, Georgetown University, Washington DC. He specializes in democracy, civil society, decentralization and governance, conflicts, elections and constitution making in Ethiopia and the Horn. He is a Member, International Advisory Board, *Journal of African History, Politics and Society* (*JAHPS*) and a Board Member of the Forum Social Studies (FSS). He is on the International Advisory Board of the *Ethiopian Journal of Social Science and Humanities* (since April 2008). He was a member of the Team of International Experts and nominee of the Intergovernmental Authority on Development (IGAD) in the Abyei Boundary Commission to determine the status of the contested Abyei Region in Sudan (April 2005 – July 2005). His publications include: 'Conflicts in the Horn of Africa and Implications for Regional Security' in Redie Bereketeab (ed.), *The Horn of Africa: Intra-State and Inter-State Conflicts and Security* (2013).

Gaim Kibreab is Professor of Research and Director of Refugee Studies, School of Law and Social Science, London South Bank University. He is the author of *People on the Edge in the Horn* (James Currey, 1996), *Eritrea: A Dream Deferred* (James Currey 2009) and, most recently, *The Eritrean National Service* (James Currey 2017).

Kuyang Harriet Logo teaches at the Institute for Peace, Development and Security Studies and the College of Law of the University of Juba. Ms Kuyang is a researcher and independent consultant working on Democratic Governance, Access to Justice and the Rule of Law with the United Nations and International organizations, including academic institutions. Prior to becoming a researcher and consultant, Ms Kuyang served with the United Nations Development Programme in the capacities of Rule of Law Analyst, Programme Analyst for the Rule of Law Cluster and Access to Justice Specialist in the Sudan, South Sudan and Timor Leste. Kuyang graduated with an honours degree in Law from the Faculty of Law at Makerere University in Uganda and proceeded to advance her studies at Ohio Northern University in the USA where she obtained a Master of Laws Degree with Distinction in Democratic Governance and the Rule of Law. She has published scholarly articles on International Humanitarian Law, Transitional Justice and Access to Justice.

Amr M. A. Mahgoub trained as a doctor specializing in community medicine and later joined the World Health Organization as Regional Advisor for Health Management support and health systems strengthening. In the past fourteen years, he has had experience in health system analysis, strategy development, institutional capacity assessment and building, and preparation and implementation of various donor-funded or co-funded (including EU, USAID, GAVI, Global Fund, JICA, DIFID, etc.) programmes in many countries. In South Sudan he has been instrumental in facilitating health plan development.

Kidane Mengisteab (volume editor) is Professor of African Studies and Political Science at the Pennsylvania State University. The focus of his current research includes the relevance of 'traditional' institutions in Africa's governance; the socio-economic implications of extractive industries and commercial farming in Africa, and alternative approaches to democratization in Africa. He is author or editor of several books on Africa. His earlier books include *Regional Integration, Identity & Citizenship in the Greater Horn of Africa* (James Currey 2012, co-edited with Redie Bereketeab) and *The Horn of Africa: Hot Spots in Global Politics* (Polity Press 2015). His most recent book is a co-edited volume titled *Traditional Institutions in Contemporary African Govern-ance* (Routledge 2017, with Gerard Hagg).

Mohamed A. Mohamoud (Barawani) is former Executive Director of the Somaliland Non-State Actors Forum (SONSAF). He was also a co-founder and the Executive Director of the largest national Youth Umbrella Organization in Somaliland (SONYO). He is a PhD candidate in Peace, Governance and Development at the United Nations University for Peace, Costa Rica. He has worked in institutional development, governance, peace-building, state-building, conflict resolution, development, democratization and elections.

Leben Nelson Moro is an Associate Professor and Director of Planning, Quality Assurance and Innovation at the University of Juba. Before assuming the current position, he was the Director of the Institute of Peace, Development and Security Studies at the same university. He received his M.Sc. in Forced Migration and D.Phil. in Development Studies from the University of Oxford. He primarily conducts research on forced displacement and resettlement, focusing on the impact of the extraction of oil on the local communities in South Sudan. He has also carried out research on local justice in South Sudan. He has published several book chapters, journal articles and working papers on a range of issues including forced migration, local justice, state-building and peace-building. He has also consulted for many governmental and non-governmental organizations.

Macharia Munene is Professor of History and International Relations at the United States International University (USIU), Nairobi, Kenya. His areas of interest include; Kenya, Constitutional History, Politics of Constitutionalism, Theories of Governance and Security and Power Politics, Foreign Policy and Diplomatic Changes, Peace Promotion and Conflict Analysis and Management. Among his many publications are *Political Testament of Nationhood* (Fig Tree Books, History Works 2017); *Historical Reflections on Kenya: Intellectual Adventurism, Politics and International Relations* (University of Nairobi Press 2012); and *Politics of Transition in Kenya, 1995–1998* (Quest and Insight 2001).

Acknowledgement

Earlier drafts of the chapters of this book were presented at a conference titled 'Alternative Approaches to Democratization in the Greater Horn of Africa'. The conference, which took place in Nairobi on 16 and 17 August 2016, was organized by the Greater Horn Horizon Forum and it was funded by the Intergovernmental Authority on Development (IGAD) and the Konrad Adenauer Stiftung (KAS). The editor and the Greater Horn Horizon Forum are grateful for the support of IGAD and KAS.

List of Abbreviations

ADFM	Amhara Democratic Forces Movement
ADLI	agricultural development-led industrialization strategy
AGR	African Governance Report
AI	Amnesty International
ALM	Afar Liberation Movement
AMISOM	African Union Mission to Somalia
ARCSS	Agreement on the Resolution of the Conflict in the Republic of South Sudan
AU	African Union
CCA	contextualized comprehensive approach
CPA	Comprehensive Peace Agreement
CSA	Central Statistical Authority
CSA	civil society agency
CSO	civil society organization
CUD	Coalition for Unity and Democracy
DfID	Department for International Development
DLDP	District Level Decentralization Program
EEBC	Eritrea-Ethiopia Border Commission
EFFORT	Endowment Fund for the Rehabilitation of Tigray
EIJM	Eritrean Islamic Jihad Movement
ENS	Eritrean National Service
EPLF	Eritrean People's Liberation Front
EPRDF	Ethiopian People's Revolutionary Democratic Front
EPRP	Ethiopian People's Revolutionary Party
ESF	Eritrean Salvation Front
ESRC	Economic and Social Research Council
EU	European Union
FDRE	Federal Democratic Republic of Ethiopia
FGD	focus group discussion
FRUD	Front for the Restoration of Unity and Democracy
FSS	Forum for Social Studies
FVP	First Vice President

GDP	gross domestic product
GHA	Greater Horn of Africa
GPLM	Gambela People's Liberation Movement
GTP	growth and transformation plan
HoF	House of Federation
HoPR	House of Peoples' Representatives
HPO	hybrid political order
ICG	International Crisis Group
ICNL	International Center for Non-profit Law
IGAD	Intergovernmental Authority on Development
IPU	Inter-Parliamentary Union
LRA	Lord's Resistance Army
MEISON	Amharic Acronym for All Ethiopian Socialist Movement
MoFED	Ministry of Finance and Economic Development
MPs	Members of Parliament
MRC	Mombasa Republican Council
n.d.	not dated
NCEW	National Confederation of Eritrean Workers
NCP	National Congress Party
NEBE	National Electoral Board of Ethiopia
NGOs	non-governmental organizations
NIF	National Islamic Front
NRA	National Resistance Army
NUEW	National Union of Eritrean Women
NUEYS	National Union of Eritrean Youth and Students
OAU	Organization of African Unity
OLF	Oromo Liberation Front
ONLF	Ogaden National Liberation Front
PFDJ	Popular Front for Democracy and Justice
PND	National Democratic Party
PSD	Social Democratic Party
R-ARCSS	Revitalized Agreement on the Resolution of the Conflict in the Republic of South Sudan
RPF	Rwandan Patriotic Front
RPP	People's Rally for Progress
RSADO	Red Sea Afar Democratic Organization
SNM	Somali National Movement
SNNP	Southern Nations, Nationalities and Peoples
SPLM	Sudan People's Liberation Movement
SPLM IG	Sudan People's Liberation Movement in Government
SPLM IO	Sudan People's Liberation Movement in Opposition
SPLM/A	Sudan People's Liberation Movement/Army
SPLM-DC	Sudan People's Liberation Movement-Democratic Change
SPLM-N	Sudan People's Liberation Movement-North
SuGDE	Sudan Group for Democracy and Elections

SuNDE	Sudanese Network for Democratic Elections
TCSS	Transitional Constitution of South Sudan
TGE	Transitional Government of Ethiopia
TGoNU	Transitional Government of National Unity
TPDM	Tigray People's Democratic Movement
TPLF	Tigray People's Liberation Front
UNCOI	United Nations Committee on Information
UNDP	United Nations Development Programme
UNECA	United Nations Economic Commission for Africa
UNMISS	United Nations Mission in South Sudan
UNSC	United Nations Security Council
UP	Umma Party
UPDA	Uganda People's Democratic Army
UPM	Union for Presidential Majority
UPR	Union of Reform Partisans
USC	United Somali Congress
WYDC	Warsai-Yikealo Development Campaign

I

Introduction: Structural and Institutional Factors in the Crisis of Democratization in the Greater Horn of Africa[1]

KIDANE MENGISTEAB

Introduction

Like many countries in other parts of the world, African countries participated in what Huntington (1991) referred to as the 'third wave' of democratization. In the aftermath of the end of the Cold War, most of them instituted multi-party political systems and adopted the election-centred liberal approach to democratization. This post-Cold War wave of democratization was a new round of attempts at such for many African countries that were not party to the first wave since they were colonies. Their first attempts took place during the early years of decolonization in the late 1950s and early 1960s, as colonial powers allowed the erection of some of the conventional procedures of democracy in the waning years of their control. Unsurprisingly, the first attempts at democratizing failed, often culminating in military coups and single-party rule, largely because most African countries at the time lacked the conditions that would enable them to sustain a democratization process. Dominated by the executive branch of government, the African state did not have the mechanisms of checks and balances to foster democratization. The African population was largely illiterate at that time and was too fragmented along ethnic lines to be able to influence the policy choices in order to advance broad social interests. The middle class, the intelligentsia, the media, and civil society at large were too weak to put strong enough pressure for accountability of the functionaries of the state. The fragmentation of the economies and institutions of governance, along with societal fragmentation along primordial lines, also did not allow inclusive representation and

[1] The Greater Horn countries are Djibouti, Eritrea, Ethiopia, Kenya, Somalia, South Sudan, Sudan and Uganda. Somaliland is not a recognized state but it has been operating as a separate entity and has developed its own approach to nation building and democratization. For these reasons, it is included in this study. Djibouti and Uganda are included in the analysis, although separate chapters are not devoted to them.

participation in the political process. Under such conditions, the likelihood of successful democratization was highly unlikely except in rare cases where there were leaders who were highly committed and competent enough to protect aspects of democratic governance. Leaders of Botswana and perhaps Tanzania might be included in the ranks of this small group of leaders. The combination of competency and commitment, however, were rare among African leaders, who, at the time, had limited experience of governing, even if they had the commitment.

Unfortunately, the second round of democratization attempts has also fizzled out in much of Africa, giving way to dominant ruling parties and elected autocrats. The failure of both rounds of democratization attempts begs for an explanation of the enduring obstacles of democratization in the continent and for the search for alternative approaches that address the bottlenecks to a sustainable democratization process. This volume is an attempt to respond to this need and has two principal objectives. One is to examine the key structural and institutional factors that have impeded a sustainable democratization process in Africa.[2] The second is to explore an alternative approach to democratization that may be more effective in addressing the underlying structural and institutional obstacles than the prevailing election-centred approach.

The countries of the Greater Horn of Africa are used as cases for the analysis. A key reason for selecting the Greater Horn as the case for the study is because the structural and institutional obstacles to democratization, such as fragmentation of economic and institutional systems and fragmentation of society and nation-building crisis, are relatively more pronounced in the region, with economic and institutional fragmentation among the deepest in Africa, as the subsistence economic sector is among the largest in the continent. With the exception of Djibouti, the region has among the highest ratio of its population engaged in the traditional peasant and pastoral economic systems in the continent. The region also has the largest pastoral communities in Africa. In addition, the region, with relative exception of Kenya, is characterized by a large number of chronic violent ethnic-based civil

---

[2] Structures and institutions are two concepts that have broad and ambiguous meanings and are often used interchangeably, with no unanimity as to whether or not the two terms have the same or different meanings. For the purposes of this study, the word 'institutions' is used to refer to formal and customary laws, rules, norms and practices that govern the behaviour and interaction of human beings. Specifically, it is used to refer to the formal laws of the state and the customary laws and norms that operate within the traditional subsistent economic systems in much of Africa. The word 'structure', on the other hand, is used to refer to social organizations and systems and how different social systems foster different institutions. More specifically, structures are used to refer to relations between different economic systems and the organizational set up of the African state.

wars and social conflicts. In addition to sharing the colonial impacts on identity-based conflicts with the rest of Africa, the region has experienced two additional conflict factors. One is the hierarchical inter-identity relations left behind by the expansionist pre-colonial empires of the late nineteenth and early twentieth centuries in the two of the largest countries in the region, the Abyssinian Empire in Ethiopia and the Mahdiya State in Sudan. Both these empires were expansionist and left behind political, economic, cultural and religious subordination of the identity groups they forcibly incorporated into their domain. Contemporary Ethiopia and Sudan have to deal with such legacies, as well as those of colonialism. Another contributor to the region's conflicts is the unending external intervention the region has experienced since the inception of the Cold War. Its strategic location has made the region a theatre of competition among world powers and their proxy wars. The region, thus, presents itself as a good case for examining the structural and institutional hindrances to democratization and for exploring an alternative approach. The fact that the region is a highly suitable case for the study, however, does not mean that the study is not relevant for the rest of Africa. Despite differences in magnitude, most African countries face similar structural and institutional obstacles to democratization as those faced by the countries of the Greater Horn.

To set the stage for the rest of the book, this introductory chapter attempts to undertake the following five tasks. First, it describes the level of participation of the countries of the Greater Horn in the post-Cold War round of democratization effort. The second explains the stagnation of the promising initial process of democratization in the countries of the region. The third task is to formulate a theoretical anchor for the book by proposing that structural and institutional factors constitute the most formidable bottlenecks for the democratization process. The fourth task is to sketch a democratization approach, with the aim of tackling the prevailing structural and institutional obstacles to democratization in transitional countries, such as those in the Greater Horn of Africa.[3] The fifth task is to briefly outline the contributions of the book and to introduce the rest of its chapters.

Participation in the post-Cold War wave of democratization

As noted, the Greater Horn of Africa consists of eight countries: Djibouti, Eritrea, Ethiopia, Kenya, Somalia, South Sudan, Sudan and Uganda.

---

[3] Transitional societies are defined here as societies that operate under multiple economic systems, such as a capitalist system coexisting with non-capitalist subsistent farming and pastoral economic systems. A fuller description of transitional societies is given later in the chapter.

Djibouti, Ethiopia, Kenya, Sudan and Uganda have participated, albeit at different levels, in the post-Cold War wave of democratization. They also have recorded noteworthy progress in implementing aspects of the institutions of liberal democracy and reforming their political systems, although again at varying levels.

Under pressure from internal forces and the global democratization environment unleashed by the end of the Cold War, the ruling elite in the reforming countries of the Greater Horn abandoned the single-party system and legalized the establishment of multi-party systems. Notwithstanding the periodic clampdowns, when regime stability is threatened, they also have undertaken notable steps towards liberalizing the press and extending other aspects of civil liberties to their populations. They also have conducted several rounds of multi-party elections of leaders and representatives in national assemblies. Kenya reinstituted a multi-party system in 1991 and conducted a multi-party election in 1992. Djibouti, Ethiopia and Uganda followed Kenya's lead in 1992, 1995 and 1996 respectively. With its April 2010 election, Sudan also reinstated the multi-party system over two decades after suspending it following the 1989 military coup, which brought to power the National Islamic Front (NIF) with General Omar al-Bashir at the helm.[4]

The remaining three countries of the Greater Horn region, Somalia, Eritrea and South Sudan have yet to participate in the democratization effort. State formation through violent armed struggle, civil wars, and inter-state conflicts have contributed in the failure to engage in the democratization process in these three countries. Somalia fell into a civil war in the early 1980s with different armed groups fighting against the despotic regime of Siad Barre. The groups succeeded in removing him from power in 1991 but they also brought about the collapse of the Somali state with some of the armed groups degenerating into clan-based groups led by warlords. Nearly three decades after the removal from power of Siad Barre, the country's civil war still rages on, despite the re-establishment of the state with massive external intervention. Given the ongoing civil war, establishing the institutions of a democratic system has not been feasible in the country.

Eritrea is one of the two new countries in the region. It gained its *de facto* independence in 1991 after a thirty-year war of independence from Ethiopia. The country has yet to engage in the democratization process, although its independence coincided with the outbreak of the democratization wave. The regime in the country has been in power since 1991, neither instituting a constitution nor conducting

---

[4] A multi-party system was briefly reintroduced in 1999 but it was abruptly ended with the declaration of a state of emergency following a power struggle between President Bashir and the then Speaker of the House, Hassan al-Turabi.

any national elections. It has also not allowed the formation of opposition political parties nor the establishment of a free press. There exists hardly any separation of powers among the component organizations of the state or even between the state and the leader in the country. The regime, which rules with little accountability, attributes the 'deferment' of constitutional rule and democratization in the country to the 1998–2000 border war with Ethiopia and the state of 'no-war-no-peace' situation that prevailed between the two countries until July 2018. The war between Eritrea and Ethiopia officially ended on 16 September, when the leaders of the two countries signed a peace and cooperation agreement, however the regime has yet to take steps to liberalize the political system. As explained in Chapter 2, the reasons for lack of democratization in the country are much deeper than the war with Ethiopia.

The region's newest country, South Sudan, gained its independence in 2011, well after the outbreak of the second wave of democratization, and in less than three years after gaining its independence, the country found itself engulfed in a civil war, which has ravaged its economy and displaced large numbers of its citizens. The war, which initially seemed to revolve around an inter-elite power struggle, quickly spread into a brutal inter-ethnic war. Given the atrocities committed across ethnic lines by the protagonists in the conflict, it is likely that finding a resolution to the conflict will be daunting. Meaningful elections and progress towards democratization are again hardly likely to take place in the country before it finds a solution to the civil war and the crisis of nation building. The warring factions signed a new peace agreement on 12 September 2018. However, it remains to be seen if the agreement holds and leads to an end to the civil war, and a democratization process. Chapter 3 examines the complex hindrances to democratization in the country.

Stagnation of the democratization process in the Greater Horn

As noted, in the previous paragraphs, the post-Cold War democratization wave in the Greater Horn of Africa has not been a wave that washed away despotic rule throughout the region. Yet, most of the countries of the region have participated in it. The liberalization reforms that took place in the five countries mentioned above are not insignificant when compared to the single-party and military or autocratic civilian rules that predominated in much of the region and the rest of the African continent during the roughly three decades preceding the outbreak of the post-Cold War wave of democratization. The principles and practice of multi-party systems, elections, and civil liberties have become widely known, and it has become difficult for regimes to command legitimacy while denying them altogether.

However, the reforms that took place in the region hardly resulted from a political victory of pro-democracy social forces. They were not spearheaded by leaders who were committed to promoting real democratization, but were, rather, concessions by the political elite, who – under internal and international pressure – chose to adopt the changes to legitimize their rule. The reforms, therefore, were bound to be limited in scope. Under the circumstances, the democratization process was not likely to advance further and was even susceptible to paring down if it threatened the prevailing order. Thus, despite the promising initial steps, the democratization process in the reforming countries has stalled. The manifestations of the stagnation of the process are many. One is the nature of elections that take place in the region. Various types of harassment of opposition parties and rigging characterize these elections. Often, the elections are also followed by violent conflicts. Ethiopia's 2005 election and Kenya's 1992 and 2007 elections were the most violent in the region. Elections in Djibouti and Uganda have also seen some low intensity violence as well as arrests of leaders of opposition parties. Most opposition parties, which alleged excessive restrictions on their campaign activities by the government, boycotted the 1995 and 2000 general elections in Ethiopia. Both the 2010 and 2015 elections in Sudan also were conducted amidst civil wars and were boycotted by the major opposition parties.[5] The more recent elections in Ethiopia (2010 and 2015), Uganda and Djibouti (2011, 2016), Kenya (2013), and Sudan (2015) were relatively less violent. However, the various types of restrictions on opposition parties and attacks on their leaders have continued in most of them. Faced with popular unrest in two of its largest regional states, the Amhara and Oromia states, Ethiopia also imposed a state of emergency that lasted from 9 October 2016 to 4 August 2017. With continued unrest, the country re-imposed the state of emergency on 15 February 2018 and lifted it again on 5 June 2018.

The multi-party systems in the region, perhaps except for that of Kenya, have also come to be characterized by dominant ruling parties, as opposition parties, for a variety of reasons, have failed to emerge as serious contenders for power. Ethiopia's ruling party, the Ethiopian People's Revolutionary Democratic Front (EPRDF), which has been in power since 1991, won 93 per cent of the seats in parliament in 2010 and 100 per cent of the seats in the 2015 election. President Museveni

---

[5] With respect to the other countries of the region, Eritrea remains a single-party state and has had no national elections since its independence in 1993. South Sudan also has not yet conducted elections following its break away from Sudan in 2011. Somalia remains too insecure for any meaningful general election. Somaliland has a working multi-party system and elections have been viewed to be generally fair. However, that country has not yet received full recognition as an independent state by any other country.

of Uganda has won the presidency in every election since assuming power in 1986. In the 2011 election he won by over 68 per cent of the vote, and his party, the National Resistance Movement, won about 80 per cent of the seats in parliament. In the February 2016 election, President Museveni garnered 60.8 per cent of the vote. In Djibouti also, President Ismail Omar Guelleh won 80 per cent of the 2011 vote, and the opposition parties, which boycotted the 2008 election, boycotted the National Assembly after winning only eight of the sixty-five seats in the 2013 parliamentary elections.[6] The President won 87 per cent of the vote in the election held on 8 April 2016. Perhaps the overwhelming dominance of the ruling parties accounts for why the more recent elections were less competitive and less violent. In any case, most of the regimes in the region have enjoyed lengthy incumbency in power, in some cases by not allowing elections, as in Eritrea, and in other cases by manipulating them to ensure their victory. Opposition parties in most countries of the region have also failed to wage serious contests by cultivating transformative platforms that would win them popular support.

Elections constitute the centrepiece of the prevailing approach to democratization. However, they have not produced change of leaders or ruling parties in any of the countries of the Greater Horn, except in Kenya and Somaliland. It seems that the leaders in most of these countries have mastered the skills of how to conduct elections with little risk of losing them. There are also no term limits, except in Kenya, since such limits, where they existed, have been removed through constitutional amendments. The leaders of Djibouti and Uganda have successfully amended the constitutions of their respective countries to subvert presidential term limits and extend their tenure in power.

President Museveni of Uganda, who came to power by military means in 1986, ruled for ten years under a non-party or 'Movement' system, which prevented political parties from fielding candidates for presidency or parliament. Following a constitutional assembly, a new constitution with a two-term limit on the tenure of the president was instituted and the first elections under this system took place in the country in May 1996 – with all candidates standing under the Movement banner. After serving two elected terms by winning the 1996 and 2001 elections, however, President Museveni managed to bring about the repeal of the term-limit provision of the constitution in 2005. After a referendum the same year, a multi-party system was restored, and the Movement became a political party. Museveni won a third elected term

---

[6] The Union for Presidential Majority (UPM) is the ruling coalition in Djibouti, comprising the People's Rally for Progress (RPP), the Front for the Restoration of Unity and Democracy (FRUD), the Union of Reform Partisans (UPR), the Social Democratic Party (PSD) and the National Democratic Party (PND).

in the 2006 election, a fourth term in 2011, and a fifth term in February 2016. All in all, he has been in power for thirty-three years at the time of writing. Late in 2017 the parliament voted to remove the presidential upper age limit.

In Djibouti, the ruling party, the People's Rally for Progress (currently a member of the coalition known as the Union for the Presidential Majority), has been in power since the country's independence in 1977. President Ismail Omar Guelleh, who succeeded his uncle in 1999, has been in power for 20 years now after repealing in 2010 the constitutional term-limit provision. He won the 8 April 2016 election with 87 per cent of the vote for his fourth five-year term in office.

Sudan's 2005 Constitution limits the president's tenure to two terms. Notwithstanding, in August 2018 the ruling National Congress Party amended the constitution to allow President Bashir to be its candidate in the 2020 elections. However, Bashir's overthrow from power by military coup in April 2019 has rendered the constitutional amendment to change the term limit irrelevant.

With its 1994 constitution, Ethiopia instituted a parliamentary system with no term limit on the post of prime minister. It also transformed itself from a unitary state into a federal system, which, in principle, allows extensive devolution of power to regional states drawn, largely but not exclusively, along ethnic lines. However, the centralizing control exercised by the ruling party, along with the concentration of power on the executive branch of government, has compromised the devolution of power. The ruling party has also succeeded in establishing itself as a dominant party, which has so far faced little risk of losing an election either at the federal or regional levels.[7] The late Prime Minister Meles Zenawi stayed in office for twenty-one years from 1991 to 2012, when he died while in office. Meles Zenawi's successor, Hailemariam Desalegn, resigned in 2018 under pressure from popular protests and has been succeeded by the current prime minister, Abiy Ahmed. The EPRDF, however, remained in control, despite notable signs of internal disharmony, until 1 December 2019, when the Prime Minister formed a new national party, the Prosperity Party (PP), by unifying three of the constituent parties of the EPRDF and its affiliated parties. The TPLF has declined to join the PP and the implications of this development to the federal system and the country's unity remains to be seen. In any case, the leaders of the countries of the Greater Horn, except for Kenya's post-Moi leaders, remain heavily infected by what Kambudzi (2004: 62) calls the 'virus of long political incumbency'. They have kept themselves in power at the expense of building state institutions of effective transfer of power, checks and balances, and accountability.

---

[7] Regional parties that are affiliated with the ruling EPRDF party, have full control of all the regional states.

As Robert Bates notes, democracy 'is a form of government in which political power is employed to serve the interests of the public rather than of those who govern' (2010: 1133). Not surprisingly, the region's haphazardly implemented procedures of democracy have done little to ensure that power is employed to serve the interests of the public, failing to empower the general population to exercise meaningful influence on the governance and policy of their countries. Democratization with civil liberties and inclusive representation would be expected to promote policies that safeguard human rights and the rule of law. It would also advance a peaceful process of nation building by allowing identities with grievances to participate in designing governance arrangements that address their concerns and resolve state-identity conflicts peacefully. Additionally, progress in democratization would produce policy measures that address the key interests of most of the population – the peasant and pastoral communities. Such policies would include respecting customary land rights and cessation of forcible land-takings by the state from peasant farmers and pastoral communities, with little compensation, to lease to foreign investors in large-scale commercial farming and mining. Land appropriation for the expansion of such industries have led to evictions of customary landholders, unemployment, poverty and pollution, which has adversely affected both the health and production of nearby communities. A democratizing process would also entail extending public service to marginalized populations that operate in the traditional economic system.

While there are noteworthy differences in the performance of individual countries, the region fares poorly on the above-identified policy measures, which would be associated with a democratizing system of governance. Violations of human rights and disregard of the rule of law are pandemic throughout the region, according to various human rights reports.[8] As indicated in Table 1.1, the region's overall democratic performance continues to be extremely poor. Marginalization of certain identities as well as large-scale land appropriations from peasant and pastoral communities remain pervasive.[9] State-identity and inter-identity conflicts also persist throughout the region (African Peer Review Mechanism 2006, 2009; Mengisteab 2014; Williams 2016). The most serious state-identity conflicts in the region, include the

---

[8] Human Rights Watch (2013) documents the litany of human rights violations by all the regimes in the region (see also Table 1.1).

[9] It is hard to find the exact amounts of land-takings, as land leases are not publicized by governments. However, the scale is quite high, especially in South Sudan and Ethiopia. South Sudan also is said to have leased about 5.15 million hectares of land (roughly 8 per cent of the country's total land area) between 2007 and 2010 (The Oakland Institute 2011). According to Malkamuu Jaatee (2016), at least 7 million hectares of agricultural land was transferred to investors between 1995 and 2016 in Ethiopia.

Table 1.1 2018 Scores of Democratic Performance of the Greater Horn Countries Relative to the Rest of Africa*

Country	Overall		Safety & rule of law		Participation & human rights		Sustainable economic opportunity		Human development	
Country	Score	Rank	Score	Rank	Score	Rank	Score	Rank	Score	Rank
Djibouti	45.1	38th	48.6	36th	35.9	43rd	42.6	32nd	53.2	29th
Eritrea	29.3	51st	35.1	47th	17.5	54th	24.1	50th	40.3	47th
Ethiopia	46.5	35th	46.4	38th	35.7	44th	49.3	20th	54.6	20th
Kenya	59.8	11th	55.1	27th	55.6	22nd	60.0	8th	68.5	7th
Somalia	13.6	54th	12.3	54th	18.3	53rd	7.4	54th	16.4	54th
S. Sudan	19.3	53rd	14.2	53rd	21.1	52nd	17.1	53rd	24.7	52nd
Sudan	30.8	49th	24.1	50th	23.4	50th	36.0	42nd	39.8	48th
Uganda	55.0	20th	58.1	24th	54.6	23rd	52.6	15th	54.5	21st

Source Ibrahim Index of African Governance Summary, October 2018, www.tralac.org/documents/resources/africa/2363-2018-ibrahim-index-of-african-governance-index-report/file.html, accessed 15 January 2019
* Scores are out of 100

Darfur, Blue Nile, and South Kordofan conflicts in Sudan; the Somali and Gambela regions, the 2016–18 unrest in the Oromia and Amhara regional states, and the conflicts between the Somali and Oromia and the Amhara and Benishangul and Gumuz regional states in Ethiopia; the Coast and the Somali-inhabited eastern regions of Kenya; and the Acholi and Karamoja areas of Uganda. As noted, South Sudan remains engulfed in a civil war, and the risks of widespread famine and ethnic cleansing remain high. A different type of conflict has been underway in Eritrea. Oppressive rule, along with forced labour under the open-ended national service, has compelled young people to abandon their country in droves. Somalia's decades-long civil war also endures, despite interventions by the African Union Mission to Somalia (AMISOM) and various other powers.

Stagnation of the democratization process: a theoretical framework
Democratization in transitional societies, such as those in the Greater Horn of Africa, faces a myriad of challenges and a sizeable literature has analysed the problems of democratization in the African continent. Low levels of economic development, low levels of industrialization and urbanization, and high rates of poverty and illiteracy are among the many challenges identified (Lipset 1959). It is reasonable that such conditions would make the process of democratization challenging, as they would weaken the social forces that would stand for democratization. However, as Rustow (1970) notes, countries having the reverse of such situations do not necessarily democratize. The explanation also

neglects the structural and institutional factors that impede democratization in transitional societies. Other explanations (Bratton and van de Walle 1994; Cheeseman 2015) also identify a number of conditions that facilitate or hinder transitions from autocratic regimes. These explanations essentially deal with the conditions that make regimes receptive or resistant to change during the struggle for democratization. Cheeseman, for instance, argues that incumbents are least likely to embark on reforms in countries with considerable natural resource wealth, weak institutions and a deeply divided society. Such explanations, however, do not tell us much about why the democratization process stagnates in many of those countries that made the initial liberalization changes.

Among the central questions for this study is why the democratization process stagnated in the countries that made the initial transition by adopting some of the procedures of liberal democracy, and why some of the countries of the region have not even made the transition from despotic rule by instituting multi-party systems and conducting elections. Rustow's 1970 study forwards an explanation that, at least in part, addresses the structural impediment to democratization. For Rustow, a single background condition for democratization is national unity. In his model the population needs to share a common national identity before it can reach an accommodative agreement on democratic governance. When this requisite is satisfied, a democratic system of governance emerges out of a struggle between the forces of democracy and those who support the status quo of elite rule. If the forces of democracy are crushed, of course, a democratic system would not emerge, even in the presence of a shared national identity. Explanations such as those of Bratton and van de Walle, and Cheeseman are useful in drawing attention to the many conditions that influence the outcome of such a struggle. However, they hardly explain the underlying structural and institutional hindrances to sustainability of the democratization process. It is often the case that the ruling elite might, under pressure, introduce some changes, even when the requisites to sustain a democratization process are not in place.

The theoretical anchor of this study builds upon Rustow's democratization model by introducing two additional requisites to his national unity requisite for sustainable democratization in transitional countries, such as those of the Greater Horn. These countries, like other transitional African countries, epitomize three characteristics. One is the fragmentation of societies along primordial ethnic and religious lines, as reflected by diversity management and nation-building crisis manifested in chronic state-identity conflicts. A second characteristic is the fragmentation of economic and institutional systems, where citizens operate under parallel economic and institutional spaces. This condition may also be viewed as a national unity problem of a different kind. A third characteristic is deformities of the state, where the structures of checks and balances and accountability are either absent or very weak.[10] This chapter contends that these three characteristics constitute fundamental bottlenecks to democratization. They hinder sustainable democratization even after the initial changes that bring about multi-party systems and elections are in place. Given this diagnostic proposition, the chapter contends that there is hardly a coherent theory of democratization in transitional societies that addresses such fundamental bottlenecks.

One modest suggestion for sustaining democratization in the African context is that repeated rounds of elections, which engender peaceful competition among the contenders for power, have the potential to promote democratic values and democratic transition in Africa (Lindberg 2009; Bratton and van de Walle 1997; Joseph 1997; Diamond 1999; Gyimah-Boadi 2004). The potential of repeated free and fair electoral competition in sustaining democratic transition is hard to refute. However, in transitional countries, with fragmented societies, fragmented economic and institutional systems, and distorted state structures, the potential of the election-centred approach to engender a sustainable process of democratization is grossly overestimated. This chapter argues that the election-centred approach lacks the necessary mechanisms to transform the structural and institutional obstacles that characterize transitional societies. Even conducting free and fair elections becomes highly challenging under the prevailing underlying bottlenecks. We now examine how each of the above-identified three characteristics of transitional societies impedes a sustainable democratization process, why the election-centred approach fails to transform these conditions, and why a different approach to democratization needs to supplement the election-centred approach.

Crisis of nation building
One critical impediment to a sustainable process of democratization in the Greater Horn of Africa is the region's dual crisis of nation building and chronic conflicts, largely related to mismanagement of diversity and the practice of politics of exclusion. With some 340 language groups, the Greater Horn is a mosaic of identities and cultures. The region also harbours many ethnic groups, partitioned into different countries by colonialism.[11] In addition, some parts of the region

---

[10] This third characteristic is more than the unfavourable position the forces of democracy can command in the balance of power relative to the elite. Even if their fortunes in the balance of power changes, the forces of democracy may not be able to transform the structures of the state to establish sustainable mechanisms of accountability.

[11] Some of the region's major conflicts revolve around colonial partitioning of identity groups: e.g. those between Eritrea and Ethiopia; Ethiopia and its Somali populations in the Ogaden; Ethiopia and its Afar population; Kenya and its Somali population; as well as Somaliland's breakaway from Somalia.

inherited hierarchical inter-identity relations that have become major sources of conflicts. Diversity and partition of ethnic identities and historical legacies of discriminatory practices, in themselves, may not condemn the region to perpetual conflicts. When managed properly through governance arrangements that accommodate the key interests and values of all identity groups, diversity and historical legacies may not necessarily hinder nation building, i.e. the creation of a community of citizens sharing common institutions of governance. However, when mismanaged by the state and citizenship rights – namely access to participation in political, economic, social and cultural life – and access to public services and other opportunities of empowerment are inequitable among identity groups, diversity of ethnic and religious identities – especially those of ethnic groups that are partitioned into different states – can foster violent state-identity and inter-identity conflicts. The risk of such violent conflicts is particularly high in countries where there is a historical memory of conflicts and subjugation by pre-colonial empires, as in Ethiopia and Sudan.[12] In other words, uneven inter-identity opportunities of empowerment, along with the state's failure to establish inclusive institutional platforms for addressing grievances hinder a peaceful process of nation building. It is also a widespread practice among the governments of the region to exclude from the political process opponent groups and individuals with alternative political and economic policies and visions.

Every country in the Greater Horn has faced various types of diversity-related civil conflicts and civil wars, which are mostly but not exclusively ethnic-based. The most significant civil wars Ethiopia experienced since the 1960s include the wars against the Eritrean liberation movements (1961–91); the Western Somali Liberation Front (1974–78); the Ogaden National Liberation Front (1984 to present); the Tigray People's Liberation Front (1975–91); the Afar Liberation Movement (ALM) (1975–97); and the Oromo Liberation Front (1975 to present). The first three wars were over demands for independence while the others were largely over demands for political, economic and cultural rights, although the agendas of the different groups often changed from time to time. The number of the civil wars and their magnitude has declined since a change of government and institution of the federal system in 1991. However, the country continues to face various communal conflicts and state-identity tensions.

Post-independence, Sudan's most significant civil wars were the two north-south wars (1955–72 and 1983–2005) that culminated in South Sudan's secession in 2011. A number of other conflicts at various

---

[12] In the late nineteenth century, both the pre-colonial Abyssinian Empire in present-day Ethiopia and the Mahdiya State in Sudan were expansionist and oppressive towards the groups they subjugated.

levels of intensity remain active, however. Among them are the Darfur Conflict, since 2003, the conflicts in the eastern part of the country led by the Beja Congress and the Rashaida Free Lions, the rebellion in the Nuba Mountains and, more recently, the Blue Nile and South Kordofan conflicts against the Sudan People's Liberation Movement-North (SPLM-N).

Somalia has been embroiled in a series of civil wars and factional violence at least since its 1977–78 war with Ethiopia over the Ogaden region. With Somalia's defeat in that war, the weakened regime of Siad Barre faced a growing number of revolts and it increasingly relied on clan support and violent suppression of opponents to stay in power. The violence perpetrated by the regime triggered more revolts by various (mostly clan and region-based) groups, including the Somali National Movement (SNM), the United Somali Congress (USC), the Somali Salvation Front, which evolved into the Somali Salvation Democratic Front, and the Somali Patriotic Movement. The groups, which aimed to dislodge Siad Barre from power and bring about political and economic changes, succeeded in removing the Barre regime from power in 1991. However, they also brought about the collapse of the Somali state and chronic violent conflicts including inter-clan and inter-sub-clan power struggles. With atrocities committed by the Barre regime during the civil war and the continued power struggle and turmoil engulfing the country, especially the former Italian colony (southern Somalia), the former British colony, Somaliland declared its independence in 1991. Somalia has since remained in perpetual violent conflicts among constantly evolving actors. The country's most significant ongoing civil war is between the United Nations and African Union-supported Transitional Federal Government and the *Al-Shebab* outfit. However, the country also faces serious problems of fragmentation, as different regions clamour for autonomy, in some cases with external encouragement.

Djibouti has also experienced a civil war as well as low intensity civil conflicts between the government (often dominated by the *Issa* Somalis) and rebel groups from the country's minority Afar population. The Afar-based Front for the Restoration of Unity and Democracy (FRUD) waged an active war against the government between 1991 and 1994. Since then the situation has remained generally calm with occasional flare-ups of low intensity civil conflicts.

Uganda has also seen a number of civil wars. Among the most notable include the state vs. Buganda conflicts in the 1960s; the war waged by the Ugandan National Rescue Front against the regime of President Obote (1980–85); and the war by the National Resistance Army (NRA), 1982–86. Others include the war of the subsequent National Resistance Movement (NRM) government against the Uganda People's Democratic Army (UPDA), a rebel group that operated in northern Uganda between 1986 and1988; the ongoing low intensity conflicts waged by the Allied Democratic Forces operating in Western Uganda; and the conflicts against the Lord's Resistance Army (LRA), 1987–2008. Since 2008, the LRA has ceased to pose a threat in Uganda, and is said to be in hiding along the borders of the Central African Republic, South Sudan and the Democratic Republic of the Congo.[13]

Kenya has seen fewer civil wars compared to the other countries of the region, although in the early 1960s it faced a brief irredentist civil war from its Somali inhabitants in the then North East Province. However, the country has faced several ethnic riots and post-election violence including that following the 2007 election, which dangerously spilled over into inter-ethnic violence. The demand for independence of the coastal parts of the country by a separatist group, the Mombasa Republican Council (MRC), is also a potential risk, although the group has not waged a notable armed struggle yet. Perhaps a more threatening risk appears to be the terrorist attacks from Somalia's *Al-Shebab* and the growing unrest among the Somali population of Kenya, in part, due to its marginalization and in part due to Kenya's involvement in the Somali civil war against the *Al-Shebab*. Kenya also faces low intensity religious tensions.

The two newest countries of the region, Eritrea and South Sudan also have experienced conflicts, especially the latter. In December 2013, South Sudan, which only gained its independence in July 2011, imploded into a civil war, revolving around power struggles within the political elite as well as inter-ethnic cleavages. In the early 1990s, Eritrea faced low intensity violent activities by the Eritrean Islamic Jihad Movement (EIJM). Two Ethiopia-based groups, the Eritrean Salvation Front (ESF) and the Red Sea Afar Democratic Organization (RSADO) also claim to have waged armed struggle against the regime, although the evidence to support the claims is scanty.

Some of the conflicts in the region involve demands for independence and fragmentation of countries, especially those involving partitioned ethnic groups. Such conflicts undermine democratization, since there cannot be an agreement on democratic governance in the absence of common national identity, as Rustow's model explains. Most of the conflicts are, however, over claims by various identity groups of real or perceived political, economic and cultural marginalization. Such conflicts also contribute to the obstruction of the processes of democratization. In ethnically fragmented societies, failure to forge institutions of diversity management leads to the formation of political organizations along identity lines and elections under such conditions tend to become mechanisms that attempt to give legitimacy to the winners to dominate power and rule without the consent of identities with

---

[13] Ongoing tensions between the state and the Buganda nation are also of concern.

grievances. Elections in such cases are more likely to create or sharpen conflicts rather than resolve them.

Fragmented economic and institutional systems

Another socio-economic condition that undermines the democratization process in the countries of the Greater Horn, as in the rest of Africa, is the fragmentation of economic and institutional systems. This condition is perhaps the least-understood obstacle to the prevailing election-centred approach to democratization in transitional societies. Parallel institutions of governance characterize the countries of the Greater Horn – one type is the state-sanctioned formal systems and the other is the traditional systems that evolved from the pre-colonial governance systems, which often are either elder-based decentralized structures or relatively more-centralized authority systems. The dichotomy of the institutional systems is related to the fragmentation of the economic systems, which range from relatively advanced capitalist systems, symbolized by modern banking and stock markets, to the traditional subsistent farming and pastoral systems. The different economic systems (sub-systems)[14] are characterized by corresponding institutional systems with divergent property rights laws and resource allocation mechanisms; disparate decision-making systems; and distinct judicial systems and conflict-resolution practices.[15]

The origins of the economic and institutional fragmentation go back to the incorporation of these countries into the global system, primarily through direct colonialism. The colonial state implanted small capitalist economic sectors, tied closely to the economies of the colonial powers. The colonial state also erected new institutions of governance that corresponded with the new economic implants. However, the colonial state did not transform the large traditional subsistent economic system. It also did not abolish the African traditional institutions of governance, which corresponded with the traditional economic systems, even though it modified aspects of them in a manner that served its interests. Instead, it relegated the traditional systems into the realm of informality.[16]

---

[14] The capitalist and traditional economic systems may be viewed as sub-systems, while the socio-economic systems that encompass both can be viewed as composite systems.

[15] The combination of these differences has created separate rural/urban cultural spaces within African societies.

[16] Ethiopia, despite managing to avoid colonization (except very briefly), did not chart a markedly different political economy than those of the former colonies around it. Starting in the late nineteenth century a small capitalist sector was introduced into its largely pre-capitalist economy, and the relations between the new and traditional systems in the country developed in a similar manner as in the other countries in the region.

Long after the end of colonialism, the traditional economic and institutional systems continue to operate side by side with the state systems. Despite state intervention and expansion of the capitalist sector, the traditional systems have largely maintained their judicial systems, their conflict resolution and decision-making practices. While the segments of the population in the subsistent farming and pastoral economic systems largely adhere to the traditional institutional system, those who operate within the capitalist sector follow the formal systems. However, the line separating the two socio-economic systems is not always clear, as many people, especially those in the informal economic sector, find it necessary to negotiate the parallel systems in their daily lives.

The parallel systems have complex relationships with each other. They are incompatible in many respects and complement each other in others. With respect to the delivery of judicial service, for instance, the two systems complement each other, even though the laws in some areas and the process of reaching judicial decisions differ markedly. The traditional systems serve rural communities, which find the state's judicial system rather inaccessible, while the formal systems serve mostly urban communities. The two types of system also complement each other in dealing with major crimes, such as murder. The formal courts adjudicate such crimes and the offenders are given their sentences. However, in the traditional systems, major criminal offenses are generally the collective responsibility of the offender's extended family (or clan) and not only of the individual offender. Under such circumstances, the parties have to be reconciled through the traditional systems' various compensatory arrangements for the conflict to end. Punishment of the offender(s) by the state is generally not sufficient to end the conflict. The punitive aspects of the formal systems and the restorative aspects of the traditional systems thus complement each other.

However, despite the complex links and areas of complementarity, the two systems remain fundamentally separate socio-economic spaces with various incompatibilities and with marked inequalities. Property rights laws, especially with respect to land, constitute one critical area of incompatibility. The customary land rights of the traditional systems, which in many cases are communal (village or kinship) ownership systems, are often either not recognized or not respected by the state, especially when viewed as hindering the expansion of the capitalist sector. The capitalist sector's expansion in important industries, such as the extractive industries and commercial farming, for example, results in land-taking from the traditional sector, which, in turn, leads to evictions, unemployment/underemployment, and often to impoverishment, and migration to urban areas of peasant farmers and pastoralists.

In some of the countries, Kenya and Uganda in particular, the state has pushed for land registration (privatization) with the aim of promoting private investments on land. However, privatization is often unworkable in pastoral and subsistent mixed farming systems.[17] These systems require a communal land tenure system, which allows seasonal mobility of livestock. Privatization of land often benefits corporations, rich investors, speculators and bureaucrats at the expense of rural communities. It also disadvantages women relative to men, since land titles tend to be in the names of husbands. When state acquisition of communal land occurs, customary holders are rarely compensated for the loss of land or loss of use of land, in some cases because the state does not recognize their ownership claim of the land they customarily hold. If compensations are given to the victims of evictions, they are grossly inadequate, as the peasant communities command little bargaining power to demand fair value for their land. The compensations also hardly involve assistance to the evicted to adjust to a new way of life.

Although accurate figures are hard to find, the colonial state appropriated large parcels of communal land from the traditional sector, despite popular resistance in various forms in different parts of the region.[18] The aim of the land-takings was in some cases to accommodate European settlers and in other cases to promote the growth of the capitalist sector. The colonial state also declared considerable amounts of land as state property, especially in Kenya, Sudan, Uganda and Eritrea (Mwebaza 1999; UNDP 2006).[19]

The post-colonial state has continued many aspects of the colonial land policy. Accurate data of how much land states have appropriated is hard to find since governments rarely publish information about the land they take from customary holders to lease to investors. Rough estimates indicate that the lease amounts in 2010 were roughly 3.5 million ha in Ethiopia, 4.9 million ha in Sudan, 1.9 million ha in Uganda, 150,000 ha in Kenya and 5.15 million ha in South Sudan (Global Land Project 2010; The Oakland Institute 2011). Land-takings by the state, along with population growth and land degradation due to environmental changes, have engendered land scarcity in several localities.

---

[17] The rural land tenure systems in the Horn are rather complex. In Eritrea and Ethiopia, all land is under state control with farming and pastoral communities given usufructuary rights. In the other countries of the region, pastoral areas and pasture land are essentially under communal ownership while the tenure system of farm land varies from communal to kinship and private holdings.

[18] One of the early rebellions against land-takings by the colonial state took place in Eritrea, when a local leader, named Bahta Hogos, led a rebellion in 1894 (Tekeste Negash 1986). The rebellion was crushed quickly, however. Perhaps a better-known rebellion is the Mau Mau in Kenya, which started in 1952.

[19] Often customary users were allowed to continue to use state appropriated land when the state did not put it to use.

Such scarcities, in turn, have led to various land-based inter-communal conflicts as well as rebellions against the state (Mengisteab 2014).

As noted already, the fragmentation of economic and institutional systems is a characteristic of transitional societies, which are between different economic systems. The Horn countries, like most other African countries, have experienced a gradual expansion of the capitalist economic sector, along with the institutional systems that correspond with it. However, the traditional economic systems of subsistent farming and pastoralism and the traditional institutional systems associated with them have also remained entrenched among large segments of the population. Table 1.2 shows the proportion of the population that operates under traditional systems in the Greater Horn region. Using the judicial system as a proxy, Table 1.3 also shows the degree to which rural communities in selected areas adhere to traditional institutional systems.[20]

Table 1.2 Ratio of Rural Population to Total Population in the Countries of the Greater Horn in 2017*

Country	Djibouti	Eritrea	Ethiopia	Kenya	Somalia	S. Sudan	Sudan	Uganda
Rural Population (percentage of total)	22.0	77.4**	80.0	73.0	56.0	81.0	66.0	77.0

Source World Bank, https://data.worldbank.org/indicator/sp.rur.totl.zs, accessed 20 February 2019
* Rural population is used as a proxy for the population that largely adheres to the traditional economic and institutional systems; the rural population in the region contains the largest cluster of pastoralists in the world. Roughly 17% of the region's population is engaged in pasture-based production systems; pastoralists also constitute 61% of the region's poor (Sandford and Ashley 2008)
** data for Eritrea are for 2015

Table 1.3 Proportion of Intra-community Disputes that are Taken to the Traditional Institutions for Settlement in Selected Areas in Three Countries*

Ethiopia (percentage)	Borona 94.2	Gambela 52.1	Gurage 91.2	Average 78.7
Kenya (percentage)	Coast 73.3	Meru 41.0	West Pokot 36.6	Average 56
Somaliland (percentage)	Borama 51.6	Cadandley 78.3	Hargeissa 54.5	Average 59.2**

Source Mengisteab and Hagg 2017; data are compiled from respondents of a 2010 survey
* The rest of the disputes are taken to government institutions, religious leaders and relatives
** The total figure for Somaliland is much lower than estimates given by key informants (roughly 80%); part of the explanation for the discrepancy is that a significant number of cases go to the sharia courts, which are not counted as part of the traditional system

[20] The sample size of nine areas in the three countries, Kenya, Ethiopia and Somaliland, is rather small but it gives a good indication of the degree to which rural communities rely on traditional institutions.

How institutional dichotomy undermines democratization

The presence of dichotomous systems of institutions, for all practical purposes, means the presence of parallel systems of governance where the institutional links between the state and the segment of the population that adheres to traditional systems are weak. The participation of the latter in the formal political process and its ability to exert influence on policy-making is also severely limited, even when it votes in elections.[21] Under such conditions, an inclusive process of democratization becomes untenable. Despite its large size, the population in the traditional sector has little impact on policy and receives a disproportionately small share of public services, such as health care, education, and a range of other productivity-raising resources. A notable manifestation of its marginalization in policy and access to public services is the disproportionately high rates of illiteracy and poverty that afflict the communities in the traditional economic sector. Alkire et al. (2014) estimate that the share of rural poverty to total poverty in sub-Saharan Africa is 73.8 per cent. Land-taking by the state from the traditional sector, with little compensation, is another indication that the traditional sector is under-represented in policy-making. The population in the traditional systems, thus, faces a vicious cycle of deprivation. Its ability to influence policy is limited in large part due to its institutional detachment from the state and due to its poverty. Its lack of influence on policy, in turn, culminates in its continued marginalization in access to public services, which perpetuates its high rates of poverty and poor knowledge and information base. Poverty and lack of familiarity with the political process further exacerbate its lack of influence on policy.[22] In other words, to the extent that it participates in elections, the population in the traditional sector affects election outcomes without influencing policy in any meaningful way. In other words, it is the largest voting bloc with the least influence on policy.

A genuine democratization process would hardly materialize when the ability of the largest voting block (the population in the traditional systems) to influence policy is limited. Reconciling the fragmented socio-economic spaces and mitigating the comprehensive marginalization of the population in the traditional sector would, thus, be essential for national unity and a sustainable process of democratization. There is, however, very little effort or strategy in the prevailing election-centred approach to democratization to reconcile the frag-

---

[21] Rural people in much of Africa turn out to vote. However, as Ninsin (2006) and Wanyande (2006) note, they are mobilized to participate often along the lines of ethnicity and promises of particular economic projects by candidates for political office. Voting in elections, thus, hardly translates to participation of this segment of the population in influencing policy to advance its interests.
[22] The traditional sector is also marginalized in access to resources allocated by the market mechanism partly due to the low purchasing power it commands and partly due to the subsistence nature of its production system.

mented institutions and thereby mitigate the institutional exclusion of the large peasant and pastoral communities from the political process. Under the circumstances, elections mask the exclusion of the populations in the traditional systems from the political process.

Deformity of the structures of the state

Another structural obstacle to sustaining the democratization process even after the initial liberalization change in transitional countries, such those of the Greater Horn, is deformity in the structures of the state. The state is the chief organizer of socio-economic life in every country. Yet, it is a rather difficult entity to conceptualize and the literature is replete with conflicting definitions (Weber 1958; Skocpol & Amenta 1986; Samatar & Samatar 2002; Wallis & North, 2010).[23] For the purposes of this chapter, a working definition of the contemporary state is that it is a complex apparatus composed of a set of interlocking organizations that collectively govern socio-economic life in a country (Wallis & North, 2010).[24] Although they differ between political systems, the set of organizations that comprise the contemporary state include the government, (the executive, legislative and judiciary branches); the constitutional court; the security forces; the bureaucracy; the central bank; the electoral commission; and the auditor general. In a democracy fostering state, the different organizations of the state would enjoy a measure of independence from each other in performing the tasks within their spheres of authority. In other words, decentralization of power allows the different organizations of the state to constitute multiple poles of power that ensure horizontal accountability by acting as checks and balances on each other. By contrast, in a political system of absolute monarchy or dictatorship the roles of all the different constituent organizations of the state would be concentrated in either a single organization (the executive branch of government) or an individual leader, forming a single pole of power. In the absence of checks and balances, as in executive monarchies and dictatorships, there would be little distinction between the state and the government, or even between the state, the government and the individual leaders.[25]

---

[23] Reasons for disagreements on the definition are many. One reason is related to the changing nature of the state over its historical development. The advanced state differs in many respects from its earlier less developed forms.

[24] This definition is adopted because it allows drawing a clear distinction between the state, the government and leaders, and allows identification of the component organizations that make up the state. Additionally, it allows explanations of how the structural relations between the component organizations of the state affect the nature of governance.

[25] This above conceptualization of the state draws a clear distinction between the state and the government and allows analysis of the structures of the state as well as the relationships among its constituent parts.

Horizontal accountability within the component organizations of the state hinders the tendencies of concentration of power in the hands of the executive branch or any individual leader. Attempts by the executive branch to restrict such a space would also be blocked or restrained by the other organizations of the state, such as the constitutional court. A state with robust structures of checks and balances would also be likely to have vertical accountability, which safeguards the space for civil society and citizens at large to engage in the political process with full access to civil liberties provided the problems of institutional fragmentation and diversity management are also addressed.

A state with well-developed structures of accountability would also be better situated to properly manage diversity within the citizenry or to, at least, provide mechanisms for identity groups or individual citizens with grievances to obtain redress through legal process.[26] When they have the necessary level of independence, the legislature, the constitutional court and the judiciary would be in a position to protect the rights of citizens granted by the constitution from possible transgressions by the executive branch of government. They can also protect vulnerable identity groups from discriminatory policies and arrangements. Similarly, the legislature would be restrained by the constitutional court from passing laws that may contravene the constitution and infringe on the rights of citizens at large or those of certain segments of the population.[27] Independence of the legislature would also enhance representation of citizens in the making of laws. If the legislature is a rubberstamp of the executive branch of government, as usually is the case with dominant parties in the countries of the Greater Horn, it can hardly represent the interests of its constituency and protect it from transgressions by the executive branch.[28] Without independence, the bureaucracy also can easily serve as a vehicle of imposition of the policies and ideology of the executive and ruling parties. Independence of the electoral commission and the courts is also essential for the protection of the integrity of elections.

A critical impediment to a sustainable democratization process in the transitional countries of the Greater Horn relates to the structures of

---

[26] As explained in the next section of the paper, the structures of accountability, while necessary, may not be sufficient to ensure proper management of diversity in divided societies. In ethnically or racially divided societies, it is possible that the different organizations of the state may be run by people from the same identity group making it possible for the different organizations of the state to collude in denying rights to other members of the population.

[27] This assumes that the rights of all citizens and rights of groups are enshrined in the constitution.

[28] As noted, most of the countries of the region are characterized by dominant parties that dominate the legislature and the presidency (or prime minister's office).

the post-colonial state, which render the state incapable of addressing the bottlenecks of democratization, such as economic, institutional and societal fragmentation, and crises of nation building. The post-colonial African state has yet to develop the structures of accountability that serve as a firewall against autocracy or dictatorship, although some countries have registered more progress than others. Absence or weakness of the structures of checks and balances has led to concentration of power within the executive branch of government. It has also made the state a guardian of the power and interests of the elite and rendered the functionaries of the state susceptible to pervasive corruption. Dominated by the executive body, the state in Africa has become a rather debilitating burden on society by advancing elite interests at the expense of general societal well-being.[29]

There are notable differences among the countries of the Greater Horn with respect to the development of the structures of checks and balances within the state. Somalia, which essentially is without a properly functioning state, Eritrea, which has yet to implement a constitution ratified in 1997, and Sudan and South Sudan, which have been engulfed by intractable civil wars and inter-communal conflicts, are characterized by the absence of or extremely weak structures of accountability. Djibouti, Ethiopia and Uganda, where dominant parties rule, also lag behind Kenya in the development of the structures of state accountability, even though ethnicization of political parties has also hampered Kenya's accountability structures. Despite the relative differences, however, no country in the region has put in place the necessary level of separation of powers within the constituent organizations of the state to establish a level of accountability sufficient to foster democracy and curb corruption.

There are several indicators of the presence of structures of accountability of a state. Among the most obvious are judicial independence from the executive, ability of the legislature to check the power of the executive branch, presence of competitive political parties and vibrancy of opposition parties in the legislature. Other indicators are autonomy of the electoral authorities (commissions) from the executive branch, fairness and competitiveness of elections, level of access of citizens to civil liberties, and ability of citizens and civil society organizations to influence policy. Direct empirical evidence on these indicators is rather sparse. However, expert opinion surveys by the United Nations Economic Commission for Africa (2013), although now dated, show that the countries of the region score very poorly on most of the identified indicators (see Table 1.4).

---

[29] Authoritarian governments in some cases have advanced a developmental state, which promotes societal economic well-being. However, authoritarian governments can also easily turn self-serving, corrupt and oppressive, as there are few mechanisms to prevent such reversals.

Table 1.4 Expert Opinion on Selected Indicators of Democratization in the Countries of the Greater Horn of Africa*

	Djibouti	*Ethiopia*	*Kenya*	*Uganda*
Percentage of experts agreeing that legislative control of the executive branch is usually or always effective	42	44	31	20
Percentage of experts agreeing that government respects due process and the rule of law mostly or fully	45	50	20	36
Share of experts agreeing that civil society organizations contribute moderately or effectively in promoting transparency and accountability	36	34	64	38
Percentage of experts agreeing that the electoral commission is independent and fairly or fully competent	23	34	81	30
Percentage of experts agreeing that national elections are mostly or always free, fair and generally transparent	44	40	18	22
Percentage of experts agreeing that political parties mostly or always have equal access to electoral resources	30	25	8	12
Share of experts agreeing that the judiciary is free from corruption	21.5	21.5	9	12.5
Share of experts agreeing that mass media is completely free or only infrequently violated by the government or ruling party	30	31	64	31
Share of experts agreeing that human rights are usually or always respected	42	48	17	24

* Eritrea, Somalia, South Sudan and Sudan are not included in the survey
Source UNECA, African Governance Report III, 2013, www.uneca.org/publications/african-governance-report-iii, accessed 4 October 2019

Kenya's relatively high score (81 per cent) on the independence of the electoral commission seems to be an exception, although the April–June 2016 protests against the electoral commission by supporters of the opposition party do not support the high score rendered by the survey of expert opinion.

As already noted, without the structures of accountability, the political elite can easily become autocratic, constitutional provisions for term limits can be amended, as in Djibouti and Uganda, ruling parties can establish dominance by suppressing opposition parties, human rights can be easily violated, elections can be rigged or manipulated, and

Table 1.5 Corruption Index in the Countries of the Greater Horn

Country	2018 Rank and score (out of 180 countries)		Average score 2014–18 (out of 100)
	Rank	*Score*	
Ethiopia	114	34	33.8
Djibouti	124	31	32.0
Kenya	144	27	26.2
Uganda	149	26	25.6
Eritrea	157	24	19.6
Sudan	172	16	13.8
South Sudan	178	13	12.8
Somalia	180	10	9.0

Source Transparency International (2014–2018), www.transparency.org/files/content/pages/2018_CPI_Executive_Summary.pdf, accessed 10 March 2019; www.transparency.org/news/feature/corruption_perceptions_index_2016#regional, accessed 10 March 2019

citizens can be silenced through denial or restriction of civil liberties. These conditions, which are regular occurrences in the countries of the Greater Horn, clearly indicate that governance advances and protects the interests of the political elite rather than the interests of the public.

Corruption by government officials is another manifestation of the absence of strong mechanisms of checks and balances. While corruption levels are hard to estimate directly, perception of corruption is very high throughout the region, as depicted in Table 1.5.

Given the state's weak structures of checks and balances, elections – even those deemed 'free' from rigging by election observers – are likely to project the facade of a democratic system while they merely serve as poor attempts to legitimize despotic rule. This is a major reason why authoritarian regimes conduct elections, as Levitsky and Way (2002) note. Elections in the Greater Horn countries have rarely brought about transfer of power. Ruling parties and incumbent leaders have not lost elections since the early 1990s, when the region's countries installed multi-party systems, except in Kenya. Even when they have, as in Kenya, they have hardly brought about the independence of the constituent organizations of the state.

It is conceivable that leaders, who are committed to state-building, can spearhead the transformation of the existing deformed structures of the state.[30] They can enhance the independence of the constituent

[30] State-building is used here to refer to the process of building the structures and capacity of the state in order to enhance its effectiveness in managing diversity as well as in providing the services that advance the interests and well-being of citizens.

organizations of the state and thereby build a system of checks and balances. They can also strengthen all the institutions of governance. However, they can play such a transformative role only if they are willing to accept checks on their own power. State-builders, thus, would have to deny the temptation of aggrandizing and perpetuating their own power and commit 'class suicide', as Cabral (1969) expected of African leaders. The Horn of Africa has not produced such leaders yet. Instead, it is known for its infamous dictators, including Idi Amin, Mengistu Hailemariam, Siad Barre and Omar Bashir. Some of the region's current leaders are not far behind the identified notorious despots, in terms of subverting institution building to perpetuate their incumbency in power (see Table 1.6).

At its core, the struggle for democracy is a struggle between the political elite, who, motivated by self-interest, want to control power and policy, and the public that wants freedom and representation in decision-making so that policy reflects its general interests rather than the interests of the ruling elite. Since the elite, perhaps with a few exceptions, are not likely to betray their core interests and become benevolent agents of democratization, the success or failure of democratization, even when the above-discussed structural and institutional requisites are available, would depend on the balance of power between the social forces that line up on one side or the other of the struggle for democracy. In other words, the weaker the general population is, due to lack of unity, education and organization, the less likely democratization, where political power serves the interests of the public, would materialize. The absence or weakness of the structures of accountability of the state is a reflection of the weakness of the forces of democracy in the democratic struggle. It is a reflection that the forces of democracy, even if they win some concessions from the elite, have not been able to establish state structures of accountability that would ensure sustainability of the democratization process. Under conditions of enduring weak structures of checks and balances, the political elite are able to keep themselves in power by preventing the rise of effective competition from opposition parties. Elections, under the circumstances, can hardly promote democratic values. It would also be unlikely that elections would be fair. It is not merely an accident that practically all the elections in the region are accompanied by irregularities and manipulations. Even in the unlikely event that an opposition party wins an election it is not likely that it would advance the structures of accountability. Instead, it is more likely that it would simply trade places with the former ruling party and maintain the deformed structures of the state to advance its own interest of keeping power so long as the forces of democracy are weak. At least there have not yet emerged transformative platforms from opposition parties in the region.

Table 1.6 Length of Incumbency of Leaders in the Greater Horn

Country	Years in power
Djibouti	20 (1999 to present)
Eritrea	28 (1991 to present)
Ethiopia	(2018 to present)*
Kenya	(2013 to present)**
South Sudan	8 (2011 to present)
Sudan	30 (1989 to 2019)
Uganda	33 (1986 to present)

* Ethiopia's late prime minister, Meles Zenawi, died in office on 20 August 2012; his successor, Hailemariam Desalegn stayed in office for six years (2012–18)
** Kenya has conducted elections regularly since 1992 with a two-term limit on the presidency

A new approach to democratization, and chapter contributions

A sizeable literature has analysed the challenges of democratization in the African continent. Yet, a coherent theory on what the structural and institutional obstacles to democratization are in transitional societies, and how to overcome these obstacles, which include divided societies, fragmented economies and institutions of governance, and deformed state structures, remains elusive. As already noted, this study has two principal objectives. One is to explain the factors that impede a sustainable democratization process in the countries of the Greater Horn of Africa. The second objective is to contribute in bridging the theoretical gap by proposing an alternative approach to democratization in transitional societies, such as those of the Greater Horn, where the election-centred liberal approach has remained ineffective in addressing the bottlenecks of a sustained process of democratization. To accomplish these two principal objectives, this book attempts to answer four critical research questions. One is what the critical factors are that have impeded a sustainable process of democratization in the countries of the Greater Horn. The second question is why the prevailing election-centred liberal approach to democratization is unlikely to overcome the foundational obstacles to democratization in the region. The third question is if there is an alternative approach to democratization that would be more effective in tackling the bottlenecks of democratization and compatible with the socio-economic realities and values of transitional societies. The last question is if there are social forces that can spearhead an alternative approach to democratization.

In addressing the second principal objective, the study proposes a four-pronged contextualized comprehensive approach (CCA) to democratization. The composition and workings of the CCA are explained in

Chapter 10. Here it suffices to point out that the CCA aims to addresses the structural and institutional obstacles and thereby to complement the election-centred approach. Given the stagnation of the liberal approach to democratization throughout Africa, the proposed approach is likely to motivate the search for more-effective approaches to democratization in transitional societies by stimulating a critical re-think of the prevailing approach.

The book consists of eleven chapters, including this introductory chapter that serves as a theoretical anchor, eight case studies, a chapter that proposes an alternative approach to democratization, and a brief concluding chapter. While the underlying structural and institutional factors constitute the primary hindrances to the democratization process in the Greater Horn, there are also various secondary factors. Chapters 2 to 7 are empirical case studies that examine the obstacles to democratization in different countries of the region. These chapters examine both the primary and secondary factors.

Chapter 2 examines how the obsessive proclivity to control, which seems to be a defining characteristic shared by former leaders of revolutions and liberation movements, have blocked any progress towards 'rule-based, participatory politics' in Eritrea. Propositions that may contribute in unblocking the process of democratization in the country are advanced, and the extent to which the suggested approaches are implementable is briefly discussed.

Complementing the arguments of Chapter 2, Chapter 3 discusses the factors for the failure of the leaders of the Sudan People's Liberation Movement (SPLM) to install basic democratic standards after assuming power in South Sudan. The chapter also discusses how the monopolization of resources through corruption, along with the weak internal democratic culture within the ruling SPLM party, contributed to civil strife, ethnic polarization and a harsh economic situation. The chapter's authors suggest that the prospects of ending the civil war that ravages the country and initiating a democratization process are linked to full implementation of the August 2015 Peace Agreement on the resolution of the conflict, and reforms within the SPLM leadership.

Chapter 4 examines how a host of factors, including the politicization of ethnicity and the blending of the ruling party and state structures, have derailed the democratization process of post-1991 Ethiopia. The author argues that centralization of power mediated by the Ethiopian ruling party's unbridled control of the political and economic commanding heights culminated in the gradual and the progressive diminishing of the public space. With this as backdrop, propositions presumed to offset the prevailing deadlock militating against efforts aimed at democratizing the workings of the Ethiopian state and state-society relations are advanced.

Chapter 5 examines the public engagement of Ethiopia's parliament and assesses the challenges and constraints it faces in strengthening democracy and repressive governance. The chapter pays special attention to how the dominant ruling party system that prevails in the country affects the basic functions of the parliament, including exercising oversight over the executive branch of government, providing representation to all citizens, and making laws that advance the general interests of the public.

Chapter 6 examines the most important factors constraining the democratization process in Sudan. Failure to manage diversity properly and to address social injustice is placed at the centre of the problem. Lack of consensus on national vision, the nature of the educational system and family, clan and ethnic organizations are said to be important contributing factors.

Chapter 7 analyses how the Sudanese patronage structure creates a serious state-based caring deficiency, distorts democratizing efforts, and causes chronic political and economic problems. The chapter argues that two types of 'spaces of autonomy' can help reforming the Sudanese clientele state and promote a democratization process. These are an institutional 'space of autonomy' between the bureaucracy and the dominant political patrons, and an economic 'space of autonomy' between Sudanese political parties and their clients.

Contending that democracy is a contested concept and that it has often become an ideological tool in geo-political competition to whip states into line with the wishes of the powerful 'master states', the author of Chapter 8 examines the impact of external influence on Kenya's democratization process, arguing that the process of democratization would have been less violent and less contested without the eagerness of powerful states to dictate policies to Kenya and to violate its interests.

Chapter 9 analyses Somaliland's approach to state-building and democratization, which revolves around the hybrid system that fuses the traditional institutions of governance with the formal systems of governance. The chapter analyses the achievements so far and the challenges the hybrid system faces.

Based on the theoretical discussion of Chapter 1 and the findings of the case studies, Chapter 10 explains how CCA becomes a better-suited approach to tackle the underlying obstacles to democratization in the countries of the Greater Horn. The concluding Chapter 11 briefly summarizes the most important factors for the stagnation of democratization in the countries of the Greater Horn of Africa, and the key components of the proposed alternative approach to democratization. It also highlights the key contributions of the book.

Bibliography

African Peer Review Mechanism. 2006, *Country Review Report: The Republic of Kenya*. Addis Ababa: African Peer Review Mechanism.

—— 2009, *Country Review Report: The Republic of Uganda*. Addis Ababa: African Peer Review Mechanism.

—— 2011, *Country Review Report: The Federal Democratic Republic of Ethiopia*. Addis Ababa: African Peer Review Mechanism.

Ake, Claude. 1991, 'Rethinking Democracy'. *Journal of Democracy* 2(1): 32–44.

—— 1993, 'The Unique Case of African Democracy'. *International Affairs* 69(2): 239–44.

Alexander, Amy C., Inglehart, Ronald and Welzel, Christian. 2012, 'Measuring Effective Democracy: A Defense'. *International Political Science Review* 33: 41–62.

Alkire, S., Chatterjee, M., Conconi, A., Seth, S. and Vaz, A. 2014, 'Poverty in Rural and Urban Areas Direct Comparisons Using the Global MPI 2014', Oxford Poverty and Human Development Initiative, www.ophi.org.uk/wp-content/uploads/Poverty-in-Rural-and-Urban-Areas-Direct-Comparisons-using-the-Global-MPI-2014.pdf, accessed 10 December 2017.Bates, Robert H. 2010, 'Democracy in Africa: A Very Short History'. *Social Research: An International Quarterly* 77(4): 1133–48.

Beetham, David. 1992, 'Liberal Democracy and the Limits of Democratization'. *Political Studies* 40 (Special Issue): 40–53.

Bowles, Samuel and Gintis, Herbert. 1993, 'Democracy and Capitalism', in Philip Green (ed.), *Democracy: Key Concepts in Critical Theory*. Atlantic Highlands, NJ: Humanities Press, 168–74.

Bratton, M. 2007, 'Formal versus Informal Institutions in Africa'. *Journal of Democracy* 18(3): 96–110.

Bratton, M. and van de Walle, N. 1994, 'Neopatrimonial Regimes and Political Transitions in Africa'. *World Politics* 46 (4): 453–89.

—— 1997, *Democratic Experiments in Africa: Regime Transitions in Comparative Perspective*. New York: Cambridge University Press.

Cabral, Amilcar. 1969, *Revolution in Guinea: An African People's Struggle*. London: Monthly Review Press.

Cheeseman, Nic. 2015, *Democracy in Africa: Successes, Failures, and the Struggle for Political Reform*, www.researchgate.net/publication/290275977_Democracy_in_Africa_successes_failures_and_the_struggle_for_political_reform, accessed 28 November 2018.

Cowen, Michael and Laakso, Liisa. 2002, 'Elections and Election Studies in Africa', in Michael Cowen and Liisa Laakso (eds), *Multi-Party Elections in Africa*. New York: Palgrave Macmillan, 1–26.

Dahl, Robert. 1993, 'Why All Democratic Countries Have Mixed Economies', in John W. Chapman and Ian Shairo (eds), *Democratic Community*. New York University Press, 259–82.

Diamond, L. 1999, *Developing Democracy: Toward Consolidation*. Baltimore, MD: Johns Hopkins University Press.

—— 2008, *The Spirit of Democracy: The Struggle to Build Free Societies Throughout the World*. New York: Times Books.

Friedman, Milton. 1962, *Capitalism and Freedom*. Chicago, IL: Chicago University Press.

Global Land Project 2010, 'Land Grab in Africa: Emerging Land System Drivers in a Teleconnected World'. GLP International Project Office, University of Copenhagen Department of Geography and Geology, www.ihdp.unu.edu/docs/Publications/GLP/GLP_report_01.pdf, accessed 15 January 2018.

Gudina, Merera. 2011, 'Elections and Democratization in Ethiopia, 1991–2010'. *Journal of Eastern African Studies* 5(4): 664–80.

Gyimah-Boadi, E. 2004, *Democratic Reform in Africa: The Quality of Progress*. Boulder, CO: Lynne Rienner.

Hayek, F.A. 1960, *The Constitution of Liberty*. London and Henley: Routledge and Kegan Paul.

Held, David. 2006, *Models of Democracy*. Stanford, CA: Stanford University Press.

Human Rights Watch. 2013, *World Report 2013*, www.hrw.org/sites/default/files/wr2013_web.pdf, accessed 20 October 2017.

Huntington, P. Samuel. 1991, *The Third Wave: Democratization in the Late Twentieth Century*. University of Oklahoma Press.

Jaatee, Malkamu. 2016, 'Land Grabbing and Violations of Human Rights in Ethiopia', *Finfinne Tribune*, 28 January, http://genocidewatch.net/2016/02/01/land-grabbing-in-ethiopia, accessed 15 January 2018.

Joseph, Richard. 1997, 'Democratization in Africa after 1989: Comparative and Theoretical Perspectives'. *Comparative Politics* 29(3): 363–82.

Kambudzi, Admore. 2004, 'Issues and Problems of Political Renewal in Africa', in Olugbenga Adesida and Arunma Oteh (eds), *African Voices, African Visions*, Uppsala: Nordic Africa Institute, 53–66.

Khan, Mahmood Hasan. 2001, 'Rural Poverty in Developing Countries: Implications for Public Policy'. *Economic Issues* (26), www.imf.org/external/pubs/ft/issues/issues26/index.htm, accessed 10 October 2017.

Kuhnhardt, Ludger. 2014, *Africa Consensus: New Interests, Initiatives, and Partners*. Washington, DC: Woodrow Wilson Center Press; Baltimore, MD: The Johns Hopkins University Press.

Levitsky, Steven and Way, Lucan A. 2002, 'Elections without Democracy: The Rise of Competitive Authoritarianism'. *Journal of Democracy* 13(2): 51–65.

Lijphart, Arend. 1969, 'Consociational Democracy'. *World Politics* 21(2): 207–25.

—— 1977, *Democracy in Plural Societies: A Comparative Exploration*. New Haven, CT: Yale University Press.

Lindberg, Stephen. 2009, 'A Theory of Elections as a Mode of Transition', in Stephen Lindberg (ed.), *Democratization by Elections: A New Mode of Transition*. Baltimore, MD: Johns Hopkins University Press, 314–41.

Lindblom, E. Charles. 1982, 'The Market as Prison'. *Journal of Politics* 44 (May): 324–36.

Lipset, Seymour Martin. 1959, 'Some Social Requisites of Democracy: Economic Development and Political Legitimacy'. *American Political Science Review* 53 (March): 69–105.

Macpherson, B. 1966, *The Real World of Democracy*. Oxford: Oxford University Press.

Mengisteab, Kidane. 2014, *The Horn of Africa*. Cambridge, UK: Polity Press.

Mengisteab, Kidane and Hagg, Gerald. (eds) 2017, *Traditional Institutions in Contemporary African Governance*. London and New York: Routledge.

Mittal, Anuradha and Mousseau, Frederic. 2011, 'Understanding Land Investment Deals in Africa, Country Report: Ethiopia'. The Oakland Institute, Oakland, CA.

Mwebaza, Rose. 1999, 'Integrating Statutory and Customary Tenure Systems in Policy and Legislation: The Uganda Case', paper presented at a Workshop on Land Tenure Policy in African Nations. DfID workshop, Ascot UK.

Ndjio, B. 2008, 'Millennial Democracy and Spectral Reality in Post-Colonial Africa'. *African Journal of International Affairs* 11: 115–56.

Ninsin, K. A. 2006, 'Introduction: The Contradictions and Ironies of Elections in Africa'. *Africa Development* 36: 1–10.

Rustow, Dankwart A. 1970, 'Transitions to Democracy: Toward a Dynamic Model'. *Comparative Politics* 2(3): 337–63.

Samatar, Abdi Ismail and Samatar, Ahmed. 2002, 'Introduction', in Abdi Samatar and Ahmed Samatar (eds), *The African State: Reconsiderations*. Portsmouth, NH: Heinemann, 1–16.

Sandford, Judith and Ashley, Steve. 2008, 'Livestock, Livelihoods and Institutions in the IGAD Region'. IGAD, LPI Working Paper 10-08, Addis Ababa, FAO.

Schedler, A. (ed.) 2006, *Electoral Authoritarianism: The Dynamics of Unfree Competition*. Boulder, CO and London: Lynne Rienner.

Schmitter, Philippe. 1995, 'Democracy's Future: More Liberal, Preliberal, or Postliberal'. *Journal of Democracy* 6(1): 15–22.

Sekyi-Out, Ato. 1996, *Fanon's Dialectic of Experience*. Cambridge, MA: Harvard University Press.

Sklar, Richard. 1987, 'Developmental Democracy'. *Comparative Studies in Society and History* 23 (4): 686–714.

Skocpol, Theda and Amenta, Edwin. 1986, 'States and Social Policies'. *Annual Review of Sociology* 12: 131–57.

Tekeste Negash. 1986, *No Medicine for the Bite of a White Snake: Notes on Nationalism and Resistance in Eritrea, 1890–1940.* Uppsala, Sweden: University of Uppsala.

The Oakland Institute. 2011, 'Understanding Land Investment Deals in Africa', Country Report: South Sudan, Oakland, CA, www.oaklandinstitute.org/sites/oaklandinstitute.org/files/OI_country_report_south_sudan_1.pdf, accessed 8 December 2018.

UN Economic Commission for Africa. 2013, *African Governance Report III.* Oxford: Oxford University Press for UNECA, www.uneca.org/publications/african-governance-report-iii, accessed 11 October 2019.

—— 2016, 'The Demographic Profile of African Countries'. UNECA, Addis Ababa, www.uneca.org/sites/default/files/PublicationFiles/demographic_profile_rev_april_25.pdf accessed 25 November 2017.

UNDP (United Nations Development Programme). 2006, 'Share the Land or Part the Nation: The Pastoral Land Tenure System in Sudan', (Study 3). Khartoum, Sudan.

van de Walle, N. 1996, 'Elections Without Democracy: Africa's Range of Regimes'. *Journal of Democracy* 13: 66–80.

Wallis, John Joseph and North, Douglass C. 2010, 'Defining the State', Working Paper 10–26, June. Washington, DC: George Mason University Mercatus Center.

Wanyande, Peter. 2006, 'Electoral Politics and Election Outcomes in Kenya'. *Africa Development* 31(3): 62–80.

Weber, Max. 1958, 'Politics as Vocation', in H. H. Gerth and C. Wright Mills (eds), *From Max Weber: Essays in Sociology.* New York, Oxford University Press.

Williams, D. Paul. 2011, *Horn of Africa: Webs of Conflict and Pathways to Peace.* Washington, DC: The Wilson Center.

2

Problematizing 'Liberation' and Democratization in Post-independence Eritrea

GAIM KIBREAB

Introduction

> To be free from dictatorial government and from the application of its arbitrary and repressive laws is what it means to be free in the most elementary political sense of the word. (Sodaro & Collinwood 2008: 173)

Contrary to conventional wisdom, democratization is a slow, protracted, participatory, consensual and multi-layered process. Its central *raison d'être* is the production and reproduction of a rule-based system of governance underpinned by shared democratic values that interconnect people across the social cleavages of faith, ethnicity, region, ideology and way of life. The single most important question that we need to ask in our beleaguered region is not whether there have been multi-party elections or whether the regimes in place are formally democratic or tyrannical. It is more important to ask the extent to which the system in place promotes or stymies the development and, over time, consolidation of the buttressing core values, such as freedom, equality, cross-cultural understanding and trust, as well as respect for the sanctity of difference, life and rule of law.

These anchors of democracy are not necessarily the result of multi-party elections because, as James Bovard observes, 'Democracy must be something more than two wolves and a sheep voting on what to have for dinner' (1994: 333). It would be foolish and dishonest to attribute more meaning and significance to the procedural elections that have been taking place in our region – with the exception of the last Kenyan experience where, in spite of the rampant and palpable divisiveness, at least there was vibrant participation of civil society organizations (CSOs), including the rabidly bigoted. This does not deny the vital role the process may play in raising public awareness and fostering dialogue across the divides in the run up to and after elections. However, this is dependent on how open, free and transparent the process is because, more often than not in multi-ethnic and multi-faith societies where there is dearth of democratic culture, elections are more likely to divide and polarize rather than unite the societies concerned. The importance of multi-party elections is not therefore measured by the fact that the government exercising power is elected or not, but rather by whether such an election leads to flourishing of freedom and greater cross-cultural understanding across the cultural and political divide permeating the society in question.

I argue throughout this chapter that the reason Eritrea is in a state of abysmal decay is not because there have been no elections since its birth as an independent country over a quarter of a century ago: the degree of democratic deficit in other countries in the region, including in those where there have been elections (save Kenya), is equally bleak. What distinguishes the sorry state post-independence Eritrea is in is that it is in the pitiless grip of an autocratic and control-freak personal ruler inimical to private enterprise, any form of freedom of speech and expression, freedom of movement, choice of means of livelihood and the sanctity of rule of law. These are the edifices of the foundation on which democratization rests. It is argued throughout the chapter that, as long as impunity and arbitrariness remain the rule of the game, there will be no democratization.

The objectives of the chapter are to discuss the meanings of democratization and democracy; to examine the state of democratization in Eritrea; to identify the major constraints on democracy; and to suggest alternative approaches that may contribute to overcoming the constraints on the process of democratization in the country. A brief attempt is also made to discuss the extent to which the proposed approaches are implementable.

The meaning of democratization
The former Secretary-General of the UN, Boutros Boutros-Ghali defines democratization as 'a process which leads to a more open, more participatory, less authoritarian society' (1996: 1). Laurence Whitehead in his book *Democratization Theory and Experience* (2002: 27) defines democratization 'as a complex, long-term, dynamic and open-ended process. It consists of progress towards a more rule-based, more consensual and participatory type of politics. Like "democracy" it necessarily involves a combination of fact and value, and so contains internal tensions.' Although democratization, as Whitehead states, is a protracted and cumulative process, it may be possible to assess whether there is evidence to demonstrate that the so-called democratizing countries in Africa in general and post-independence Eritrea in particular have been progressing towards more 'rule-based, consensual and participatory politics' over time. In the absence of such phenomena, democratization is inconceivable.

Whitehead identifies the stages when the process of democratization begins and ends in which he states, 'democratization begins with the exit of an authoritarian regime and ends after competitive elections have given rise to two successive peaceful transfers of government between contending parties' (2002: 26). Nevertheless, although the end of the democratization process may, under favourable conditions, usher in a possibility of rule-based, consensual and participatory politics, this cannot be taken for granted. Since some countries that have experienced two successful transfers of power through peaceful and competitive elections may still be far from completing the process of democratization, Whitehead states, 'democratization is complete when all significant political actors accept (with good grace or ill) that the electoral process has become "the only game in town" for reallocating public office' (27). As Whitehead argues, this stage is unlikely to be reached after two successful consecutive elections in countries where tyranny and impunity have been the rule of the game for a long time.

Democracy and its determinants

The meaning of the concept of democracy is highly contested. According to Aristotle, 'democracy exists when the free and the poor, being a majority, have authority to rule' (1984). For Joseph Schumpeter, 'democracy is a political method, that is to say, a certain type of institutional arrangement for arriving at political – legislative and administrative – decisions and hence incapable of being an end in itself' (1976: 242). He defines method as an 'institutional arrangement for arriving at political decisions in which individuals acquire the power to decide by means of a competitive struggle for the people's vote' (269). In the Schumpeterian sense, democracy is a means and not an end, while for Robert Dahl (1971) democracy is a complex system underpinned by participation and liberalization. In his work, *On Democracy*, Dahl defines poliarchy as a 'modern representative democracy with universal suffrage' (1998: 90). For a system to qualify as democratic, it requires effective participation, equality in voting, access to information, control of the agenda and inclusion of adults. Dahl perceives democracy as a process that is continuously evolving rather than being 'invented once and for all, as, for example, the steam engine was invented' (*ibid.*: 9).

In the same vein, Larry Diamond observes, 'if ... we think of democracy in *developmental* terms, as a political system that emerges gradually in fragments or parts, and is always capable of becoming more liberal, inclusive, responsive, accountable, effective, and just, then we must see democratization not simply as a limited period of transition from one set of formal regime rules to another, but rather as an ongoing process, a perpetual challenge, a recurrent struggle' (1997, emphasis original). For Sodaro and Collinwood (2008: 171), the 'essential idea of democracy is that the people have the right to determine who governs them. In most cases they elect the principal governing officials and hold them accountable for their actions. Democracies also impose legal limits on the government's authority by guaranteeing certain rights and freedoms to their citizens'. They identify on the one hand, democratic values, such as 'freedom, inclusion, equality, equity, respect, tolerance, compromise and trust' and on the other, the 'principle of the rule of law, the legal foundation on which democracy rests' (172).

These two steps (democratic values and rule of law) are tightly interconnected in which the 'values underlie the law, and the law implements the values' (2008: 172). It is the responsibility of democratic governments to act on the basis of these ideals and implement them. 'To these ends', Sodaro and Collinwood state that 'democratic governments have three essential functions to respect popular sovereignty [in terms of people having the right to govern themselves]; to guarantee specific rights and liberties; and to enhance the economic well-being of the population' (*ibid.*). They refer to these 'three pillars of the Temple of Democracy' as the *'functional components* of democracy' (*ibid.*, emphasis added). These three pillars of democracy are so fundamental that any democratic government worth the label should act upon them. They argue that 'democracies must provide people with effective opportunities to escape poverty and improve their quality of life, while also providing basic social welfare benefits' (*ibid.*). They further state that these three functional components of democracy – namely, *popular sovereignty, rights and liberties* and *economic well-being* – must be firmly grounded in democratic values and the rule of law.

The 'ten conditions for democracy' identified by Sodaro and Collinwood are 'state institutions, elites committed to democracy, national unity, national wealth, private enterprise, a middle class, support of the disadvantaged for democracy, citizen participation, civil society and a democratic political culture, education and freedom of information and a favourable international environment' (2008: 221–40). We shall see later the extent to which these pre-conditions for democracy exist in post-independence Eritrea.

Marc Bűhlmann et al (2007: 14) argue that democracy relies on 'three fundamental principles: *equality, freedom and control*' (emphasis added). They summarize:

> we define freedom, equality and control as the three core principles of democracy. To qualify as a democracy, a given political system has to guarantee freedom and equality. Moreover, it has to optimize the interdependence between these two principles by means of control. Control is understood as control *by* the government as well as control *of* the government. (Emphasis added)

Only in polities where there are well-developed institutional arrangements and enforcement mechanisms are these possible.

Since the demise of the Soviet Union, there has been an immense surge of research interest on the determinants of democratization and democracy (see Barro 1999; Fish and Brooks 2004; Merkel and Weiffen 2012; Acemoglu et al 2005; Debs and Morrison 2015; Gerring, Zarecki and Hoffman 2016; Özbudun 2005; Ishkanian 2007; Wheatley 2003). Some of the determinants of democratization and democracy are discussed briefly in the following to lay the ground for the analysis of whether there is an ongoing democratization process leading towards democracy.

One of the key determinants of democratization and democracy is education. Most analysts agree that *education* is one of the indispensable pre-conditions for democratization and democratic consolidation. This is because democratic choices require a certain degree of awareness and knowledge about the world, as well as rational and critical thinking, in order to compare and contrast the political, economic and the agenda of the parties competing for ascendance to power. It is not due to coincidence that democracy thrived in Western Europe when newspapers and affordable books became available. According to John Dewey (1997), a high level of education cultivates a 'culture of democracy' and engenders prosperity, which provides a convivial environment for the process of democratization to unfold and democracy to flourish. Martin Lipset (1959: 79) further advanced this view by arguing that education and economic growth are prerequisites for economic development and democracy. He argued: 'The more well-do-do a nation, the greater the chances it will sustain democracy' (56). To underscore the significance of education for the development and consolidation of democracy, Lipset states: 'Education presumably broadens men's outlooks, enables them to understand the need for norms of tolerance, restrains them from adhering to extremist and monistic doctrines, and increases their capacity to make rational electoral choices' (79). Lipset's assertion is confirmed by different studies (e.g. Barro 1999). Robert Barro's study based on time series cross-country data analysis shows that countries at higher levels of economic development are more likely to sustain democracy than those at lower levels of development (1999: S163). A study by Acemoglu et al. shows 'a statistically significant correlation between education and democracy' (2005: 45).

Economic growth and preponderance of the middle class are also said to be indispensable to democratization and democracy. Barrington Moore, for example, states that 'a vigorous and independent class of town dwellers has been an indispensable element in the growth of parliamentary democracy', emphatically declaring: *'No bourgeois, no democracy'* (1966: 418, emphasis added). It is argued that a 'large middle class tempers conflict by rewarding moderate and democratic parties while also penalizing extremist groups' (Lipset 1963 quoted in Özbudun 2005: 98). An independent middle class is able to hold those who exercise power accountable. This is one of the reasons why the Eritrean head of state loathes the middle class and has adopted economic policies that have eliminated them from the scene.

Another reason autonomous middle class is consequential to democracy is in its absence, the state is likely to 'control a vastly greater share of the most-valued economic opportunities (jobs, contracts, licences, scholarships and development largesse)' (Lipset in *ibid.*) while, as argued by Mosca, democracy requires, 'a large [middle] class of people whose economic position is virtually independent of those who hold supreme power' (1939: 144 quoted in *ibid.*). We shall see later when we look at the Eritrean case in which the democratization process was nipped in the bud how edifying this observation is. Samuel Huntington's observation is also consistent with this in which he states that 'in virtually every country the most active supporters of democratization came from the urban middle class' (quoted in Barro 1999: 163).

Another question, which has been the major focus of analysts, is the nexus between heterogeneity and democracy. Not only is heterogeneity perceived to represent a potential threat to democracy in transitional and emerging democracies, but also to mature democracies as well (Merkel & Weiffen 2012: 388). The assumption that coherent and homogenous political communities are *sine qua non* requirement for stable and sustainable democracy is an old one. John Stuart Mill, for example, wrote in 1861,

> Free institutions are next to impossible in a country made up of different nationalities. Among a people without fellow-feeling, especially if they read and speak different languages, the united public opinion, necessary to the working of representative government cannot exist. (cited in *ibid.*: 395)

Robert Dahl's observation in this regard is not substantially different either in which he observes, 'as the strength and distinctiveness of a country's sub-cultures increase, the chances for polyarchy should decline' (1989: 255). These observations are not necessarily always true. As we shall see later, notwithstanding the fact that Eritrea is home to disparate nine ethno-linguistic groups, during the liberation struggle, they were able to set aside their differences in pursuit of a common goal – national independence – by bonding across the cleavages of religion, ethnicity and region. Had the liberation struggle produced good government, this scarce social resource would have provided auspicious grounds for a democratization process to be unleashed, as well as democracy to thrive. As most other things, this opportunity was squandered when the personal ruler, President Isaias Afwerki, adopted a destructive approach based on 'my way or the high way'.

Nothing can be more adverse to democracy than such a stance. The phenomenon Mill identifies as the dearth of 'fellow-feeling' that allegedly permeates multi-ethno-linguistic societies is not immutable. The condition is not fixed and therefore can be overcome through cooperation, negotiation and building trans-ethnic and trans-faith bridges, which can lead to development of solidarity, mutual trust and coop-eration. There was clear evidence to show that the Eritrean liberation movements, especially the Eritrean People's Liberation Front (EPLF) was able to achieve these goals with remarkable success. Unfortu-nately, the leaders of the EPLF and later the People's Front for Democ-racy and Justice (PFDJ) solely concentrated on controlling every aspect of Eritrean politics by ignoring the connection with the past.

A common feeling of nationhood – sentiment and commitment that transcend sub-national and sub-cultural loyalties and belongings – can offset the potential dangers that may be posed by ethno-linguistic heterogeneity. Switzerland is a classic case in point. Gerring et al. (2016: 284), after extensively referring to the literature which paints a bleak picture of the effect of heterogeneity on democratization and democracy, state: 'Yet, on balance, and *ceteris paribus*, the consensus seems to be that social diversity has either a negative or – at best – no relationship to democracy'.

The reason why ethno-linguistic diversity is favourable to democ-racy is because of the potential diversity of interests, which on the one hand, constrain the ability of an authoritarian ruler to co-opt the opposition and on the other, allow the opposition leaders to mobilize distinct constituents which may undermine the hegemonic control of an authoritarian leader. 'In such a situation, it will be difficult for a single faction to successfully monopolize power' (Horowitz 1985 in Gerring et al. 2016: 5). At the heart of the argument is the postulation that ethno-linguistic diversity is auspicious to democracy is because cooperation is considered to be an essential element in democracy and that, in a highly fractionalised society, it would be difficult for a small clique to dominate and monopolize power. Eritrea seems to be an outlier in this theorizing or generalization. As we shall see later, despite the nine ethno-linguistic groups inhabiting Eritrea, the personal ruler, Isaias Afwerki, and his small inner circle have been able to exercise absolute power without being accountable to anyone. The personal ruler is unimpeded by the multiplicity of identities that permeate the Eritrean cultural and social landscape.

With regard to violent conflict which equally applies to democratiza-tion and democracy, Paul Collier and Anke Hoeffler argue that countries where there is 'ethnic dominance', reflected in the fact that a single ethnic group represents between 45 and 90 per cent of the population, the probability of major civil conflict is higher than in societies that are either homogenous, reflected in one group constituting more than 90 per cent of the population, or 'those highly fractionalised countries where each group comprises less than 45 per cent of the population' (cited in Fish & Brooks 2004: 160). The same is true with democracy.

However, as opposed to ethno-linguistic heterogeneity, religious diversity may damage the prospects for democracy (Gerring et al. 2016;

Barro 1999). Another prerequisite for democratization and democracy is the existence of independent and vibrant civil society associations and organizations, including non-governmental organizations (NGOs), which on the one hand, may hold governments accountable and on the other, protect the interests of individuals and groups. Since Alexis de Tocqueville accentuated the importance of vibrant associational life to the development of democracy, the vital roles civil society associations play in counteracting the power of the state has been the major preoccupation of analysts (see Putnam 1993, 2000; Kibreab 2008). Armine Ishkanian, for example, argues that successful transition to democracy is only possible 'if civil society or "something like it" either pre-dates the transition or is established in the course of a transition from authoritarian rule' (Perez-Diaz 1993 in Ishkanian 2007: 3).

National liberation, democratization and democracy

> Robespierre, with his cruel moral relativism, embodied the cardinal sin of all revolution, the heartlessness of ideas. (Paul Johnson, *The Spectator*)

If we were to ask ourselves the simple question: how many of those who have taken over state power after leading successful revolutions and national liberation struggles do not share Robespierre's heartlessness, we may struggle to find one. Callousness and obsessive proclivity to control seem to be the defining character traits shared universally by former leaders of revolutions and liberation movements. These character traits do not die when the shooting stops, culminating in the defeat of the enemy and establishment of an independent and/or a revolutionary government. On the contrary, they tend to flourish subsequently long after the shootings stop. There seems to be no exception to this general observation. I will try to explain this phenomenon later by referring to the Eritrean experience, which is by no means unique. Over time, people who have been accustomed to resolving differences through the use of force rather than discourse, deliberation, negotiation, compromise and reconciliation, tend to become habituated to the use of suppressive measures to deal with their enemies, including their former comrades under different pretexts. Democratization and democracy are inconceivable without the willingness and ability to resolve differences through dialogue, compromise and negotiation based on mutual respect and understanding.

> Nationalism is one of the most powerful legitimizing forces of our age, strong enough to compel even human sacrifice, yet its extraordinary power requires leaders of the movement to be neither democratic nor self-effacing functionaries. Once victorious, moreover, nationalism

can lend a regime an overwhelming aura of legitimacy, again without internal democracy or a democratic leadership style. (Friedrich 1963: 245)

Although the demand for self-determination is essentially democratic, the feelings it stirs and the consciousness it engenders on the way and the means by which it is achieved tend to sow seeds of intolerance and dictatorship, as well as undermine the democratic process not only during the fighting, but also when the shooting stops. That may be the reason why most revolutions and liberation struggles are succeeded by autocratic regimes in spite of the lofty promises they make and the expectations they arouse. The available evidence seems to suggest that in the majority of cases, nationalism and democracy make hostile bedfellows. (On the relationship between nationalism and democracy see Lecours & Moreno 2010). This observation also seems to be true with regard to the relationship between revolution and democracy.

The ground-breaking observation Alexis de Tocqueville made in his book, *Democracy in America* (1956), after he returned from his visit to the United States and after witnessing what had become of France after Louis Napoleon Bonaparte's coup d'état, still remains fundamentally true. His critical assertion that democracy's future would largely depend on the 'habits of the heart' and the environment, which forms or deforms the heart, such as families, neighbourhoods, classrooms, congregations, voluntary associations, workplaces and other venues of public life where "the company of strangers" gathers' (quoted in Palmer 2011) is edifying. One may add to this list national liberation movements, political parties and mass organizations, which have the potential to form or deform the 'habits of the heart' of their leaders, members and sympathizers. It is these habits and the places where they are shaped or transformed that form the invisible infrastructure of democracy or autocracy on which the quality of political life depends. The habits of the heart are formed and deformed by what individuals, groups or even populations experience and internalize in everyday life.

The track records of liberation movements, in terms of instilling and cultivating democratic values and norms which constitute the edifice of the foundation on which the 'habits of the heart' are cultivated and reside in the Tocquevillian sense, have been bleak throughout history. Some of the common features shared by most liberation movements are authoritarianism and unfathomable antipathy to dissent, and averseness to listening with openness and respect to the alternative voice. Ironically, these were the defining features of the autocratic structures of the regimes such movements abolished. This meant that, not only were the repressive characters of the regimes they once abhorred and abolished reproduced during the liberation struggles but also, once in power, the liberators also emulated the dictatorial proclivities of their predecessors. As Ranger and Vaughan state:

> The most convincing legitimation of new states has lain in the plausibility of their indictments of their predecessors. Their own positive legitimations – however strenuously worked at and for a time convincing – have not worn well. Indeed, the collapse of the hegemony of one form of state has routinely been attended by nostalgia for its once-reviled predecessor. (1993: 1)

This misfortune has been common in most post-liberation states and Eritrea is no exception. Examples of national liberation dreams turned sour can be found in Angola (see Global Witness 1998), Ethiopia (see Aelen et al. 2002; Abbink & Hagmann 2013), Namibia (Leys & Saul 1995; Melber 2003b) Rwanda (Prunier 1998) and Zimbabwe (Kriger 1992; Melber 2004; Moyo 2004; Ranger 2004), to name a few. (For brilliant accounts of what went wrong in Southern Africa see Melber 2002; 2003a; 2003b; 2006.)

Jonathan Moyo, before he barefacedly changed sides, wrote a scathing attack on the war of liberation (*Chimurenga*) in Zimbabwe, stating:

> There can hardly be any doubt that the armed struggle in Zimbabwe was a pivotal means to the goal of defeating oppressive and intransigent elements of colonialism and racism. However, as it often is the case with protracted social processes of a conflict with two sides, the armed struggle in this country had a deep socio-psychological impact on its targets as well as on its perpetrators. *For the most part, the armed struggle in this country lacked a guiding moral ethic beyond the savagery of primitive war and was thus amenable to manipulation by the violence of unscrupulous nationalist politicians and military commanders who personalised the liberation war for their own selfish ends. This resulted in a culture of fear driven by values of violence perpetrated in the name of nationalism and socialism.* (Melber 2006: 264, emphasis added)

In Rwanda, according to Filip Reyntjens: 'Rather than liberation, inclusiveness and democracy, the RPF [Rwandan Patriotic Front] has brought oppression, exclusion and dictatorship' (2006: 1103, abstract). He further observes that 'the transition has been one from one dictatorship to another, and a more ruthless one at that' (1113). This and Moyo's descriptions are fitting not only to most liberation struggles, but also to many post-liberation governments in Africa and elsewhere, including in Eritrea. Christopher Clapham (1998: 12) insightfully argues that in some cases:

> insurgency ... has provided a means of establishing fragile and exploitative forms of rule which owe more to pre-colonial patterns than to any model of 'modern' statehood. Often, it has contributed immeasurably to the level of human suffering to which many parts of Africa

have been prey, without offering any evident means through which the basic human needs of peace and welfare could be attained. In looking at insurgency, we are, ultimately, taking one particular slant on the complex process through which Africa is – for better or worse – adapting to the decay of the post-colonial continental order.

Although this may sound paradoxical, the phenomenon reproducing the tyrannical features of the past is neither new nor specific to the anti-colonial liberation movements in Africa. Nicholas Kittrie observes perceptively:

> The French Revolution of the late eighteenth century is recorded as an uprising against privileged, insensitive, and tyrannical authority. Yet the reign of terror imposed by France's revolutionaries exceeded the abuses of Louis XVI and the evils of Bastille. The American Civil War, popularly depicted as a struggle for the liberation of African Americans from the inhumanity of slave labour, was followed by political powerlessness and continuing social degradations for new subject class of 'freemen.' Similarly, the 1917 Russian Revolution, portrayed as a workers' and peasants' uprising against a thoroughly abusive authority, quickly created its own and even more terrifying reign of terror. (1995: 58–9)

The same is true of most national liberation movements throughout the developing societies of Africa, Indo-China and Central America. For example, of Nicaragua Paul Staines (1989: 13) writes: 'The 1979 revolution brought the Sandinistas to power with five commitments: a market economy, respect for human rights, democratic political pluralism, religious freedom and a non-aligned foreign policy. Not one of those commitments has been honoured.' Staines further states that in the process of creating a 'New Nicaragua' the Sandinistas have carried out political killings, disappearances, torture, arbitrary arrests and imprisonment – all the hallmarks of 'conventional' totalitarian regimes (13). Henning Melber writing on Southern Africa (2003: 149) states:

> The track records of liberation movements are at times dubious and far from setting positive examples, victims turned liberators often turned into perpetrators. Supported by international solidarity movements basing their actions upon moral and ethical imperatives, they were fighting against systems of institutionalised violation of basic human rights. At the same time they were not always sensitive to human right issues and the cultivation of democratic virtues within their own ranks.

The so-called liberators turned into perpetrators use the same repressive methods and practices to silence and/or obliterate dissenting forces, including those who were in the trenches with them, and this has become a common occurrence. Norma J. Kriger's work – *Zimbabwe's Guerrilla War: Peasant Voices* (1992) shows that popular support during the struggle was at times based more on coercion among the colonized than on genuine resistance against the colonial state – and this was by no means unique to Zimbabwe.

According to Melber:

> the anti-colonial wars were hardly a suitable environment to instil and cultivate the internalisation and implementation of democratic values and norms. The organisation of armed resistance, especially, had much in common with the authoritarianism and hierarchical organisation inherent in the totalitarian structures of the colonial system opposed. (2003: 150)

More poignantly, he observes: 'To this extent, *features of the colonial character were reproduced in the fight for their abolition and the emerging concepts of power applied in the post-colonial reconstruction phase*' (*ibid.*, emphasis added). As mentioned earlier, this has been one of the most significant discernible patterns of the legacies of revolutionary movements throughout history. De Tocqueville, for example, argues that 'the French revolutionaries in the process of implementing the structures of the new system maintained the mentalities, habits, even the ideas of the old state while using them to destroy it. And they took the rubble of the old state to establish the foundation of the new society' (cited in Melber 2003: 150). Rephrasing de Tocqueville, Melber writes:

> To understand the revolution and its achievement, one has to forget about the current society but has to interrogate the buried one. His ultimate reasoning ends in the suggestion that freedom has been replaced by another repression. *Revolutionaries in the process of securing, establishing and consolidating their power base sacrificed the declared ideals and substantive issues they were fighting for in the name of the same revolution. (Ibid., emphasis added)*

The brief exposé above demonstrates that democracy is the single most significant Achilles heel of revolutionary political organizations both during their fight for political changes and after their ascendance to power through violent means. Their propensity to use force to maintain their power and to suppress their opponents, including their former comrades-in-arms who refuse to toe the line is unmistakable. The available evidence shows that whoever seizes power through violent means are strongly inclined to employ force to consolidate and remain in power. This unmistakable and discernible pattern has prevailed all over the countries where there have been regime changes through violent means.

Whether the former Eritrean liberators have turned into perpetrators by falling prey to the discernible common pattern of malaise that is commonly displayed by leaders of revolutions and liberation movements or have been able to break the mould will be discussed in what follows.

Structural and institutional constraints on democratization in Eritrea

> Meet the new boss
> Same as the old boss
>
> The Who – *Won't Get Fooled Again*

Many Eritreans hoped that the 'new boss' that ascended to power in the aftermath of the victorious liberation struggle would be a law-abiding democrat markedly different from his predecessor, the tyrant, Mengistu Hailemariam, 'the old boss'. To their dismay, down the line, they discovered that the 'new boss' is as intolerant and tyrannical as the 'old boss'. The Russian revolutionary, Victor Serge, after witnessing the betrayals and the tragedies unfolding in the Soviet Union in his celebrated book, *Memoirs of a Revolutionary* (2012) [1951] wrote:

> What with the political monopoly, the Cheka and the Red Army, all that now existed of the 'Commune-State' of our dreams was a theoretical myth. The war, the internal measures against counterrevolution, and the famine (which had created a bureaucratic rationing apparatus) had killed off Soviet democracy. How could it revive, and when? *The Party lived in the certain knowledge that the slightest relaxation of its authority would give way to reaction.* (Emphasis added)

The fit between Serge's description and the current reality in post-independence Eritrea is astonishingly high. This reality is also true of most post-revolutionary and liberation struggles. The unhappy scenarios that have been unfolding in post-independence Eritrea are due to a combination of multiple and complex factors, among which, President Isaias Afewerki's unfettered obsession of exercising power without institutional constraints is only one. The political developments in post-independence Eritrea are consistent with the common discernible observations made by different analysts – that 'revolutions devour their own children'. The way the Eritrean president has been treating his former revolutionary comrades is a vivid testimony to the parable. As we shall see next, not only has the Eritrean head of state – the chairman of the executive and of the effectively defunct National Assembly which has not met since 2002, and the commander-in-chief of the military, as well as the chairman of the *de facto* defunct ruling party, the PFDJ – failed to break the mould, but also he has excelled in the art of perpetuating repression and tyranny.

In what follows, first, the policies and actions of the longest serving provisional government in the world has been taking to prevent the process of democratization from unfolding are discussed. In light of the institutional and structural determinants of democratization and democracy discussed above, this is an attempt is made to analyse the extent to which democratization is feasible in the context of the post-independence government's policies and actions, as well as the institutional and structural conditions pervading the Eritrean polity, and the major constraints on democratization and democracy are discussed.

Violation of human rights

The sanctity of human and individual rights and the rule of law constitute the edifice of the foundation on which the democratization process in any society rests. Without respect for the sanctity of the principles of human rights and rule of law, no democratization process is conceivable. Post-independence Eritrea's human rights records have been indefensibly poor. For example, the US-based independent advocacy group, Freedom House, has classified Eritrea among the 'world's most repressive regimes' in terms of freedom, civil liberties and political rights. Its rating score in the spheres of freedom, civil liberties and political rights in 2018 was 7 on a scale where 1is the best score and 7 the worst (Freedom House 2018). Eritrea was listed fourth with a press freedom score of 94 among the 50 worst of the violators of press freedom. Only North Korea, Turkemenistan and Uzbekistan (97, 96 and 95 press freedom scores respectively) were worse than Eritrea (Freedom House 2016) while, in Freedom House (2018), Eritrea's score of 84.2 (179th of 180) was the worst next to North Korea. Among sub-Saharan African countries, Eritrea's score in freedom was the worst, with Sudan's and Ethiopia's ratings being nearly equally bleak (*ibid.*) Throughout its reign, the post-independence government's human rights performance by all measurable standards has been horrific (see Amnesty International 2006; HRW 2016).

Although the Eritrean post-independence government's violation of human rights pre-dates the incarceration of the eleven members of the G-15 opposition group and most of the journalists who worked in the privately owned newspapers in September 2001 (see Kibreab 2009), since then arbitrary detention without trial has become normal. In 2013, Amnesty International reported that there were '10,000 political prisoners in unimaginably atrocious conditions' (cited in BBC 2013). Given the closed nature of the country, it is difficult to verify the extent to which these figures are accurate. The exact number could be more or less than the stated figure. However, the presence of large numbers of political prisoners with no charges brought against them is common knowledge. Some of those who are arbitrarily detained without being charged are journalists, critics of the government, practising members of prohibited faith groups, draft evaders and deserters from the indefinite national service.

A few, such as his Holiness the Archbishop of the Orthodox Church and the father of the former Minister of Information, Ali Abdu, are in their late 80s or older. Such acts in the Eritrean cultural context are anathema. Most of the detainees are held in unknown places and their families and friends are kept unaware of their whereabouts. Claire Beston of Amnesty who researched the human rights situation in Eritrea wrote: 'The government has systematically used arbitrary arrest and detention without charge to crush all opposition, to silence all dissent, and to punish anyone who refuses to comply with the repressive restrictions it places on people's lives' (cited in BBC 2013). Democratization is inconceivable in such a bleak context.

Excessive securitization
Since the border war and its aftermath, the Eritrean government has been excessively preoccupied with securitizing every aspect of the Eritrean polity. The government's obsession with security issues and the ill-conceived decisions it has been taking allegedly to avert the imagined or exaggerated external threats to 'national security' have jeopardized human security and nipped in the bud the democratization process in the country. More importantly, the alleged threat to national security is used as a pretext to suppress internal dissent. Provision of a political space for political dissent is *sine qua non* for democratization. Without a political space for dissent, neither democratization nor democracy is conceivable. In a country where excessive securitization is a norm, there is no room for democratization. Not only do the government's paranoid and misconceived security policies and goals act as a drain on the country's scarce manpower and other national resources, but they have also risked the security of the citizens and the state itself. It is in this sense Robert Mandel perceptively argues:

> Generally security appears to represent a universal good that all in society strive to achieve. However, drawbacks can emerge when security becomes a primary or all-consuming emphasis: this focus can foster (1) paranoia and a counter-productive focus on constantly unearthing potential threats to security or (2) a drain of resources away from her societal values (such as economic well-being) deemed important. Portraying concerns as security issues can elevate them into crisis requiring extreme emergency measures that may be unwarranted and may provoke similar harsh responses from others. (1994: 16)

The narrative that dominates official discourse in government circles and their supporters, including in the diaspora, can be summed up as: 'before solving the existential problem facing our country and our people, it is irresponsible to talk about democracy and human rights'. The corollary is that in the light of perceived existential threats posed by the Ethiopian Government and its powerful Western allies, democratization is an indulgence that should be put on the back burner.

The Eritrean government is aware of the high premium national security commands in the Eritrean psyche, given the fact that they paid a very high price in terms of lives, property and forgone opportunities during the thirty-year war (1961–91) and the border war (May 1998 to May 2000). It is also worth noting that the memory of the loved ones who paid the highest price to achieve independence is still fresh. The government knows this and exploits it without moral constraint.

The threat to national security is invoked to ensure the political and economic power of the incumbents and the survival of the regime. By invoking the threat to national security, not only has the Eritrean Government been able to stifle the demand for political and economic change, but it has also used this alleged threat to introduce draconian measures that would under 'normal circumstances' be unjustified or illegal. As elsewhere in the region and in the rest of the world, tyrannical political power is exercised in the name of averting 'a clear and present' danger to national security. It is not unusual for governments to invoke such imagined or manufactured risk to national security either to conceal malign intentions or to justify oppressive policies and practices.

Once an issue is framed in security terms, it justifies any measure that can prevent the imagined threat from unfolding. In the absence of such a threat, the measures would be regarded as gross violation of international and national human rights standards. Waever, for example, defines security

> as a practice, a specific way of framing an issue. Security discourse is characterised by dramatizing an issue as having absolute priority. Something is presented as an existential threat: if we do not tackle this, everything else will be irrelevant ... and by labelling this a security issue, the actor has claimed the rights to deal with it by extra-ordinary means, to break the normal political rules of the game ... Something is presented as existentially threatened, and on this basis it is argued that 'we' must use extraordinary means to handle the threat. (Cited in Kibreab 2000: 271)

The assumption is that in the absence of such measures, the security of the state and the people will be imminently threatened or in an extreme case scenario, both the people and the nation may be wiped out. For example, the Eritrean head of state, Isaias Afwerki, in an attempt on the one hand, to emphasize the extent to which the change-seeking forces such as the G-15 and their supporters represented an existential threat to national security and on the other, to underscore the necessity of taking uncompromising and draconian measures to avert the 'danger', said: 'If the vertical tension (*tikulawi mtfnan*) [caused by the G-15] in the society unfolds, as what we have been witnessing in Somalia, in which people are incited to fight against each other, there will neither be a people nor a country' (Amare and Seyoum 2003). In saying this, the president aims to achieve two things simultaneously. By framing the demands of the G-15 and the other change-seeking forces in security terms, not only does he want to delegitimize the demands for democracy, justice, fairness and rule of law, but he also wants to justify the draconian measures taken against them and other change-seeking forces.

His message, no matter how misplaced, is straightforward and simple: 'If we don't take the illegal measures, e.g. incommunicado incarceration of those who allegedly represent danger to our country, not only would the security of the nation be endangered, but there may even be no people and country at all'. Once an issue is framed in such a chilling manner, any means taken to avert such calamity is justifiable in the eyes of nationalists. That is precisely the picture which the Eritrean government and its supporters have been trying to present since the government's clampdown on the change-seeking forces, journalists, religious minorities, businessmen, elders, etc. The imagined or manufactured threat to national security stems from fear or from the need, on the part of those at the helm of power, for a pretext to stifle dissent and the process of democratization in the bud. Those who are scared or those who intend to thwart any opposition to their oppressive rule want to be free from such fear and opposition. It is in pursuit of these ostensible goals that the Eritrean government has severely constricted the space that would allow democratization and democracy to unfold.

The ascendance to power of Dr Abiy Ahmed in Ethiopia on 2 April 2018 has brought about some fundamental changes not only in the country, but also in the whole region, including in the relations between Eritrea and Ethiopia. In July 2019, the two heads of state declared the end of the state of 'no war no peace' or hostilities between the two states. In September 2019, the border between Eritrea and Ethiopia was re-opened enabling citizens of both countries to travel and interact with each other freely without restraint. The euphoria and prompt elation that accompanied the re-opening of the border showed that the fight was between the two governments rather than between the two peoples of Eritrea and Ethiopia.

The only Eritrean nationals who cannot leave the country legally in spite of the peace deal are those who are affected by the open-ended national service and those approaching the age of conscription. All those who are seven years and older are said to fall within the category of 'approaching the age of conscription' and therefore cannot leave the country legally. Before the peace deal, the single most important reason the Eritrean government gave to justify the open-ended national service was the risk of another war with Ethiopia. (On the Eritrean national service, see Kibreab 2017.) Ten months have passed since the alleged threat of war and national security that previously held democracy at bay has ceased. In spite of the cessation of the alleged threat to national security, there has been no change whatsoever in the realms of governance, justice, freedom of speech, due process and free enterprise in Eritrea. The thousands of citizens who were incarcerated without due process, including minors, under the pretext of safeguarding national security still remain unaccounted for notwithstanding the fact that the ostensible threat to national security and sovereignty have ceased to exist. The open-ended Eritrean national service continues unabated in spite of cessation of hostilities between the two countries. The so-called people's militia introduced under the pretext of an external threat of war in 2012 persists unabated.

The alleged threat, used by the Eritrean President Isaias Afwerki as a pretext to hold democratization and democracy at bay, blew up in his face. The prevailing reality on the ground demonstrates beyond any shadow of doubt that the so-called threat of war was a ploy to arrest political change and transformation in Eritrea.

Self-reliance and refusal of international aid
The incumbents in post-independence Eritrea pride themselves in turning down international aid because they perceive the latter as a conduit for external influence and pressure. They see international aid as being a key leverage for Western governments and organizations to impose conditionalities on recipient countries. Such a tenacious stance is espoused, irrespective of the consequence on the well-being of the Eritrean people in general and the poor in particular. The Eritrean head of state is aware that compliance with rule of law, democracy and human rights are the *sine qua non* requirements for receiving international aid with the consequent establishment of links with the globalized world. The corollary is that a government that receives foreign aid willy-nilly becomes an integral part of the global economic and political system, which requires compliance with the values and norms based, *inter alia*, on the sanctity of the principles of human rights, formal democracy and rule of law. Nothing can be more objectionable to the Eritrean President and his inner circle than such principles.

What is unique about Eritrea, no matter how depressing and repugnant the post-independence political development has been, is that, unlike in other countries in the region and elsewhere, at least in the realm of democracy, what you hear is what you get. The incumbents do not talk democracy and then practice tyranny. Their rhetoric about democracy is scornful and their political practice in the public sphere is tyrannical and they are not embarrassed about it. There is neither pretence nor posturing. The reason they have been able to speak and act consistently is because they can afford it. They owe nothing or little to the outside world and hence the international community is unable to bring pressure to bear on them. Eritrea's personal ruler, Isaias Afwerki, in an interview conducted in New York in 2011 stated:

> Anyone who takes aid is crippled. Aid is meant to cripple people ... Governments in Africa and elsewhere are not allowed to write their own programs. And when it comes to implementing programs, it deprives you of building institutions and the capacity to implement your programs ... [We] need to write our own programs in the first place. We need to articulate on the projects we write. We need to have a comprehensive strategy, plans on how to implement those programs ... Unless we do that on our own, we can't possibly imagine that we are achieving any of the goals – millennium or non-millennium. (Quoted in Danto 2015)

Notwithstanding its refusal of aid, the government has neither been able to build institutions nor feed its own citizens. At the heart of its isolationist policy and its rejection of democratization lays the obsession with the desire to control every aspect of the polity, and the hollow policy of self-reliance enables it to do so. Democracy is inconceivable in a country where the incumbents are unwilling to provide a political space to its opponents.

Repressive policies and actions: old habits die hard

Notwithstanding the fact that the leaders of the EPLF have always a displayed cavalier attitude towards the basic rights of fighters and civilians in the areas they controlled during the liberation struggle, many Eritreans, including intellectuals in the diaspora, expected the process of democratization to unfold and democracy to flourish in post-independence Eritrea. As we shall see later, there were no grounds for such naïve optimism. Neither President Isaias Afwerki nor the EPLF ever promised to govern the country democratically. Besides, in view of the fact that there was ample evidence to show that organizations that seize power through violent means are anathema to democracy, such optimism was ill-founded. Even those who were aware of the bleak common history of revolutionary organizations and national liberation movements hoped against hope that the Eritrean experience would be unique and, would break new grounds by following a different path.

The late luminary Professor Tekie Fessehatzion, who was a highly regarded scholar and an ardent advocate of justice, human rights and Eritrean independence, for example, wrote:

> The question for all Eritreans is whether an organisation whose predecessor (EPLF) was founded to lead Eritrea to independence and national sovereignty, which it did, is equipped structurally and programmatically, to move the country into the ranks of the economically and politically developed family of nations during the next few decades. Can an organisation initially formed along military lines and

the politics of command to achieve what has already been achieved (independence) be reprogrammed to deliver within the frameworks of a civilian government whereby consensus and thorough consultation with the public is the norm? Simply put, can yesterday's liberationists become tomorrow's democrats given the dismal record on democratisation in the post-liberation world? (Cited in Kibreab 2009: 361)

Although Tekie undoubtedly knew better, like most of his compatriots in the diaspora, he ended his remarks with an unrealistic but well-meant optimistic note: 'there is no predetermined reason why Eritrea should not break the mould'.

Now that the incumbents have been in power for nearly three decades, we can safely conclude that they are not any different from other leaders of national liberation movements or from other leaders who ascended to power through the use of force. In view of the evidence presented in the first part of the chapter and Tekie's observation, this is not surprising as, hitherto, there has not been a single leader in modern history that seized power by force and allowed substantive as opposed to procedural democracy to thrive, or a leader that abandoned violence in favour of democratic dialogue and consultation as a means of winning hearts and minds of citizens, including dissidents.

Given the small size of the country in terms of geography and population in comparison to its southern neighbour, Ethiopia, against whom it waged a bitter thirty-year war of independence, the May 1991 military victory of the Eritrean people was indeed awesome. However, as history is rarely made to order, the successive unhappy and wretched scenarios that have been befalling the country and its citizenry have taken most Eritreans, including a substantial proportion of the former combatants, into disbelief. This is not because the leader of the liberation struggle, the EPLF and its successor, the PFDJ, Isaias Afwerki and his inner circle, have betrayed the democratic agenda. Although their betrayal of the democratic agenda is subject to no controversy, except in one or two opportunistic moments, the head of state has never promised the Eritrean people a government whose politics would be governed by a constitution and the rule of law. Since the early 1970s, i.e. after he became the chairman of the secret party, the Eritrean People's Revolutionary Party (EPRP; see Connell 2004), he made it crystal clear by his deeds, if not words, that whatever political decision he took on behalf of the secret party, the Front and, after he became head of state, the country, required no consultation or tolerated opposition. This has been his guiding principle throughout his political career and herein lies one of the most important constraints on democratization.

In theory, the EPLF as a front was an amalgamation of different classes, groups and individuals with different interests and aspirations. This heterogeneity notwithstanding, however, the Front operated as a monolith where the rules and procedures were constructed, deconstructed and enforced arbitrarily without recourse to the principle of rule of law or constitutional limitation by the chairman of the secret party and the Secretary-General of the Front and later head of state, Isaias Afwerki. Rhetoric notwithstanding, the EPLF, later the PFDJ and the Eritrean government never exercised a collective leadership. From 1973 to the present, Isaias Afwerki has been running the EPLF/PFDJ and later the country in his capacity as a personal ruler exercising power without constraint with an iron fist (Kibreab 2008, 2009a).

Whoever stood/stands on the way or questioned his way was/is removed by different means. These removal mechanisms included *mdskal* (freezing), humiliation/demonization, torture and incarceration in the dungeons of the notorious Halewa Sowra (guardians of the revolution) during the war of independence and in unknown places, including hundreds of underground cells, shipping containers and prisons in the post-independence period. Many of the 'non-compliant' were physically eliminated during the war of independence (see Markakis 1990; Pool 2001; Kibreab 2008). These brutal mechanisms of suppressing dissent have become institutionalized and normalized over time. The corollary of all this is that an environment permeated by such idiosyncrasies is hostile to democratization.

Militarization of education, and youth exodus

Not only are the absolute dearth of human rights and rule of law reflected in the arbitrary and indefinite detention without trial of thousands of innocent citizens, but also the adult population between the ages of seventeen and seventy are subjected directly or indirectly to endless servitude in the national service and people's militia. The Proclamation of the National Service was among the first acts the Provisional Government of Eritrea enacted, requiring citizens with some exceptions and exemptions to undertake eighteen months of national service – i.e. six months military training at the Sawa military camp in western Eritrea and twelve months participation in post-conflict (re)-construction and nation building. Given the devastation the country and the society suffered during the thirty-year war, with the exception of few, most Eritreans happily embraced the programme. Military training was introduced for the first time in mid-1994.

Before the border war broke out between Eritrea and Ethiopia in May 1998, the government observed the limitation of the duration and consequently demobilized the first four cohorts accordingly. However, after the border war, the government used the pretext of the threat of another war to keep those who joined before and after in arms indefinitely. It also adopted a new policy known as the Warsai-Yikealo Development Campaign (WYDC) to turn the Eritrean national service into indefinite open-ended obligation, and consequently it has degenerated into forced labour or a modern form of slavery (see Kibreab 2009b, 2017; HRW 2009, 2014).

The situation has not been helped by the Ethiopian Government reneging on its declared commitment to border demarcation made in the presence of Witnesses to the Algiers Agreement of 12 December 2000, namely, Algeria, the African Union, the European Union, the United States and the United Nations (see Council of the European Union 2006). The Ethiopian Government's defiance of the terms and conditions of the Algiers Agreement and its defiance of the supposedly final and binding decision of the Eritrea-Ethiopia Border Commission (EEBC) has given the government in Asmara a pretext to hold democracy and human rights at bay. Democratization is impossible and unthinkable when the whole adult population is in arms and under unforgiving military discipline permeated by a gruesome punishment regime (see Freedom House 2015; Amnesty International 2015).

The counterfactual is not amenable to empirical scrutiny and therefore it is important to guard against the unwarranted assumption that had the Ethiopian Government accepted the decision of the EEBC and consequently the borders between the two countries were demarcated accordingly, the process of democratization would have been unleashed and democracy would have flourished in the country. Undeniably, Ethiopia's compliance with the EEBC's decision and the consequent demarcation of the borders between the two countries would have promoted the cause of peace, security, trade and commerce, as well as development in both countries and in the region. In the short term, the impact of the stalemate on democratization is less obvious. What is clearly certain, however, is the fact that the state of 'no peace, no war' provided the Eritrean President and his small inner circle with the golden opportunity to securitize every aspect of Eritrean society, including democracy. The government argues that democracy is a luxury that a state and people who face existential threat cannot afford to indulge in. Nevertheless, the peace accord signed between the Eritrean head of state, Isaias Afwerki and Ethiopia's Prime Minister, Dr Abiy Ahmed, has caused the explosion of the alleged threat of war in the former's face. In spite of the elimination of the threat to Eritrea's national security the Eritrean head of state has refused to budge from his intransigent stance – business as usual.

As seen in the first part of the chapter, the education system has an important role to play in the development of the core values that underpin the process of democratization and consolidation of democracy. Education also broadens learners' world outlook and develops their critical faculties, which are vital to the development of rational, analytical and problem-solving skills. They are critical to the growth and development of learners' ability to scrutinize and question the policies and practices of governments and political parties. These values are enhanced in educational systems that recognize learners', parents', teachers' and other stakeholders' rights, so that they are able to influence the decisions that affect them. Participation and freedom of expression are important for the development and consolidation of democratic values, which are necessary conditions for the realization of other rights. This implies that education is the cause and effect of democracy.

It is important to note, however, that these expected outcomes are not necessarily intrinsic in all educational systems. Only an educational system that contributes to the development of learners' independence, self-esteem, and values such as freedom, inclusion, equality, equity, tolerance, compromise, non-discrimination and respect for human dignity, trust and deference to the principle of rule of law promotes democratization and democracy. Over time, these core values enable learners to realize the importance of holding governments accountable for their actions and inactions. As we saw earlier, many analysts have confirmed John Dewey's ground-breaking observation that democratic culture is a function of high-level education. The findings of Ayşe Demirbolat (2018), for example, show that 'well educated citizens and an economic system supporting participation are needed for a developed political democracy'.

How about the educational system in Eritrea? Does it promote democracy by engendering the core values that make democracy work and prevail? During the independence war, tens of thousands of students and schoolteachers joined the liberation movements, while many others fled the country in search of international protection. The system also suffered from lack of investment in infrastructure and skill development of schoolteachers and learning materials. Most school buildings were dilapidated. When independence was achieved, most Eritreans hoped that the post-independence government would prioritize education and adopt a rights-based policy promoting learners' autonomy, critical thinking, evaluative capability, freedom, equality and respect for the rights of others. There was also an expectation that independence would stem the flow of asylum seekers and encourage the return of those who fled during the liberation struggle. Contrary to this expectation, Eritrea has become one of the major refugee-producing countries in the world (Kibreab 2009a, 2013).

As seen earlier, contrary to these expectations, soon after their ascendance to power, the incumbents in the post-independence government introduced a policy that required all citizens between the ages of eighteen and forty years to perform eighteen months of national service. Initially, the majority of the Eritrean people embraced the national service, but after it became open-ended and the severe punishment regime became unbearable, *inter alia*, due to non-compliance, tens of thousands fled the country to Ethiopia and Sudan en route to

Western Europe and Israel where many of them faced death in the Mediterranean Sea attempting to cross into the EU countries in boats that were not seaworthy. Many also died in the Sinai desert at the hands of merciless traffickers, avaricious smugglers and corrupt police and security officers in the neighbouring countries and in Libya and Egypt. Ironically, Eritrea has become one of the major refugee producers in the world.

To minimize the risk of desertion of large numbers of students, the government extended the duration of secondary school education by one year and transferred all year 12 students to Sawa military camp in 2003 to perform national service in combination with rigorous military training and education under strict military discipline (see Kibreab 2009b, 2013; HRW 2009). At Sawa, students are subjected to rigorous indoctrination and political socialization in order to instil them with the values of the revolution – patriotism, sacrificial nationalism, dedication, commitment to public causes, relinquishment of self-interest and obedience to authority without questions asked. These values are the exact opposite of the values that promote citizenship and democracy based on critical, evaluative and questioning ability, rather uncritically embracing what is on offer.

In 2006, the government went further, closing down the only university in the country and transferring all university students to militarized colleges scattered in different parts of the country. The students were regimented in companies, units, platoons, battalions and divisions headed by military commanders both at the Sawa military camp and the militarized colleges. Throughout the country they were subject to military discipline, including severe punishment regimes. The transfer of final year secondary school students to the Sawa military camp, closure of the only university in the country and establishment of militarized colleges run by the military marked the total militarization of the educational system in the country. As if this was not enough, the government has also recently closed down the Halhale College of Business and Economics. The site was turned into a dairy farming institution without warning or consultation.

Not only did the high level of militarization stifle the potential development of democratic values that would have been instrumental in the future democratization process, but its detrimental impact on the social fabric of the society also caused the exodus of hundreds of thousands of the motive force of the democratization process: the youth. The United Nations estimates that, excluding those who have been perishing in the Sinai and Sahara deserts, the Mediterranean Sea and elsewhere, about 400,000 Eritreans representing about 9 per cent of the whole population have fled in recent years. Eritreans 'accounted for a majority of the 3,000 people who have drowned in the Mediterranean [in 2015]' (Stevis and Parkinson 2015). According to UNHCR, during October 2014 more than 5,000 Eritreans were said to have crossed into Ethiopia, more than doubling the figures of the preceding months of that year. The haemorrhage continues unabated. The fact that the single most important driver of these displacements is the open-ended national service, which has degenerated into forced labour or modern form of slavery (see Kibreab 2009b) is evidenced by the fact that '[a]bout 90 per cent of those who arrived [in EU countries] in October [2014] are between 18–24 years old' (UNHCR 2014).

The militarization of education in the country has had serious implication on democratization. This is because military service and the values it engenders are irreconcilable with democratic citizenship. In national service, conscripts' fundamental rights are regularly violated or, in the best-case scenario, restricted. More importantly, military education's aim is to instil discipline, compliance, respect and unquestioning obedience to authority. Military education encourages subordination to authority, among other things, by breaking the willpower, autonomy and self-esteem of the servers concerned. Nothing can be more inimical to democracy and democratization.

Dearth of middle class
As we saw in the first part of the chapter, another determinant factor of democratization and democracy is an independent middle class embedded in a growing economy. The Eritrean economy is devoid of a middle class because the government's economic policy is inimical to private enterprise (see Kibreab 2009a, Chapters 5 & 6). The state and the ruling party, using unpaid labour of conscripts, dominate the little economic activities there are in the country. Because of the government's hostility to private enterprise and foreign investment, the level of economic activity is very low and so is the rate of economic growth. Since 2011, there has been growth in the mining industry, but extractive industries do not promote democratization because they are dominated by the state rather than by domestic private enterprise. This is particularly the case in Eritrea.

In any post-war economy, the most vibrant sub-sector is construction. Under favourable conditions, a vibrant middle class can emerge and consolidate and over time play a vital role in the process of democratization and consolidation of democracy. In Eritrea, the private sector is banned from participating in construction. In April 2006, the government adopted a policy that required all contractors, civil engineers, architects, surveyors, decorators, etc. to return their licenses and to close down their business activities without prior warning (Kibreab 2009a). Most of the ongoing projects were abandoned and have become derelict. Nearly all of the professionals who were deprived of their livelihoods fled the country and some of them are working in South Sudan, Uganda, the Gulf States and elsewhere. The rest are scattered throughout the world, including in the US and Western Europe. Therefore, the government has deliberately targeted and stifled the emergence and development of one of the vital drivers of democratization, the middle class. The middle class has become stillborn. The hostility of the Eritrean government to private enterprise can be demonstrated by the fact that Eritrea is the worst country, save South Sudan, to do business. In 2014, its rank was 184 out of 189 countries (see World Bank 2013). The absence of the middle class is therefore one of the major constraints on democratization in the country.

The question of heterogeneity and democratization
Eritrea in spite of its small size in terms of geography and population is home to nine ethno-linguistic groups and two major religions. This diversity has never stopped Eritreans from cooperating with each other and setting aside their differences in pursuit of their common interest. Without the ability to work together, setting their religious and ethnic differences aside, the Eritrean people would have been unable to wage the thirty-year war of national liberation successfully against sub-Saharan Africa's largest army (see Welch 1991). During the liberation struggle, at least in the EPLF, invoking religion and ethnicity or asking and speaking about one's or someone else's religion and ethnicity was considered a taboo.

This was to a large extent helped by the fact that all the ethno-linguistic groups were facing a stronger external enemy, which necessitated the relegation to the background the differences that permeated the society at large. What was introduced, or one may even say imposed, initially to defeat an external enemy over time, became a habit and substantially weakened sub-national and religious identities and contributed to the construction of a common Eritrean national identity. Under an auspicious system of government, this prized social capital would have provided lifeblood to a democratization process in post-liberation Eritrea. Unfortunately, the post-independence government has not built on this scarce social resource, instead it has squandered a rare opportunity due to its failure to establish democracy based on inclusion.

Civil society and democratization
The incumbents are excessively preoccupied with the exercise of political and economic power without any constraint. They are inimical to any kind of autonomous CSOs and NGOs. The government has made the country so hostile to civil society NGOs that they have substantially undermined the pre-existing social institutions and stifled the emergence of new ones. The government adopted a blatantly inimical policy in 1997 and kicked out all international NGOs and withdrew the licenses of the handful of national NGOs (Kibreab 2009a; see also HOA Political Scene n.d.; Danto 2015; U.S. Department of State 1998).

In May 2005, the government issued its proclamation prohibiting all NGOs, both national and international, from receiving funding for relief, including rehabilitation activities from any United Nations organizations and their affiliates, as well as from other international organizations and through bilateral agreement (Government of Eritrea 2005: arts. 8(5), 9(3); see also International Center for Not-for-Profit Law 2006: 76, 80). The prohibition applies to all NGOs without exception. The minimum budgetary requirement for NGOs to operate in the country is that they have to have 'at their disposal in Eritrea one million US Dollars or its equivalent in other convertible currency' (Government of Eritrea 2005: art. 8(1)(c)). After the draconian proclamation was issued, CIVICUS (2005), an international organization that worked in Eritrea at the time insightfully stated: 'if the new proclamation results in the closing down of the few independent local NGOs and the departure of the few remaining international NGOs, there will be no independent civil society left'. According to the UN, between May 2005 and March 2006, the number of NGOs operating in the country declined from 37 to 13 (Kibreab 2009a; UNOCHA 2006). In 2006 and 2007, there were only 11 NGOs registered in the country (Kibreab 2009a).

The post-independence government has also suppressed the religious freedom of the minority churches, such as the Jehovah's Witnesses, Pentecostal Christians, Baha'is and the Medhanie Alem Orthodox Church. The National Union of Eritrean Women (NUEW), National Union of Eritrean Youth and Students (NUEYS) and the National Confederation of Eritrean Workers (NCEW), which wrongly refer to themselves as NGOs, are affiliated to the government and the ruling party, the PFDJ, and therefore cannot be considered NGOs or CSOs. Therefore the dearth of such organizations is another factor that represents a major constraint on democratization in the country.

What is to be done?

How can the impasse to democratization be overcome in the country? Inasmuch as the process of democratization is meandering, complex, multi-faceted and protracted, there is no simple answer to this challenging question. As we saw in the first part of the chapter, democratization and democracy are the function of inextricably interwoven composite factors, which reinforce and counteract each other depending on varieties of structural, institutional and motivational factors. Post-independence Eritrea had all the requisites for the democratization process to unfold and over time pave the way for democratic governance. This potential process was nipped in the bud politically, not in terms of eliminating the factors that were readily available to buttress democracy, but in terms of preventing the complex and protracted scenario of democratization from unfolding. Hence what is suppressed politically by design can only be resuscitated through political means.

In the immediate post-independence period, there was a short-lived semblance of a formal democratization process reflected, *inter alia*, in constitution making which involved top-down-engineered popular participation. In March 1994, the Provisional Government of Eritrea established a Constitutional Commission under the chairmanship of the well-renowned scholar on African law and government, Bereket Habte Selassie, to draft a new constitution. In May 1997, i.e. twenty-seven months after, a draft constitution was presented to the so-called National Assembly, i.e. a body comprising seventy-five members of the EPLF central council and seventy-five representatives elected by regional assemblies rather than by the Eritrean people. Although the draft constitution was ratified in May 1997, the president has since then refused to implement it and, as a result, the two promised elections have not taken place even though the election law was enacted in 2002.

Worse still, the so-called National Assembly has not met since 2002 because the president who is also its chairman refuses to convene such a meeting, and many of its members are in incommunicado detention without being charged while many others are in exile. The personal ruler, President Isaias Afwerki, has been ruling the country with an iron fist by exercising executive and legislative powers without any constraint. He also appoints and demotes judges arbitrarily. For example, when the eminent former Chief Justice, Teame Beyene, criticized the president's office for incessant interferences in the work of the judiciary (see Teame Beyene 2001), he was fired by the Minister of Justice, Weizero Sophia Hashim, at the behest of the president. This most able former Chief Justice has been unemployed since September 2001 and his attempt to obtain a license for private practice has not been approved by the government. A government that tolerates no dissent is anathema to democratization.

Democratization or formal democracy is inconceivable without: toleration; division of powers between the executive, legislative and judiciary; and the principle of *Habeas corpus* and rule of law – the former provides remedy against arbitrary detention without trial and the latter is the single most important principle that distinguishes a free country from a country ruled arbitrarily. F.A. Hayek observes on the rule of law:

> Stripped of all its technicalities this means that government in all its actions is bound by rules fixed and announced before hand – rules which make it possible to foresee with fair certainty how the authority will use its coercive powers in given circumstances, and plan one's individual affairs on the basis of this knowledge. (2003 [1944])

Eritrea is ruled by the arbitrary caprice of the president, unconstrained by the rule of law such that citizens are unable to determine the basis of their actions within the existing framework of law. Where the rule of law reigns, citizens are able to predict where the red line lies. This limits the powers of the government and enables citizens to predict what is expected of them.

Where there is no rule of law, there is neither human rights nor democratization. In Eritrea the other requisites for democratization, such as freedom of speech and expression and recognition of rights of citizens to fend for themselves and their families by selling their labour power in the labour market freely, are absent. This is partly because most of the able-bodied citizens are tied to the open-ended national service, and the firms of the ruling party and the public sector monopolize economic activities and assets in the country (Kibreab 2009a, 2009b, 2017). Without opportunities to escape poverty, no democratization is conceivable. The pillar of democratization, namely freedom of association, is also absent in the country.

Alternative approaches to democratization: in lieu of a conclusion

In Eritrea, as noted earlier, most of the requisites of a successful democratization process are either absent or are systematically eroded by the government to facilitate the smooth functioning of dictatorship with impunity. Even if we were to assume that the determinants of democratization existed in the country, it would still be naïve to think that the large majority of citizens would benefit from formal or procedural democracy, namely, free and fair elections, institutions such as independent judiciary, separation of powers of the executive, legislative and judiciary, as well as vibrant civil society, freedom of expression, association and access to alternative sources of information. These institutions are *sine qua non* for the institutionalization and consolidation of formal or procedural democracy.

Given the fact that Eritrean society is predominantly rural, it is imperative to ask the extent to which these institutions are likely to promote democratization. According to the World Bank, 65 per cent of Eritrea's population lives in the rural areas where 80 per cent depend on subsistence farming for their livelihoods (World Bank 2015). The level of illiteracy is unacceptably high. The overwhelming majority of the population has no access to transistor radio, television or newspapers. Even for those who are able to read and write, there are no alternative sources of information as the government has absolute monopoly over both print and broadcast media geared towards disinformation and brainwashing rather than providing objective and balanced information to encourage debate and influence public decisions. Eritrea is also devoid of a middle class. Many theorists and analysts consider the latter as the engine of democratization. Notwithstanding the flawed assumption of the EPLF and later the government, Eritrea is bereft of classes. The (Ethiopian) *Derg* nipped the process of differentiation and hence class formation in the bud in the urban areas in the mid-1970s. Life in rural Eritrea, where smallholding and pastoralism are dominant, is permeated by relative equality where poverty is widespread and most people live on a knife-edge, permanently worried about making ends meet in adverse circumstances.

The specificity and adversity of the circumstances that characterize people's lives and living conditions make it also almost impossible for their interests to be represented by individuals, be it in the executive, legislative or judiciary, who do not share their life experiences and perspectives. The realities of people living in cities, separated from the means of production and dependent for their survival on the sales of their labour power in the service of the government, and to a lesser extent manufacturing sectors, are fundamentally different from those who live in rural areas and derive their livelihoods directly from environmental resources. For the latter segment of the Eritrean polity, representative democracy where the representatives are most likely to be urban dwellers whose perspectives, aspirations and lived experiences are fundamentally different is inconsequential.

If procedural democracy is inconsequential in rural Eritrea, what is the alternative? Given the fact that rural Eritrea, especially the communities in the Plateau and to a lesser extent in parts of the lowlands, had a sophisticated culture of substantive or direct democracy based on participation of all male members of the communities concerned in debates and decisions that directly or indirectly affected their lives on the basis of equality without any distinction, any democratization process that is not anchored in this rich tradition regulated by detailed provisions of customary laws (see Pollera 1996; Russell 1959; Kemink 1991; Nadel 1945, 1946; Habte Selassie 2003; Favali and Pateman 2003; Campbell 2005) is a foreign import oblivious to traditional Eritrean institutions and hence is doomed to fail or at least is unlikely to succeed in the short and medium terms.

The EPLF as a super modernist organization was from the outset hostile to Eritrean customary laws, practices and traditions. From their perspective, anything based on customary practice and tradition was perceived to represent backwardness, which should be eliminated or transformed. That was the reason the EPLF systematically undermined the long-standing customary laws and the single most important mechanism of enforcement, the *baito* (the village assembly) where all male adult members convened to participate in all decisions that affected their lives directly or indirectly. Although the EPLF and later the government formally usurped the institution of the *baito*, they hollowed it of its democratic values and inhabited it by hand-picked loyalists who lacked the legitimacy derived from traditional authority.

From the time the EPLF operated in the liberated areas in the mid-1970s, its sole preoccupation was to control the communities by imposing its own rules at the expense of pre-existing traditional arrangements and customary laws. As a modernist political organ-ization excessively preoccupied with control of every aspect of the society in the areas they operated, the EPLF looked at Eritrean tradi-tions and the customary laws with some degree of disdain, which had to be undermined rather than preserved and promoted. Excessively concerned with the need to exercise unfettered control over the society, the post-liberation government deliberately ignored the connection with the past. In the EPLF leaders' conception, a return to local institu-tions was perceived to be regressive. Recognition of the country's rich indigenous institutions would have provided an opportunity for the rural inhabitants to practice decentralized substantive democracy.

Bibliography

Abbink, J. and Hagmann, T. 2013, *Reconfiguring Ethiopia: The Politics of Authoritarian Reform*. London and New York: Routledge.

Acemoglu, D., Johnson, S., Robison, J. and Yared, P. 2005, 'From Educa-tion to Democracy'. *The American Economic Review* 95(2): 44–9.

Aelen, L. and Tronvall, K. 2008, 'The 2008 Ethiopian Local Elections: A Return to Electoral Authoritarianism'. *African Affairs* 108(430): 111–20.

Aelen, L., Pausewang, S. and Tronvoll, K. 2002, *Ethiopia Since the Derg: A Decade of Democratic Pretension and Performance*. London: Zed Books.

Amare, E. and Seyoum, M. 2003, 'Kalemeteyik ms President Isaias Afwerki', Shaebia Interview. *Barentu* Special Issue (23 January).

Amnesty International. 2006, 'Amnesty International Report 2006 – Eritrea', 23 May, www.refworld.org/docid/447ff7a62.html, accessed 20 October 2019.

—— 2015, 'Just Deserters: Why Indefinite National Service in Eritrea has Created a Generation of Refugees', December, www.amnesty. org/download/Documents/AFR6429302015ENGLISH.PDF, accessed 25 July 2017.

—— 2016, 'Eritrea 2015/2016', https://freedomhouse.org/report/ freedom-press/freedom-press-2016, accessed 20 August 2017.

Aristotle. 1984 [fourth century BCE], *The Politics*, Book 1, The City and the Household. *The Complete Works of Aristotle*, Vol. 2, Revised Oxford Translation, Jonathan Barnes (ed.), Princeton NJ: Princeton University Press, 1984.

Balázs, J. 1985, 'A Note on the Interpretation of Security'. *Development and Peace* (6): 143–50.

Barro, Robert J. 1999, 'Determinants of Democracy'. *Journal of Political Economy* 107(S6): 158–83.

BBC News. 2013, 'Eritrea: "10,000 Political Prisoners in Awful Conditions"', 9 May, www.bbc.co.uk/news/world-africa-22460836, accessed June 2016.

Boutros-Ghali, B. 1996, *An Agenda for Democratization*, New York: United Nations.

Bovard, J. 1994 [1956], *Lost Rights: The Destruction of American Liberty*. New York: St Martin's Press.

Bǔhlmann, M., Merkel, W. and Wessels, B. in collaboration with Lisa Mǔller. 2007, 'The Quality of Democracy: Democracy Barometer for Established Democracies', Challenges to Democracy in the 21st Century, Working Paper 10. National Centres of Competence in Research Democracy (NCCR-D), University of Zurich Social Science Research Centre, Berlin.

Campbell, D. F. J. 2008, 'The Basic Concept for the Democracy Ranking of the Quality of Democracy'. Democracy Ranking,Vienna.

Campbell, P. J. 2005, 'Gender and Post-Conflict Civil Society: Eritrea'. *International Feminist Journal of Politics* 7(3): 377–99.

CIVICUS. 2005, 'New NGO Law Threatens the Existence of Civil Society in Eritrea', 26 August, www.civicus.org/new/content/ERITREAN-GOlaw.htm, accessed 13 January 2016.

Clapham, C. 1998 'Introduction: Analysing African Insurgencies', in C. Clapham (ed.), *African Guerrillas*. Oxford: James Currey, 1–18.

Connell, D. 2004, *Conversation with Political Prisoners*. Trenton, NJ: Red Sea Press.

Council of the European Union. 2006, 'Ethiopia-Eritrea: Statement by the Witnesses to the Algiers Agreement', 22 February, New York, www.consilium.europa.eu/uedocs/cms_data/docs/pressdata/en/er/88497.pdf, accessed 20 July 2014.

Dahl, R. 1971, *Poliarchy, Participation and Opposition*. New Haven, CT: Yale University Press.

—— 1998, *On Democracy*. New Haven, CT: Yale University Press.

Danto, E. 2015, 'U.S. NGOs Kicked Out of Eritrea: Foreign Aid Is Meant To Cripple People', 5 April, www.globalresearch.ca/u-s-ngos-kicked-out-of-eritrea-foreign-aid-is-meant-to-cripple-people/5441367, accessed 25 August 2017.

de Tocqueville, A. 2004 [1835, 1840], *Democracy in America*, a new translation by Arthur Goldhammer. New York: Library of America.

Debs, A. and Morrison, K. M. 2015, 'Income, Middle Class and Democracy', 26 May, www.pitt.edu/~kmm229/DebsMorrison(2015).pdf, accessed 15 October 2016.

Demirbolat, A. O. 2018, The Relationship Between Democracy and Education. Sharjah, UAE: Bentham Science Publishers, http://

ebooks.benthamscience.com/book/9781608053711,   accessed   13 January 2019.

Dewey, J. 1997 [1916], *Democracy and Education*. New York: The Free Press; Simon & Schuster.

Diamond, L. 1997, 'Civil Society and the Development of Democracy'. Estudio/Working Paper 1997/101, June. Seminars: 'Developing Democracy: Toward Consolidation', Center for Advanced Study in the Social Sciences of the Juan March Institute, Madrid, November 1996.

Favali, I. and Pateman, R. 1991, *Blood, Land and Sex: Legal and Political Pluralism in Eritrea*. Bloomington, IN: Indiana University Press.

Fish, M. S. and Brooks, R. S. 2004, 'Does Diversity Hurt Democracy?' *Journal of Democracy* 15(1): 154–66.

Freedom House. 2015, 'Eritrea' report. Washington, DC, https://free-domhouse.org/report/freedom-world/2015/eritrea, accessed 17 May 2017.

—— 2016, 'Freedom of the Press 2016: Sub-Saharan Africa'. Washing-ton, DC, https://freedomhouse.org/report/freedom-press/freedom-press-2016, accessed 17 May 2017.

—— 2018, 'Freedom in the World 2018'. Washington, DC, https://freedomhouse.org/report/freedom-world/2018/eritrea accessed 10 February 2018.

Friedrich, C. J. 1963, *Man and His Government*. New York: McGraw-Hill.

Gerring, J., Hoffman, M. and Zarecki, D. 2016, 'The Diverse Effects of Diversity on Democracy'. *British Journal of Political Science* 48(2): 1–32,

Global Witness. 1998, 'A Rough Trade: The Role of Companies and Government in the Angolan Conflict'. Global Witness, London, https://site-media.globalwitness.org/archive/files/pdfs/a_rough_trade.pdf, accessed 8 January 2018.

Government of Eritrea. 2005, 'A Proclamation to Determine the Administration of Non-Governmental Organizations', 145/2005, 11 May,   www.ilo.org/dyn/natlex/docs/ELECTRONIC/81435/88425/ F975805266/ERI81435.pdf, accessed 23 September 2019.

Habte Selassie, B. (2003). *The Making of the Eritrean Constitution: The Dialectic of the Process and Substance*. Trenton, NJ: Red Sea Press.

Hayek, F. A. 2003 [1944], *The Road to Serfdom*. London and New York: Routledge.

HOA Political Scene. n.d., 'Eritrea and NGOs ... No is Just No and there Might Be No Grounds!' www.hoa-politicalscene.com/eritrea-and-ngos.html, accessed 20 November 2017.

Horowitz, D. L. 1985, *Ethnic Groups in Conflict*. Berkeley: University of California Press.

HRW (Human Rights Watch). 2009, 'Service for Life: State Repres-sion and Indefinite Conscription in Eritrea', www.hrw.org/

report/2009/04/16/service-life/state-repression-and-indefinite-conscription-eritrea, accessed 20 November 2017.

—— 2014, 'World Report 2014: Eritrea Events 2013', www.hrw.org/world-report/2014/country-chapters/eritrea, accessed 20 November 2017.

—— 2015, 'World Report 2015: Eritrea Events 2014', www.hrw.org/world-report/2015/country-chapters/eritrea, accessed 20 November 2017.

—— 2016, 'World Report 2016: Eritrea Events 2015', www.hrw.org/world-report/2016/country-chapters/eritrea, accessed 13 July 2017.

International Center for Not-for-Profit Law. 2006, 'Recent Laws and Legislative Proposals to Restrict Civil Society and Civil Society Organizations'. *International Journal of Not-for-Profit Law* 8(4), www.icnl.org/research/journal/vol8iss4/art_1.htm, accessed 23 September 2019.

Ishkanian, A. 2007, 'Democracy Promotion and Civil Society', in M. Albrow, M. Glasius, H. Anheier and M. Kaldor (eds), *Global Civil Society 2007/8*. London: SAGE.

Kemink, F. 1991, 'The Tegreñña Customary Law Codes'. *Paideuma: Mitteilungen zur Kulturkunde* 37: 55–72.

Kibreab, G. 2000, 'Resistance, Displacement, and Identity: The Case of Eritrean Refugees in Sudan'. *Canadian Journal of African Studies / Revue Canadienne des Études Africaines*. 34(2): 249–96.

—— 2008, *Critical Reflections on the Eritrean War of Independence: Social Capital, Associational Life, Religion, Ethnicity, and Sowing Seeds of Dictatorship*. Trenton, NJ: Africa World Press.

—— 2009, *Eritrea: A Dream Deferred*. Oxford: James Currey; Uppsala: Nordic African Institute.

—— 2013, 'The National Service / Warsai-Yikealo Development Campaign and Forced Migration in Post-independence Eritrea'. *Journal of Eastern African Studies* 7(4): 630–49.

—— 2017, *Servitude for Our 'Common Good': The Eritrean National Service and Youth Exodus*. Woodbridge: James Currey.

Kittrie, N. 1995, *The War Against Authority:From the Crisis of Legitimacy to a New Social Contract*. Baltimore and London: Johns Hopkins University.

Kriger, N. J. 1992, *Zimbabwe's Guerrilla War: Peasant Voices*. Cambridge, UK: Cambridge University Press.

Lecours, A. and Moreno, L. 2010, *Nationalism and Democracy: Dichotomies, Complementarities, Oppositions*, Studies in Nationalism and Ethnicity. New York: Routledge.

Leys, C. and Saul, J. S. 1995, *Namibia's Liberation Struggle: The Two-Edged Sword*. London: James Currey; Athens, OH: Ohio University Press.

Lipset, S. M. 1959, 'Some Social Requisites of Democracy: Economic

Development and Political Legitimacy'. *American Political Science Review* 53(1): 69–105.

—— 1963, *Political Man: The Social Bases of Politics*. Garden City, NY: Doubleday/Anchor.

Mandel, M. 1994, *The Changing Face of National Security: A Conceptual Analysis*. London: Greenwood Press.

Markakis, J. 1990, *National and Class Conflict in the Horn of Africa*. London: Zed Books.

Melber, H. 2002, 'From Liberation Movements to Governments: On Political Culture in Southern Africa'. *African Sociological Review* 6(2): 161–72.

—— 2003a, 'Liberation and Democracy: Cases from Southern Africa', *Journal of Contemporary African Studies* 21(2): 149–53.

—— 2003b, 'From Controlled Change to Changed Control: The Case of Namibia', *Journal of Contemporary African Studies* 21(2): 267–84.

—— 2004, 'Inside the "Third Chimurenga": Media Repression, Manipulation and Hegemony in Zimbabwe – Some Introductory Notes', in Melber, H. (ed.), *Media, Public Discourse and Political Contestation in Zimbabwe*, Current African Issues 27. Uppsala: Nordic Africa Institute, 7–11.

—— 2006, '"Where There's No Fight for it There's No Freedom": On Scholars and Social Commitment in Southern Africa – Which Side Are We On?' *Journal of Contemporary African Studies* 24(2): 261–78.

Merkel, W. and Weiffen, B. 2012, 'Does Heterogeneity Hinder Democracy?' *Comparative Sociology* 11: 387–421.

Mill, J. S. 1861, *Representative Government*, http://aecau.ro/userfiles/files/ebooks/518/RepresentativeGovernment.pdf, accessed 25 January 2018.

Moore, B. 1966, *Social Origins of Dictatorship and Democracy: Lord and Peasant in the Making of the Modern World*. Boston, MA: Beacon Press.

Mosca, G. 1939, *The Ruling Class (Elementi di Scienza Politica)*, trans. Hannah D. Kahn. New York and London: McGraw-Hill.

Moyo, D. 2004, 'From Rhodesia to Zimbabwe: Change without Change? Broadcasting Policy Reform and Political Control', in H. Melber (ed.), *Media, Public Discourse and Political Contestation in Zimbabwe*, Current African Issues 27. Uppsala: Nordic Africa Institute, 12–28.

Nadel, N. F. 1945, 'Notes on Beni Amer Society'. *Sudan Notes and Records* 36: 51–94.

—— 1946, 'Land Tenure on the Eritrean Plateau'. *Africa* 16(1): 1–21.

Özbudun, E. 2005, 'The Role of the Middle Class in the Emergence and Consolidation of a Democratic Civil Society'. *Ankara Law Review*, 2(2): 95–107.

Palmer, P. 2011, 'Parker J. Palmer's Five Habits of the Heart', adapted from Parker J. Palmer, *Healing the Heart of Democracy: The Courage to Create a Politics Worthy of the Human Spirit*. Centre for Courage and

Renewal, Seattle, WA, www.couragerenewal.org/habitsoftheheart, accessed 20 March 2018.

Perez-Diaz, V. 1993, *The Return of Civil Society*. Cambridge, MA: Harvard University Press.

Pollera, A. 1996 [1935], *The Native Peoples of Eritrea* (*Le popolazioni indigene dell'Eritrea*), trans. Linda Lappin. Bologna: Capelli / University of Asmara.

Pool, D. 2001, *From Guerrillas to Government: The Eritrean People's Liberation Front*. Athens, OH: Ohio University Press.

Prunier, G. 1998, *The Rwanda Crisis: History of a Genocide*. New York: Columbia University Press.

Putnam, R. 1993, *Making Democracy Work: Civic Traditions in Modern Italy*. Princeton NJ: Princeton University Press.

—— 2000, *Bowling Alone: The Collapse and Revival of American Community*. New York: Touchstone Books / Simon & Schuster.

Ranger, T. 2004, 'Nationalist Historiography, Patriotic History and the History of the Nation: The Struggle Over the Past in Zimbabwe'. *Journal of Southern African Studies* 30(2).

Ranger, T. and Vaughan, O. (eds). 1993, *Legitimacy and the State in Twentieth-Century Africa: Essays in Honour of A. H. M. Kirk-Greene*. London: Macmillan.

Reporters Without Borders. 2018, '2018 World Press Freedom Index'. Paris, https://rsf.org/en/ranking/2018, accessed 12 February 2019.

Reyntjens, F. 2007, 'Post-1994 Politics in Rwanda: Problematising "Liberation" and "Democratisation"'. *Third World Quarterly* 27(6): 1103–17.

Russell, F. F. 1959, 'Eritrean Customary Law'. *Journal of African Law* 3(2): 99–104.

Schumpeter, J. 1976 [1943], *Capitalism, Socialism and Democracy*. New York: Harper Perennial.

Serge, V. 2012 [1951], *Memoirs of a Revolutionary*. New York Review Books Classics.

Sodaro, M. J. and Collinwood, D. W. 2004, *Comparative Politics: A Global Introduction*. McGraw-Hill.

Staines, P. 1989, *In the Grip of the Sandinistas: Human Rights in Nicaragua, 1979–1998*. London: International Society for Human Rights.

Stevis, M. and Parkinson, J. 2015, African Dictatorship Fuels Migrant Crisis: Thousands Flee Isolated Eritrea to Escape Life of Conscription and Poverty. *The Wall Street Journal*, November, www.wsj.com/articles/eritreans-flee-conscription-and-poverty-adding-to-the-migrant-crisis-in-europe-1445391364, accessed 12 February 2019.

Teame Beyene. 2001, 'The Eritrean Judiciary: Struggling for Independence. A Paper Submitted to the International Conference on Eritrea on the 10th Anniversary of Eritrea's Independence, May, Asmara, Eritrea'. *Eritrean Law Society Occasional Papers*, 7 November.

UNHCR. 2014, 'Sharp Increase in Number of Eritrean Refugees and Asylum-Seekers in Europe, Ethiopia and Sudan', 14 November, www.unhcr.org/news/briefing/2014/11/5465fea1381/sharp-increas e-number-eritrean-refugees-asylum-seekers-europe-ethiopia.html, accessed January 2015.

UNOCHA (UN Office for the Coordination of Humanitarian Affairs). 2006, 'Eritrea: Authorities Expel Three Foreign NGOs', 23 March, www.irinnews.org/report.aspx?reportid=58532, accessed 25 May 2016.

U.S. Department of State. 1998, 'Eritrea Country Report on Human Rights Practices for 1997', Bureau of Democracy, Human Rights, and Labor, 30 January, Washington, DC, https://1997-2001.state.gov/ global/human_rights/1997_hrp_report/eritrea.html, accessed 12 February 2016.

Waever, O. 1993, 'Securitization and Desecuritization', Working Paper 5. Centre for Peace and Conflict Research, Copenhagen.

Welch, C. E. 1991. 'The Military and Social Integration in Ethiopia', in H. Dietz, J. Elkin and M. Roumani, *Ethnicity, Integration, and the Military*. Boulder, CO: Westview Press: 151–78.

Wheatley 2003, 'Deliberative Democracy and Minorities'. *European Journal of International Law* 14(93): 1–21.

Whitehead, L. 2002, *Democratisation Theory and Practice*. Oxford: Oxford University Press.

World Bank. 2013, *Doing Business 2014: Understanding Regulations for Small and Medium-Size Enterprises*. Washington, DC: World Bank Group.

—— 2015, 'The World Bank in Eritrea: Overview', 22 September, Washington, DC, www.worldbank.org/en/country/eritrea/overview, accessed 16 September 2016.

3

Prospects for Democracy
in Africa's Newest Country, South Sudan

LEBEN NELSON MORO & KUYANG HARRIET LOGO

Introduction

This chapter argues that democracy has not taken root in the ruling
Sudan People's Liberation Movement (SPLM), and in the whole of South
Sudan, because the liberators or former rebel leaders, who now rule the
new country, do not have an interest in embracing it as their continued
hold on power could be threatened. Like leaders of the now defunct
Sudan or former Sudan, the liberators or former rebel leaders have often
preached democracy but in practice are determined to claim or cling to
power through undemocratic means, a legacy of the long years of armed
struggle. The ideologies of liberation in Southern Sudan, which centred
on strong men with guns, have nurtured leaders determined to hold on
to power after the end of the war in 2005 and the subsequent emergence
of the state of South Sudan (Lyman 2015).

Southern Sudan's political causes and grievances were championed
by SPLM for over two decades of armed struggle. The 2005 Comprehensive Peace Agreement (CPA) eventually provided a political settlement, which included a promise for a democratic transformation of the
country. In reality, the CPA put power largely in the hands of former
rebel leaders or military strongmen, who later had no qualms about
resorting to violence to retain or gain power. Professor Mahmoud
Mamdani has observed, correctly, that the CPA's lamentable approach
to the array of armed groups in the future state of South Sudan was to
assume that only those with the capacity to wage war had the right to
determine the terms of the peace (Mamdani 2016). Quite clearly, the
legacies of the liberation struggle were perpetuated in the CPA, and
furthered the SPLM refusal to countenance internal reforms while
endorsing the power of the gun at the expense of reforms and democratic governance.

Ironically, the political reality that developed after the former rebel
leaders assumed power in South(ern) Sudan was different from that
which existed in the Southern region (1972–1982) – which was ruled

by popularly elected leaders, before the former Sudan reverted to war in 1983 – and from that promised by the former rebel leaders.

Although SPLM had emerged to resolve the problems of marginalization, discrimination and injustice of the former Sudan, the movement – epitomized by power structures in an armed liberation – failed to radically restructure and transition into a democratic organization.[1] It was no longer a national project for building a true and sustainable citizenship state capable of accommodating the multiple diversities of South Sudanese society. While the concept of a sustainable citizenship state was a desired outcome of the liberation struggle, the concept itself became an intellectual and scholarly contribution to the unfolding political discourse on rebuilding the South Sudanese state. Unlike the African National Congress in South Africa, which had a political wing to advocate for reforms and an end to apartheid, SPLM lacked such a formation and this explains the several bloody splits within it.

While undermining the very values for which it was founded, SPLM clung to the liberation struggle syndrome of self-rewards. While the post-independence legislative frameworks subscribe to the tenets of a democratic state, the party practices are in stark contradiction with the aspirations of a democratic state enshrined in the Transitional Constitution of South Sudan (TCSS – 2011). While the Constitution provides for the separation of powers, the concepts of electoral democracy and fundamental human rights for all, the SPLM reduced these values to mere words on paper.[2]

Decisions on a national census, constitution and elections began to revolve around support for or opposition to the president's rule and eventually stalled. SPLM dominance, and the conflation of party with state, meant that whoever commanded the former also controlled the latter. The then-approaching 2015 elections increased the urgency to make decisions and also increased the political divide (International Crisis Group 2014). The political crisis of the past and long-standing divisions in the Sudan People's Liberation Army (SPLA) became visible and, in the absence of strong institutions and protocols on power sharing and transfer, the SPLA became the largest important institution in South Sudan (*ibid.*).

The divisions within the Sudan People's Liberation Movement/Army (SPLM/A) are not devoid of ethnic loyalties; in fact, ethnicity was a sole tool to garner support in the 1991, 2013 and 2016 conflicts. The

---

[1] Access more information on SPLM ideology and policies from https://en.wikipedia.org/wiki/Sudan_People%27s_Liberation_Movement, accessed 25 Sep 2019.
[2] See, for more information, The Transitional Constitution of South Sudan (GSS 2011).

key leaders involved in these struggles turned to their ethnic groups for fighters, who targeted the members of the 'enemy' groups. In 1991, when three commanders attempted to oust Dr John Garang from the leadership of SPLM/A, Dinka civilians were targeted by Nuer fighters. Dr John Garang's fighters responded in kind against Nuer civilians. In December 2013, many Nuer people were targeted because of their ethnicity and by 2016, the entire nation has been embroiled in an ethnic conflict, with massacres of the Nuers, the Equatorians and the Fertit. In the same vein, all these groups have risen in self-defence, and innocent Dinka civilians have paid the price simply because of their ethnicity (*ibid.*).

The following section discusses the calls for democracy by rebel leaders during the years of the long armed struggle and how these significantly diverge from their actions. The third section discusses how the constitutions written after the end of the war concentrated power in the presidency, undermining the dreams for real democracy. The next, delves into the rampant corruption and how it consolidated power in few hands. The fifth section analyses the flawed Sudanese elections of 2010 and the political troubles that followed and is followed by a section concentrating on the disputes over reform of SPLM and the consequent split of the movement and return to violent conflict in 2013. The next section delves into the failure of peace-making and resumption of fighting in July 2016, leading to warnings of looming genocide. The penultimate section looks into the prospects of democracy in the wake of return to widespread violence and is followed by the Conclusion.

Southern Sudan's independence struggles and democracy

The Southern Sudanese people waged two deadly wars against regimes in Khartoum between 1955 and 2005. These wars were fought for as long as the Southern Sudanese demands for autonomy, development, democracy and recognition of their unique cultures were ignored by the Northern Sudanese political elite. Southern Sudanese demanded to be treated as equal citizens and not second class people in their own country, but ended being citizens of a new country partly because the Northern political elite made promises but routinely broke them (Alier 1990).

In the 1972 Addis Ababa Peace Agreement, the Northern elite, led by then-President Jaffar Nimeiri, granted the demand of the Southern Sudanese for autonomous rule in a united country. A regional government with an executive and legislature was established. As a result, peace prevailed in the country between 1972 and 1983, when the war resumed after Nimeiri reneged on the agreement.

The period of relative peace in Southern Sudan was unique in the way Southern Sudanese governed themselves. There was a vibrant democracy in the region at the time when the Northern region was governed by a single-party dictatorship, at whose helm was President Jaffar Nimeiri. Leaders of the autonomous Southern Sudan region were freely chosen by the people, and disputes were peacefully settled in the courts.[3] Even, a member of the tiny Madi tribe in Equatoria, Joseph Lagu, was elected the president of the region, defeating Abel Alier, a member of the dominant Dinka tribe.

The key institutions in the region did what was expected of them as the political elite empowered them. The regional assembly had power to hold to account all leaders, including the president of the region. Indeed, Joseph Lagu, a former leader of the *Anyanya* or the rebel group that waged the war from 1955 to 1972, was dragged before the assembly when he was president and nearly got impeached over accusations of corruption, later found to be false. The courts also performed adequately and people trusted them. Indeed, they settled election disputes, and so there was no reason for candidates who felt cheated to turn to the gun.

This period of peace and democracy in Southern Sudan was brought to an abrupt end with the resumption of war in 1983 after the Addis Ababa Agreement was abrogated, and Islamic law imposed on the whole county by President Jaffar Nimeiri (Zapata 2011). He abandoned the agreement so as to win support of Islamists and other opponents of the deal who posed a threat to his rule.

The Southern cause was picked up by SPLM/A in 1983 and waged a costly war against successive regimes in Khartoum. The founding leader of SPLM/A, Dr John Garang de Mabior, was not only a veteran military man, who took part in the first war, but also was an accomplished politician who championed effectively against the injustices Sudanese suffered at the hands of their leaders, including dictatorial rule. He promised a different kind of leadership if SPLM/A won the war.

The SPLM manifesto released in July 1983 set out the vision of the armed struggle. It stated that the armed struggle aimed to establish a 'united, democratic and secular New Sudan'. During the Second SPLM Convention in 2008, the leaders who took over after the demise of Dr John Garang in 2005 further articulated the SPLM vision. Among other things, the revised manifesto of 2008 stated:

> The transformation of Sudan envisaged by the SPLM, thus, represents a political and socioeconomic paradigm shift from hegemony in all its forms to the recognition of Sudan's political, cultural and social diversity, within a framework of a vibrant multi-party democracy with

---

[3] One of the authors, Leben Nelson Moro, participated in elections following the Addis Ababa Agreement.

a meaningful Bill of Rights that recognizes and upholds natural as well as political, socio-economic, cultural and environmental rights and obligations. That democracy shall also ensure peaceful transfer of power and separation of powers among the executive, judicial and legislative organs of the state. (SPLM 2008)

It was, however, clear that the rhetoric of democracy was an empty one. Dr John Garang, and subsequent leaders of SPLM, talked about democracy but did different things. Indeed, many people, including his subordinates, accused Dr John Garang of dictatorship and running the movement alone (Nyaba 1997). In 1991, three SPLM/A commanders tried to oust him from the leadership of the movement. Among the reasons they gave for their action was the dictatorial rule by Garang, who argued that democracy could not be practised in the midst of armed struggle but would be implemented when the war was won. The coup did not succeed. While the split weakened the SPLM, no lessons were picked from that occurrence, the movement instead became most restrictive on any talks of a democratic transition.

To shore up his support base, Garang organized the 1994 SPLM Convention which correctly addressed the issue of self-determination as a people's right, not contradicting the SPLM objective of a united democratic New Sudan, but on the contrary enhancing it. The ensuing debate during the Convention, therefore, reaffirmed the fact that the realization of the vision of the New Sudan, brought about either through a combination of armed struggle and urban popular uprisings or a politically negotiated settlement, was the key for the attainment of freedom, equality and justice for the South Sudanese people.

In the beginning of the 2000s, peace talks between the Sudanese government and SPLM picked up pace. In 2002, the Machakos protocol was signed, resolving disputes over the role of religion in politics. Shortly after, sharp differences emerged between Dr John Garang and his deputy, Salva Kiir Mayardit. In a rare meeting of the top commanders of SPLM/A in 2004 in Rumbek, Dr John Garang's leadership of the movement was roundly criticized by his colleagues. Kiir reportedly faulted Garang for running the movement alone. He told the meeting: 'The Chairman is everything, from a finance officer to one at the lowest level'.[4] Dr John Garang promised to deal with the grievances verbalized by his colleagues but he died a year later, after the CPA was signed. There was fear that a power struggle would emerge. It was felt that no person could represent the interests of the party in the manner that Dr John Garang did. While a possible power struggle was averted with the appointment of Salva Kiir as leader of SPLM/A, First Vice President of Sudan and President of the Southern Sudan region, the simmering tensions remained.

[4] Minutes of Meeting of SPLM/A commanders in Rumbek in 2004 (on file).

The CPA provisions spelled out ways of resolving outstanding problems of the Southerners – leading to the inclusion of the right to self-determination of the people of Southern Sudan, power sharing among all parties, regional autonomy for Southern Sudan, security arrangements, and human rights provisions including religious freedoms, constitutional review processes, wealth sharing and reconciliation. The agreement seemed to have finally addressed all the outstanding obstacles to stability and democracy. However, as the region got embroiled in many difficulties, this was not to be.

No doubt, the current predicaments facing South Sudan are linked to the way the CPA was negotiated and framed. Political parties other than the National Congress Party (NCP) and SPLM were denied participation in the peace process, and this fact alone became the tool used by the SPLM leaders to advance its own interests and not to work for a democratic state. These noteworthy developments meant that the leaders did not accept the principle that they were accountable to constituencies, as a democratic practice and beyond SPLM party interests (Young 2007). Due to the foregoing situation one commentator noted the following.

> Civil society influence on the Naivasha process that led to the CPA was ultimately very limited. Like the northern opposition political parties, civil society was marginalized, perceived by the government as backing SPLM/A positions on the main stumbling blocks in the negotiations: religion and the state, wealth redistribution, democratic transformation and accountability. Moreover, the other IGAD [Intergovernmental Authority on Development] countries shared similar views to Sudan on the roles and rights of civil society, whose engagement in briefings and informal sessions was only made possible after the wider international community became involved. Various civil society meetings and fora created for civil society actors, such as the series of meetings convened by Justice Africa in Kampala from 1999, were to a significant extent a response to the exclusion of civil society groups from the peace talks. (Abdel Ati 2006)

When the former rebel leaders assumed their leadership positions in the country after the agreement was signed, monopolization of power and not democracy was their main concern. This is evident in the way the constitutions of South(ern) Sudan were crafted and implemented, as discussed in the following section.

Democracy on paper and concentration of power through constitutions

In essence, the CPA was a bilateral arrangement between the regime of President Omar al Bashir and SPLM/A. As pointed out earlier, other stakeholders did not play any significant role during the negotiations even though they were expected to join in the implementation of the agreement. The two parties that negotiated the agreement fronted their interests, and hence dominated the political dispensation that surfaced. Power in the South was solidly in the hands of SPLM/A leaders, especially Salva Kiir and those close to him.

The perfect starting place for South Sudanese democracy was the two documents identified above. The constitutional texts embodied the aspirations of the people of South Sudan and potentially ensured anything that was perceived as discrimination in the past would be corrected through a new constitutional order and dispensation. Article 1(4) of the Constitution (TCSS 2011) states that South Sudan will be governed on the basis of a decentralized democratic system and will be an all-embracing homeland for its people. The Constitution recognizes South Sudan as a multi-ethnic, multi-cultural, multi-lingual, multi-religious and multi-racial entity where such diversities can peacefully co-exist (see TCSS 2011 Art 1(4)).

The bill of rights, in its entirety, lays down all rights and aspirations of the people of South Sudan. Past issues of contention such as religious rights, cultural rights and ethnicity have all been included as areas of human rights to be accorded full state protection (see the Bill of Rights within TCSS 2011). These constitutional provisions are an indication that, at the onset of the interim period and at independence, South Sudan aspired to become a democratic country and was committed to uphold the rule of law.

The Constitution of 2011 lays down the separate branches of government, clearly indicating that South Sudanese institutions of the judiciary, the legislature and the executive shall function on the model of separation of powers as entrenched in the Constitution, and as in other democracies.

The interim period was a very interesting phase for all South Sudanese. Hilde Johnson's book, *South Sudan: The Untold Story* is relevant when it comes to capturing what transpired during that phase. She noted in several instances that, while the ruling elite did not want to replicate Khartoum's system of governance, the experience of administering liberated areas during the civil war was not the same as running an inclusive government. Governance structures, strong institutions, transparency and accountability – central to effective civilian government – were beyond the scope of a liberation movement (Johnson 2016).

Military credentials and ranks became the sole process of decision-making rather than political competence and technical skills when allocating any positions or when constituting any committees such as constitutional reviews, and including ministerial positions and commissions.

Decision-making after the war ended in 2005 was always determined by the influence of the past rather than competence of the present and, in the absence of alternatives, the leadership always ended up structuring relations between the state and the citizens around traditional roles from the liberation struggle and ethnic representation. For the entire transitional period, South Sudan never really took off as a state (Johnson 2016).

The 2005 constitution-making body is an illustration of how the whole concept of state-making was never taken seriously. The committee was full of people who lacked the technical skills to draft a constitution, let alone frame the provisions. Upon the attainment of independence, a similar committee was reconstituted and at best managed to delete texts that made references to old Sudan and adopted those relevant to South Sudan.

The constitution-making processes in South Sudan – the Interim Constitution (The People of Southern Sudan 2005) and the Transitional Constitution (TCSS 2011) – suffered from lack of inclusivity, participation and political will. After independence, South Sudan pledged to undertake another constitutional review process to promulgate a constitution that would be longer in duration, more comprehensive in scope, more inclusive and participatory in nature (USIP 2012). This is yet to happen.

There was always the danger that the liberators or rebel leaders would become complacent beneficiaries of state power and the clearest sign was the practice of resorting to ethnicity and patronage as the governing framework – and just as quickly the government was full of liberators and ethnic numbers had to be met regardless of efficiency or skills, and that was really one of the roots of the current crises. Also, linked to politicization of ethnicity is rampant abuse of power in the pursuit of personal gain. This is covered in more detail in the following section.

Monopolization of resources through corruption

While the central government in Juba was beginning to function with planning and budgeting systems to facilitate decision-making, there were barely any legislative and policy frameworks in place and that is why the financial management systems became worse. The Ministry of Finance and Economic Planning was characterized by very weak capacities and underdeveloped structures. The government could barely contain the flourishing corruption amid a severely lacking political will to curb the vice (Johnson 2016). Clearly, there was no political will to institute strong and effective institutions to curb corruption and promote transparency and accountability. The president repeatedly pronounced zero tolerance to corruption but abuses flourished without any concerted effort to punish the guilty. One former Minister of Finance and Economic Planning had one time stated:, 'When there are no systems in place, stealing becomes very easy'.[5]

Much of the conflict is driven by elites attempting to re-negotiate their share of the politico-economic power balance through violence. Understanding the financial drivers of the conflict and the motivation of the major players is essential to negotiating a peaceful settlement to the conflict. Government transparency initiatives are severely under-funded and usually receive a fraction of their allocated budgets. In 2014, South Sudan was ranked 171 out of 175 in the corruption perception index and, taking the first quarter of 2015 fiscal year alone, the Anti-Corruption Commission received only 64 per cent of its budget and the national audit chamber, which published honest and detailed audit reports, received 17 per cent of its budget (The Sentry Project 2015).

Upon the attainment of a semi-autonomous status, the then Government of Southern Sudan plunged into a spending spree – senior government officials were booked into fancy tent hotels and paid US $300 per night; government officials enjoyed countless joy rides from one country to the next in the name of study tours and yet the outcomes of such initiatives hardly showed. The culture of extravagance and corruption extended during the interim period and throughout the two years of relative stability at independence. To date, and despite the economic crisis, government officials live in hotels and procure the most expensive cars. Moreover, spending on security forces continued to rise as the security of ordinary people became precarious. The liberators or former rebel leaders were determined to enjoy the fruits of the liberation struggle, but at the expense of ordinary people and stability.

Flawed 2010 elections

Between 11 and 15 April 2010, the former Sudan held its first multi-party elections in almost 25 years – a milestone set forth in the 2005 CPA that ended the twenty-two-year civil war. The elections were the first real democratic test for South Sudan. Dr Lam Akol, a prominent politician, had already fallen out with SPLM and formed the Sudan People's Liberation Movement – Democratic Change (SPLM-DC). His team contested the elections alongside the other major parties, SPLM and NCP, under a very difficult environment for anybody standing against the dominant party.

A range of human rights violations marred the historic vote, and threatened to jeopardize the referendum on self-determination that

[5] Hon. Tisa Sabuni, former Minister of Finance and now presidential advisor.

Southern Sudan was scheduled to hold in January 2011. Human Rights Watch documented numerous human rights abuses perpetrated by the two main partners in the Government of National Unity (GoNU): the ruling NCP and SPLM. These include arbitrary arrests and intimidating opponents, voters and election observers before and during the election period, with Human Rights Watch and domestic election observers reporting numerous electoral irregularities (Human Rights Watch 2010). These reports led the National Elections Commission (NEC) to hold new elections in many constituencies.

Political intolerance, repression and violence eroded the legitimacy of the elections across former Sudan, and violated the right of the Sudanese people to elect their government in genuinely free and fair elections. They contributed to a worsening human rights situation throughout the country by emboldening NCP and SPLM – neither of which have been made to account for their actions – in their clampdown against opponents. Indeed, for some years, Dr Lam Akol had to live in exile for his safety.

The 2010 elections raised the spectre of growing instability in states such as Central Equatoria, Jonglei, Unity and Western Bahr el Ghazal. They also set a worrying precedent for Southern Sudan's forthcoming referendum on self-determination.

The Human Rights Watch report on the elections noted that, despite widespread electoral irregularities, ballot stuffing, arbitrary arrests, detention and mistreatment of opponents, the international observers and diplomatic missions failed to explicitly and resolutely criticize these documented human rights and electoral abuses, or to call for accountability and reform. The USA and European Union were relatively muted in their criticism, and transiently expressed concern about voting 'irregularities', circumscribed political freedoms, and elections that fell short of international standards. But they neither condemned the widespread abuses as detailed in both the Human Rights Watch report and the reports of the national observers, nor did they press for accountability and reforms (Human Rights Watch 2010).

The Arab League (also known as the League of Arab States), the African Union (AU), the EU, the USA and the Intergovernmental Authority on Development (IGAD) – a seven-country regional organization based in East Africa – issued statements that failed to mention gross election-related abuses such as fraud, arbitrary arrests and detention and the mistreatment of opponents, etc., and merely ambiguously reported that electoral irregularities were observed. The whole world turned a blind eye to the gross electoral malpractices in Sudan and only pointed out minor irregularities.

Nationwide political repression and human rights abuses marred the elections. Human Rights Watch and domestic election observers reported widespread logistical and administrative problems; faulty ballots; fraud, including multiple voting and ballot-stuffing; incorrect voter lists; late supply of voting materials; ballot papers being taken to the wrong locations; and inconsistent identification requirements at polling stations. In some cases, these problems led to polling places being suspended or closed. They also prompted the NEC to extend voting by two days, and to later announce its intention to repeat voting in more than thirty-three constituencies.

Sudanese civil society organizations deployed about 8,000 observers across Sudan. These included 2,000 observers from the Sudanese Network for Democratic Elections (SuNDE) (in the South) and Sudanese Group for Democracy and Elections (SuGDE) (in the North), and 772 observers from the group Sudan Domestic Election Monitoring and Observation Programme (SuDEMOP) in the South. Several other networks of civil society groups deployed throughout Northern states and Darfur. Many observers told Human Rights Watch that security forces had intimidated them on several occasions, including ordering them out of polling places and, in some cases, confiscating their accreditation cards (Human Rights Watch 2010).

In their final report on the elections, SuNDE and SuGDE noted 'serious shortcomings in the administration of the elections at the polling stations observed'. They recorded 194 incidents of intimidation, harassment or violence in Southern states during the seven-day period in the polling stations observed. The former received reports of incidents of intimidation in all ten Southern states (*ibid.*). The lack of appetite for democracy on the part of the top leaders of SPLM was also evident in the way they dealt with internal matters within their own party.

Flawed internal SPLM democracy and return to war

A weekend meeting in December 2013 of SPLM's National Liberation Council (NLC) fuelled wrangles among key leaders. This was partly because of lack of agreed democratic ways of choosing the party's leaders. On 15 December, fierce fighting erupted between rival units of the SPLA in Juba, South Sudan's capital. The next day President Salva Kiir, dressed in military uniform, announced on national television that former Vice President Riek Machar had attempted a coup. Within days, eleven senior political figures were arrested for alleged involvement. Machar, who escaped from Juba, denied involvement in a coup or the initial fighting and accused the president of using the ploy of a coup to crack down on leaders who called for internal party reforms (International Crisis Group 2014). He soon declared himself the leader of an armed opposition movement that became SPLM/A in Opposition (SPLM/A IO), which quickly took control of significant parts of Jonglei, Upper Nile and Unity states, while fighting spread to other areas as well.

The government, whose faction of SPLM came to be known as Sudan People's Liberation Movement in Government (SPLM IG), and the Sudan People's Liberation Movement in Opposition (SPLM IO) have fundamentally different views of what happened on 15 December, leading to deeply divergent understandings of the core problem and how to resolve it. Most government officials maintain Riek Machar was planning to take power by force and believe the failure of the wider international community to condemn the claimed coup attempt has encouraged him. It is claimed by SPLM IO that there was no coup attempt and that Kiir and a small group of Dinka hardliners from Warrap and Northern Bahr el Ghazal used the fighting as an excuse to arrest and purge rivals and allowed Dinka units of the Presidential Guard, SPLA, National Security and police to carry out atrocities against Nuer civilians in Juba, leading to retaliations against the Dinka by the Nuer in the other states of Unity, Upper Nile and Jonglei (Logo 2015). In reality, it was a contest over power that degenerated into violence as a way of capturing power or retaining power.

The regional body, IGAD, led efforts to peacefully end the fighting. In August 2015, the parties signed an agreement, called the Agreement on the Resolution of the Conflict in the Republic of South Sudan (ARCSS). It required the SPLM IO leadership to join SPLM IG in Juba to implement the peace agreement. After several logistical hitches, the SPLM IO leadership arrived in Juba in April 2016, and Riek Machar was subsequently sworn in as the First Vice President (FVP) of a Transitional Government of National Unity (TGoNU) as per the terms of the peace agreement. As the parties made several gains in the implementation of the agreement there were sticking points, especially the status of the eighteen new states[6] controversially decreed by the president, transitional justice, and the reconstitution of the Legislative Assembly and cantonment areas for rebel forces.

In essence, ARCSS failed to address rivalries, political contestations and bad blood between the opposing parties, which persistently differed on key issues. It always took the intervention of a third party before the two could come to an agreement on any matter. In July 2016, soldiers from both sides got embroiled in fighting at the Presidential Palace in Juba. It only stopped after all the bodyguards of Riek Machar deployed outside the palace had been killed. The true narrative of this incident is yet to be known, however. But the official version put forth by SPLM IG was that Machar had attempted another coup. Of course, SPLM IO rejected this, claiming that people allied to

[6] Oblivious to grave concerns, the president has continued to decree more states, bringing the number to the present thirty-two states, plus Abyei, which is treated separately because it is a contested area between Sudan and South Sudan, an issue that remains unresolved at the time of writing.

the president were bent on sabotaging the agreement and attempting to kill Machar.

As South Sudanese reeled from yet another traumatic war in Juba, and the rest of the other parts of Equatoria, Upper Nile, Unity and Jonglei, the president replaced Riek Machar as FVP with Taban Deng Gai, another member of SPLM IO who had been dismissed by Riek Machar, and appointed new ministers. These appointments have been rejected and contested by the SPLM IO leadership and, for a while, the international community as well.

In a series of meetings on the South Sudan situation both AU and IGAD initially called for the reinstatement of the former FVP and the deployment of a protection force so that the parties could proceed with the implementation of the agreement. These propositions have been resisted by the government. The United Nations Security Council (UNSC) enforced the deployment of the protection force and proposed a robust United Nations Mission in South Sudan Mandate.

Under US pressure, AU and IGAD agreed to work with Taban Deng Gai and isolate Riek Machar, who was confined in South Africa. Determined that Riek Machar stays out of South Sudan politics, the US pushed for UN sanctions against him and others it accused of fanning the flames of war. Unfortunately, the US efforts did not address the worsening fighting on the ground.

In a change of tack, IGAD worked for the release of Riek Machar from confinement and participation in renewed efforts to end the fighting, leading to the conclusion of the Revitalized Agreement on the Resolution of the Conflict in the Republic of South Sudan (R-ARCSS) in September 2018. Under the terms of the agreement, Riek Machar was appointed FVP in a new transitional government, the formation of which was due by 12 November 2019. The 12th November 2019 date passed and another set for February 2020.

Ethnic mobilization and warnings of genocide

South Sudan is plagued with a recurrent problem of ethnicity. In the past, there were visible ethnic tensions between the two dominant tribes, the Dinka and the Nuer, but after July 2016, the Equatoria sub-group that consists of several ethnic groups has been drawn into an already bad ethnic situation. The escalating mobilization and violence along ethnic lines has led to concerns of a looming genocide (Logo 2015).

South Sudan's politics, allegiances and conflicts have always been mobilized along ethnic lines and usually, as the political infrastructure portrays a united front in national and regional matters, behind the scenes ethnicity is the first consideration because it defines inclusion, participation and the distribution of resources.

The histories of conflicts in the former Sudan and in many African countries are presented as ethnic or tribal. In Rwanda for instance, the genocide pitted the Hutu against the Tutsi and that is true for South Sudan where ethnic identities are relevant in conflicts and political participation. While the distinguishing mark of nationalism is a definitive relationship with the state, in South Sudan ethnicity is a primary factor and plays a significant role in national politics to the extent that an ethnic group would seek greater participation in national affairs at the expense of the other ethnic groups and that is extremely problematic (Paglia 2006).

Take the example of the December 2013 conflict, where Nuer were pitted against Dinka and several ethnically targeted killings occurred against the Nuer in the first days of the conflict, with a similar retaliation by the Nuer against the Dinka in days that followed. In 1991, when Riek Machar left the mainstream SPLM, the Nuer ethnic group from which he hails, sided with him and the Dinka, from which John Garang hails, quickly rallied their support behind their own. The web of ethnicity is extensive in South Sudan, and its role in determining governance issues and political participation cannot be understated.

In 2013, political tensions among the key South Sudanese leaders erupted in violence and, while the political dispute that triggered the crisis was not based on ethnic identity, it overlapped with pre-existing ethnic fault lines. The outcome was ferocious ethnic killings, sexual violence and other crimes committed against civilians by the belligerent parties. After the August 2015 peace deal, and the subsequent return of Riek Machar as FVP, clashes that took on an ethnic characteristic reoccurred in Juba in July 2016. As with other conflicts in South Sudan, civilians were once more targeted on the basis of their ethnicity. The current crisis has increased the underlying tensions and mistrusts among the South Sudan leaders and ethnicities, tensions that date back to the 1983–2005 war epoch, only this time engulfing the entire nation. There is no single ethnicity that has not been targeted based on their ethnicity. The same post-independence ethnic manoeuvring is taking the shape of the past ethnic squabbles that nearly derailed the Southern Sudan bid for independence (Blanchard 2016: 5).

Does ethnicity affect South Sudan's prospects for democracy? As much as that is debatable, the general consensus is that it does, because the nature of South Sudan's ethnic loyalties and belief in personalities rather than institutions supersedes the overall outlook towards reforms and transitioning into a country governed on the basis of the rule of law and democracy. As Hilde Johnson notes in her book, competence is both substituted for ethnic loyalties, past military prominence and acquaintances, and not based on professional skills (Johnson 2016). While SPLM was not properly prepared to run a country, its ethnic loyalties are derailing a democratic transition in South Sudan.

As noted by Mahmoud Mamdani, two main ethnic groups dominate South Sudan – the Dinka and the Nuer. Juba the capital is settled along ethnic lines and all political objectives are geared towards dividing the country along ethnic lines and destroying any basis for consensus, polarizing the citizens into 'us' and 'them' (Mamdani 2016). So in July 2013, when the president, a Dinka, dropped his deputy, a Nuer, as his vice president, mobilization along ethnic lines ensued, setting the stage for confrontation. The Jieng Council of Elders, a Dinka tribal group chaired by the former Chief Justice, embarked on a secret mobilization drive to decide the people that would protect the president – confined to the Dinka only. The force, 'Dot key Beny' (Rescue the President), were recruited with the guidance of that Council. No wonder, when violence broke out in December, initially Nuer civilians were the main victims in Juba, and followed shortly after by Dinka civilians targeted in reprisals elsewhere in the country.

For a democratic transition to occur, stability and an inclusive government is a pre- requisite, but that is barely the case because even the armed forces that could have protected citizens and instilled a sense of safety have killed and committed other crimes based on ethnicity. The policy of exclusion by the current leadership is so endemic that even the government-allied militia, the 'Mathiang Anyore', is predom- inantly Dinka and fights an ethnic war against any dissenting voices. Since July 2016, the ethnic tensions have risen to unprecedented levels and acts of brutal killings and ethnic targeting have spread beyond the realm of the pre-existing Nuer and Dinka ethnic issues.

Future of democracy after 2013 and 2016 conflicts

There are ongoing proposals on how to save South Sudan from the brink of another wave of civil war, and put the country on the path of peace and democratic rule. This will importantly entail implementing the August 2015 ARCSS, which was revitalized in September 2018, and installing democratic rule, the prospects of which in the near future have become bleak. Unlike the CPA, ARCSS involved other actors besides the two warring parties, including other political parties, civil society, women, faith-based leaders and eminent personalities. Interestingly, while the warring parties signed this peace agreement, and with government initially raising a number of reservations about some provisions of the agreement, the overwhelming majority of South Sudanese welcomed the agreement as the only option for ending violence and economic problems. The national parliament also unanimously passed the peace agreement without reference to the reservations raised by the government.

Threats to the peace are on the rise, as witnessed by the July 2016 violence in the national capital and human rights abuses. The political manoeuvring by SPLM IG continued after the July violence that caused Riek Machar to again flee the country. Initially, IGAD and AU insisted on the reinstatement of Riek Machar to his old position in TGoNU. They later succumbed to US pressure to support Salva Kiir and Taban Deng Gai and to isolate Machar. Recognizing that the US move was ill advised, IGAD persuaded SPLM IG to re-engage Riek Machar, leading to the conclusion of the Revitalized Agreement on the Resolution of the Conflict in the Republic of South Sudan (R-ARCSS) in September 2018, and reviving hopes for an end to the fighting.

A UNSC meeting approved a UN Regional Protection Force for South Sudan to enhance stability and foster the means and environment to implement the peace agreement. However, hardliners and spoilers in SPLM IG vigorously opposed it on the grounds that it would infringe on the sovereignty of the country. Under intense pressure, however, they did accept the force, which (at the time of writing) is yet to deploy to Juba.

The political stability of the new state will rest on the SPLM leadership as the ruling party, through democratic reform within itself and providing space and a conducive environment for other political parties, civil society organizations and other stakeholders. Robust democracy will require that the SPLM-dominated government provide the legal framework and environment for a multi-party system, a key issue during the liberation struggle. Nonetheless, all must recognize that, in the short term, even with elections in the next few years, the foundation for the country's democracy must first be seen and practised internally by SPLM itself as it is expected to remain the dominant party for a number of years yet to come.

Conclusion

The prospects of the current leaders, most of them former rebel commanders, leading the new country to a democratic future are bleak. This is the case because democracy is not in their interest as it could foil their quest to cling to power. Thus, their determination to hold on to power at all costs has had catastrophic consequences for the country.

South Sudan risks return to a full-scale war. South Sudanese have been leaving the country on a daily basis to find safer havens in neighbouring countries. Over one million of them have voted with their feet and sought refuge in Sudan, Uganda, Kenya and other countries. They fled because the belligerent parties have directed fire at them and also committed other gruesome abuses. The trajectory of the fighting has been marred by a total disregard of international law – the Geneva Conventions to which South Sudan is a signatory – and good governance based on democratic principles.

The wavering commitment of the government to allow the deployment of the proposed protection force to Juba is extremely worrying, and the reasons advanced by opponents of the force are far from convincing. In contrast to what they say, it is war that will threaten the sovereignty of South Sudan and not the deployment of the UN force.

South Sudan is already experiencing further violence in many parts, which, according to UN officials, could degenerate into genocide if the world does not consistently push the parties to return to honest implementation of the 2015 Peace Agreement, as revitalized in September 2018. This should also include an accounting for the events of July 2016 and the subsequent abuses against civilians and aid workers. Moreover, the liberators or former rebel leaders should be persuaded to practise the democracy they promised their people throughout the years of war.

While a national government was formed at independence, it neither developed into a strong democracy capable of meeting the needs of citizens nor did it allow for divergent opinions and free political allegiances to flourish. The leaders in Juba, the capital, and those who wielded power elsewhere were not interested in democratic rule or nation building (Zambakari and Kang 2014). Instead, they centralized power, rewarded themselves through looting government coffers, and manipulated ethnicity, consigning the country to its current sorry state.

The persistent political crises are rooted within SPLM, which was a militarist body rigidly dedicated to the liberation armed struggle. After the war, it hardly shed militarism. All elites who sought to initiate reforms were either dubbed rebels, or did so just to get to the helm of power. The militarist elite or former rebel leaders with a dominant influence in decision-making have been devoid of democratic thinking and practice.

The failure of SPLM to embrace democratic institutions and organs, responsive to citizen's concerns, inhibited democratic transition in the whole nascent country. The entrenched autocracy, that shows no signs of loosening its grip on the country, has led to the emergence of power-hungry ethnic or tribal organizations, such as the Jieng Council of Elders, which works for narrow interests against national cohesion. The constant wars are an expression of the underlying discontentment with the system of governance and ethnic domination and manipulation of resources by the elites closer to the centre of power (Zambakari and Kang 2014).

Bibliography

Abdel Ati, Hassan. 2006, 'Untapped Potential: Civil Society and the Search for Peace'. *Accord* 18: 68–71, https://rc-services-assets.s3.eu west-1.amazonaws.com/s3fs-public/Peace_by_piece_Addressing_

Sudans_conflicts_Accord_Issue_18.pdf, accessed 24 September 2019.

Alier, A. 1990, *Southern Sudan: Too Many Agreements Dishonored.* Exeter, Ithaca Press.

Blanchard, L. P. 2016, 'Conflict in South Sudan and the Challenges Ahead', 22 September. Congressional Research Service, Washington, DC, www.hsdl.org/?view&did=795792, accessed 29 July 2019.

GSS – Government of South Sudan. 2011, *The Transitional Constitution of the Republic of South Sudan, 2011*, www.sudantribune.com/IMG/pdf/The_Draft_Transitional_Constitution_of_the_ROSS2-2.pdf, accessed 25 September 2019.

Human Rights Watch. 2010, 'Democracy on Hold, Rights Violations in the April 2010 Elections', 30 June. www.hrw.org/report/2010/06/30/democracy-hold/rights-violations-april-2010-sudan-elections, accessed 29 July 2019.

International Crisis Group. 2014, 'South Sudan: A Civil War by Any Other Name', Report 217 / Africa, 10 April. www.crisisgroup.org/africa/horn-africa/south-sudan/south-sudan-civil-war-any-other-name, accessed 29 July 2019.

Johnson, H. F. 2016, *South Sudan: The Untold Story, From Independence to Civil War.* London and New York: Bloomsbury.

Logo, K. H. 2015, 'Challenges of Regulating Non-International Armed Conflicts – An Examination of Ongoing Trends in South Sudan's Civil War'. *Journal of International Humanitarian Legal Studies* 6(2).

Lyman, P. N. 2015, 'Independent South Sudan: A Failure of Leadership'. Testimony before the Senate Foreign Relations Committee, 10 December. US Government Publishing Office.

Mamdani, M. 2016, 'Who is to Blame in South Sudan?' *Boston Review*, 28 June, http://bostonreview.net/world/mahmood-mamdani-south-sudan-failed-transition, accessed 25 September 2019.

Nyaba, P. A. 1997, *The Politics of Liberation in South Sudan: An Insider View.* Kampala: Fountain.

Paglia, P. 2006, 'Ethnicity and Tribalism: Are these the Root Causes of the Sudanese Civil Conflicts? African Conflicts and the Role of Ethnicity: A Case Study of Sudan', Africa Economic Analysis. John Cabot University, Rome.

SPLM. 2008, 'The Manifesto of the Sudan People's Liberation Movement', Sudan People's Liberation Movement, http://theirwords.org/media/transfer/doc/1_sd_splm_spla_2008_43-6de1f0c9c1cd573f4e71b8acf4af0b55.pdf, accessed 25 September 2019.

The People of Southern Sudan. 2005, *The Interim Constitution of Southern Sudan, 2005*. www.wipo.int/edocs/lexdocs/laws/en/ss/ss012en.pdf, accessed 4 November 2019.

The Sentry Project 2015, 'The Nexus of Corruption and Conflict in South Sudan'. The Sentry, Enough Project, Washington, DC, https://

thesentry.org/reports/south-sudan, accessed 14 August 2016.

USIP (United States Institute of Peace). 2012, 'Constitution Making in Sudan and South Sudan', Washington DC, USIP, www.usip.org/programs/projects/constitution-making-in-sudan-and-south-sudan, accessed 11 August 2016.

Young, J. 2007, 'Sudan IGAD Peace Process: An Evaluation', 30 May, www.sudantribune.com/IMG/pdf/Igad_in_Sudan_Peace_Process.pdf, accessed 25 September 2019.

Zambakari, C. and Kang, T. K. 2014, 'Negotiating Peace in South Sudan: Democracy, Politics and Armed Movements', 14 January 2014, *African Arguments*, http://africanarguments.org/2014/01/14/negotiating-peace-in-south-sudan-democracy-politics-and-armed-movements-by-christopher, accessed 10 November 2016.

Zapata, M. 2011, 'Sudan: Independence through Civil Wars, 1956–2005', 13 December, Enough Project, Washington, DC.

4

The Quest for Alternatives in Overcoming the Democratization Deficit in Ethiopia

KASSAHUN BERHANU

Introduction

Ethiopia experienced two regime changes in the last four decades: the coercive ousting of imperial rule and its replacement by a military dictatorship in the mid-1970s, followed by the military victory over the military dictatorship and seizure of power by the Ethiopian People's Revolutionary Democratic Front (EPRDF) in May 1991. While EPRDF's initial seizure of power was facilitated by its armed victory over the military regime, its perpetuation in power since then was mediated by the outcomes of five successive electoral contests held since 1995. The rule of EPRDF commenced by introducing a series of liberal reforms aimed at bringing about betterments in the socio-cultural, economic and political spheres of life. These were underpinned by the quest for reconfiguring the alignment of the country's social forces, altering the ideological orientation and structure of the state, recasting the major strands of state-society relations, and overhauling the workings of political economy. The formation of EPRDF in 1989 was spearheaded by the Tigray People's Liberation Front (TPLF), a conglomeration of ethno-nationalist insurgent groups aspiring to unseat the military dictatorship led by Mengistu Hailemariam. The success of these movements organized under EPRDF's umbrella laid the foundation on which ethnicity was elevated to the status of an overarching principle for organizing the Ethiopian political system serving as the cornerstone of the workings of political economy and state-society relations in post-1991 Ethiopia.

Although the EPRDF-led government retained some of the military regime's institutions and governance structures, it also endeavoured to reconfigure the major aspects of socio-economic and political life through a plethora of policy instruments. Perhaps the most dramatic development that accompanied the 1991 regime change was the process of ushering in a form of constitutionalism that had far-reaching implications for subsequent developments. By resorting to a more radical move, EPRDF abolished the unitary form of the Ethiopian state and reconstituted it as a federation comprising nine self-governing regional states and two autonomous city administrations, premised on ethno-linguistic considerations. Most controversially, the constitution contains, albeit with strong safeguards attached, a clause guaranteeing the right of the country's ethnic groups to secede.[1] This provision became a major bone of contention in Ethiopian political life, pitting the proponents of ethno-nationalism who harboured centrifugal tendencies (ICG 2009) against those who feared that this could be a recipe for disintegration. The constitution stipulated that the constituents of the Federal Democratic Republic of Ethiopia (FDRE) would formally enjoy devolved powers and functions.

With the foregoing as backdrop, this article examines how elevating ethnicization of politics to the status of sacrosanct principle and blending of state and ruling party structures constrained the quest for democratic transformation. To this end, the factors that prevented EPRDF from delivering on its promise of steadfastly embarking on a wide range of measures for entrenching societal freedoms and liberties are highlighted. Moreover, attempt is made to identify the looming deficits that militate against democratization in Ethiopia and propose alternatives that could address the entrenched systemic bottlenecks. Drawing on established experiments on means and ways of entrenching democracy through reviewing pertinent literature and analysis thereof, the chapter seeks to shed light on what state and non-state actors (opposition political parties, civil society organizations, professional associations, and concerned individuals) should consider in the effort aimed at creating the requisite conditions for entrenching a democratic dispensation.

Signposts of post-1991 democratization drives

The major drives that were presumed to serve as building blocks for entrenching democratization in post-1991 Ethiopia are discussed in this section.

Decentralization
EPRDF promoted ethnicity as an overarching principle of political life by steadfastly arguing that failure in recognizing the rights of Ethiopia's ethnic groups to self-determination would result in the disintegration of the polity. The Transitional Charter (TGE 1991) and the 1995 Constitution (FDRE 1995) affirmed this. Accordingly, it was declared that these

---

[1] See Article 39 of the Constitution of the Federal Democratic Republic of Ethiopia for the details (FDRE 1995).

shall be practically expressed by the right of ethnic groups to promote their culture, history and language; administer their own affairs; effectively participate in the central government on the basis of freedom and fair and proper representation; and exercise self-determination in accordance with established rules and procedures.

The constitution defined the powers and functions of regional governments in their respective areas of jurisdiction and competence. Structuring the different levels of government within the purview of a federal political system was thus predicated on the principle of self-rule and shared-rule signified by devolution of powers and functions as an aspect of decentralized governance (TGE 1992). Article 50 (4) of the federal constitution stipulated that regional states are empowered to organize their respective administrative units as deemed necessary and appropriate. For nearly a decade after the early 1990s, the decentralization-cum-devolution initiative was limited to the self-governing regions. However, practical measures were taken since 2001 towards empowering local governments by introducing the District Level Decentralization Programme (DLDP). In this manner, the nine regional states and the two autonomous city administrations were instituted.[2] Accordingly, structuring of government in present-day Ethiopia is on the basis of hierarchical tiers comprising federal, regional, zonal, local, and grassroots administrations in descending order respectively. It is to be recalled that Article 46 of the constitution stated that these are established by considering settlement patterns, language, identity and consent of the concerned people. As indicated in Chapter 5, the constitution and other pertinent legislations stipulated that assumption of leading positions of government ranging from federal to grassroots levels is to be realized on the basis of periodic electoral outcomes.

In spite of the presumed positive ramifications of ethnic politics in entrenching self-rule and shared-rule, an overemphasis on distinctiveness has triggered hosts of unintended outcomes. These were expressed in negative developments like proliferation of inter-ethnic polarization, unhealthy competitions over territorial claims and counterclaims, conflicts over scarce resources and positional goods, and mounting tensions between majority and minority ethnic groups in most of the self-governing regional states. In spite of betterments experienced in a number of ways resulting from the decentralization measures, a close examination of the state of affairs in this regard does not warrant

---

[2] The nine regional governments that are constituent members of the Ethiopian Federal Democratic Republic are: Tigray, Afar, Amhara, Oromo, Somali, Benishangul-Gumuz, Southern Nations, Nationalities, and Peoples' Region (SNNPR), Gambella and Harari, and the two city administrations are Dire Dawa and Addis Ababa.

asserting that these have led to the taking shape and entrenchment of democratization as expected. This is evidenced by EPRDF's adherence to democratic centralism (revolutionary democracy) as enshrined in the Front's official document (EPRDF 2006), which emphasizes the ruling party's vanguard role and centrality in spearheading socio-economic and political processes by blending ruling the party and state structures. Aalen (2002) argued that EPRDF's disposition in this regard runs counter to the principle of empowerment of the self-governing regional and local governments in formulating and implementing policies. Hence, what actually takes place in practice under the guise of formal decentralization that is subordinated to the preferences and programmatic positions of EPRDF is tantamount to centralization.

Constitutional engineering as a basis for policy-making

Upon seizing power, EPRDF did not bother to put legislation in place to nullify the previous People's Democratic Republic of Ethiopia (PDRE) Constitution, unlike the move taken by the military in suspending the 1955 Constitution of the Imperial government. The annulment of the military regime's constitution is rather indirectly inferred from Article 18 of the Transitional Charter, which was declared to serve as Ethiopia's interim supreme law for the duration of the transitional period (Ta'a & Kenea 2007: 31). The July 1991 Conference, which adopted the Transitional Charter, ushered in radical changes in the Ethiopian political landscape as expressed in the establishment and composition of the Transitional Government of Ethiopia (TGE). The coalition of political groups that formed the TGE under the leadership of EPRDF was a conglomeration of assorted political groups of various persuasions that participated in the initial phase of the transition. Many of these were novices in terms of clearly understanding the workings of the ever-present power play in Ethiopian politics that is characterized by the 'winner-takes-all' game.[3]

The Transitional Charter recognized unrestricted respect for human rights as adopted in the December 1948 UN Declaration, comprising freedom of conscience, expression, and association, the right of citizens to engage in unrestricted political activities, the right of nations, nationalities and peoples to self-determination and self-rule, and freedom from undue discrimination, fear and persecution. The different provisions of the Charter also provided the legal grounds for the proliferation of political parties of varying persuasions. Around the

---

[3] Some Pan-Ethiopian political groups such as the Ethiopian People's Revolutionary Party (EPRP) and *Meison* (the All Ethiopian Socialist Movement) that had longer years of experience in political engagement than many members of the TGE were prevented from participating in the July 1991 conference that led to the establishment of the Transitional Government of Ethiopia.

time when the end of the transitional period was approaching in 1994, the transitional legislative assembly (the Council of People's Representatives) appointed a commission charged with the task of drafting a new constitution on the basis of which the *modus operandi* of the then-forthcoming Federal Democratic Republic was to be determined. In due course, public discussions on the major provisions of the draft constitution were held throughout the country. In view of the opposition boycotting the drafting process, EPRDF dominated the entire scene, as a result of which its socio-economic and political programmes were incorporated in the draft without any meaningful debate (Pausewang et al. 2002: 38, Berhanu 1995).

The Constituent Assembly approved the draft constitution, which entered into force in 1995, heralding the inauguration of what came to be known as the Federal Democratic Republic of Ethiopia. With regard to constitutional development, the constitution has some significant implications for issues surrounding socio-political engineering like recognition of fundamental rights and freedoms, introducing a parliamentary political system, and effecting changes in the unitary form of government. In addition, the new constitution provided for formal separation of powers of the federal and regional governments (FDRE 1995: Art. 51–52) by affirming that regional states shall exercise all powers that are not expressly given to the federal government or concurrently to the federal and the regional states (Art. 52/1). Preponderance of the EPRDF was crystallized in the 1995 Constitution in the making of which meaningful participation and contribution of different stakeholders outside the EPRDF mainstream remained marginal at best. Hence the era of broadening the democratic space, allowing for unhindered participation of citizens in the socio-economic and political processes unfolding in the country on the basis of fair play, began to fade in due course.

In regard to policy-making, EPRDF's cardinal organizational principles, anchored in its Marxist-Leninist past espousing the vanguard role of the party, remained intact, albeit with some modifications. This is evidenced by its adherence to democratic centralism (revolutionary democracy) emphasizing the ruling party's centrality in spearheading socio-economic and political processes. Aalen (2002) argued that this resulted in the entrenchment of upward accountability to the higher party organs to the detriment of downward accountability. This took place despite EPRDF's official pledges favouring popular initiatives and participation in decision- making. Rahmato (2008: 147) opined that the policy formulation process in the country is characterized by the absence of broad-based consultation involving major stakeholders. The ruling Front's unbridled power in the realm of decision-making is further cemented by the different provisions of the constitution that allow the federal government to formulate and implement overall economic, social and development policies (FDRE 1995: Art. 51). As mentioned in Chapter 5, the EPRDF-dominated House of People's Representatives is legally allowed to legislate on all matters falling under the jurisdiction of the federal government (Art. 55/2a), implying that prospects for ensuring institutional checks and balances and legislative oversight of the executive could be rendered ineffective.

Party and electoral politics
Party politics is a recent phenomenon that commenced in Ethiopia following the overthrow of imperial rule in the mid-1970s. In the aftermath of the monarchy's termination, semi-clandestine and clandestine political organizations that engaged in mutual antipathy came on the scene. The tribulations associated with this culminated in one-party rule spearheaded by the military regime.

As indicated in the foregoing and Chapter 5, the 1991 Transitional Charter recognized for the first time the right of Ethiopians to establish political parties in accordance with their preferences and ideological orientations. This move was subsequently endorsed by the incumbent constitution thereby leading to the proliferation of several political organizations with diverse ideological persuasions. During the last two decades following, the unravelling of the new dispensation, many ethnic-based and multi-ethnic political groups have come and gone: the Ethiopian political landscape concerning political parties constantly depicted features of mergers, splits and complete disappearances as the major traits witnessed so far. It is worth noting here that TPLF, which spearheaded the formation of EPRDF, managed to prevail on the Ethiopian political scene as a very powerful actor as compared to all other political formations. Following its seizure of power in 1991, EPRDF claimed victory in all the successive national and regional elections conducted to date.

In spite of legal recognition as regards the rights of citizens to exercise political and associational life, many blame EPRDF for exhibiting exclusionary tendencies by barring unwanted political organizations from participating in the political process under various pretexts (Berhanu 2003). The ruling Front justified its move of alienating targeted organizations by labelling them as inimical to the highly sought transformation drive anchored in peace, stability and democracy. Moreover, several among those that were legally recognized at the onset of the transitional period were forced to opt out as a result of security threats, undue pressure and intimidation exerted on them by the ruling Front.

According to the different legislations governing political parties, Ethiopians above the age of eighteen years can form a political party. The legislations in question also set a number of criteria that must be met in seeking registration as nation-wide and regional organizations. In order to qualify as a pan-Ethiopian political entity, a party is required to present a list of a minimum of 1,500 founding members of which residents of a single region cannot exceed 40 per cent of the total. In each of at least the remaining four regions, the number of those enlisted should be 15 per cent of the total number of founders. To register as a regional party, a political organization is required to enlist at least 750 founding members who are eligible residents of the concerned region. The laws in question stipulated that parties that foment conflict, animosity and hatred among social, ethnic and religious groups, mobilize supporters to promote objectives through use of force of arms, and enlist foreign nationals as members would be denied registration. Moreover, professional associations, trade unions, and mass organizations formed to advance commercial, industrial, welfare, mutual self-help and religious activities cannot register as political parties. The law also makes it incumbent on political parties to submit basic documents like memoranda of association and by-laws in order to qualify for legal recognition.

The electoral system that is currently at work in Ethiopia is based on simple plurality or first-pass-the-post system whose ramifications in sustaining multi-party electoral competition is questioned for favouring stronger parties at the expense of smaller ones. In order to win elections under a simple plurality system in single-member constituencies (electoral districts), a candidate does not need to obtain the majority (50 per cent plus one) of the votes cast. Instead, candidates who get more votes than other contestants (also known as plurality majority) qualify as winners under the first-pass-the post electoral system. It is not important whether the electoral system is based on either proportional representation or simple plurality model in so far as the political system is deficient in terms of providing avenues that ensure free and fair elections. However, Lijphart (1994: 20–21) argues that elections based on plurality majority systems deny smaller parties chances for being represented, given that the model favours bigger and well-established parties. Political parties in Ethiopia are either multi-ethnic or ethno-regional in their composition, with espousal of ideologies ranging from neo-liberal to revolutionary in terms of their orientations and programmes.

New developments in Ethiopia have been signified by the emergence of a pro-reform leadership from within the EPRDF mainstream in 2018, followed by the introduction of series of institutional and legislative reforms. Among these, amendment of the electoral law took place in 2019 with a view to broadening the political space which was one of the demands of the widespread popular protests between 2015 and 2018.

Most political parties in Ethiopia that emerged after the fall of the military dictatorship are not rooted in and organically linked to the grassroots in general and rural communities in particular both during their formative years and thereafter. Urban-based academics, ex-civil servants, businessmen and others, who seized the opportune moment of the liberalized political environment of the early 1990s, played crucial roles in the formation of most political parties that are currently operational. Similar to that perpetrated by the mainstream political establishment, hampering the initiated democratization, decision-making in several opposition parties is dominated by personalities with overwhelming powers to the detriment of proactive participation of rank-and-file members. This is reminiscent of the workings of Ethiopian political culture as a whole, underpinned by a rigid chain of command and hierarchical authority. In this connection, Adebo (1996) and Tronvoll and Aadland (1995) argue that the autocratic mentality bequeathed by the entrenchment of politics of command still persists as was the case in the past. Derailment of democratic governance in the mode of operation of political parties in this manner has thus entailed adverse consequences for the democratization project. As a result, forging coalitions among opposition parties have failed in many instances due to factional squabbles and personality clashes. Taking note of this and other related mishaps, Berhanu (1998: 93) argued that what commenced as a pluralist affair with an attractive democratic semblance is in the process of degenerating into the consolidation of unbridled power of individual strongmen. Hence it could be argued that, in so far as the thriving political parties are unable to extricate themselves from such and other similar behaviours and practices indicating domineering dispositions, it is hardly possible to unfurl the democratization process in a manner that is all-inclusive. In spite of the odds that curtail their efforts, there are signs that many opposition parties seem to have recently drawn lessons from the deficits that impeded their performance to pose as viable options to the status quo.

Since the holding of the first local elections in 1992 and thereafter, a number of political groups that participated in the formation of the TGE had opted out, citing deficits that underpin the mode of operation of the political system. This was attributed to the progressive weakening of the broad-based character of the democratization drive initiated in the aftermath of the 1991 regime change. The transitional period that was hoped to bring about a dispensation premised on a burgeoning democratic order was, in due course, transformed into an overall situation where political life in Ethiopia is dominated by holders of mainstream power under a semblance of multi-party competitive elections. As described in Chapter 5, EPRDF has overwhelmingly won all the national and regional elections conducted in the country since 1995. This is largely attributed by a mix of factors like the inherent weakness of the opposition on the one hand and undue use of advantage of incumbency by the party in power on the other.

In the national and regional elections held in May 2000, several opposition parties participated, unlike in 1995. In this regard, Clapham

(2002: vii) noted that 'the May 2000 elections were the first seriously contested elections that the country experienced in its long history', despite several alleged irregularities. Opposition parties managed to secure some representation although EPRDF remained in control of the overwhelming majority of seats in parliament. The next elections, held in May 2005, were marked by lively debates and unconstrained operational and campaign space, although controversies and unrest on the outcomes ensued in the immediate aftermath of polling day, culminating in a government response that led to considerable blood-letting and incarceration of the leaders of the major opposition party, the Coalition for Unity and Democracy (CUD). Subsequently, EPRDF dominated all branches of government at the federal level, including all the constituent regions, through the agency of ethnic-based regional parties affiliated to it.[4]

Despite that, the several elections held in Ethiopia following the 1991 regime change are marred with contentions and controversies as regards processes and outcomes, EPRDF's move in making elections important instruments of representative democracy is a positive development for a country characterized by paucity of meaningful electoral contests in the past. Detractors attribute the experienced shortfalls in election management to the hurdles surrounding the defective institutional arrangements expressed in the partisanship of the electoral commission and the courts. According to Pausewang and Tronvoll (2000: 21), EPRDF's sole proprietorship of state power undermined efforts towards entrenching unconstrained exercise of democratic liberties and respect for human rights. This allegedly resulted from the ruling Front's quest for regime security and power consolidation buttressed by the fusion of party and government structures that are too hazy to differentiate. The unabated persistence of this phenomenon is believed to have undermined incentives for competitive politics under a seemingly multi-party framework. EPRDF's privileged access to public resources by virtue of its incumbency and control of the political and economic commanding heights is also in the process of weakening multi-party competitive elections.

The continuous overwhelming presence of EPRDF members in parliament thus served as a major instrument for fortifying centralized rule in present-day Ethiopia, despite the existence of a series of decentralization schemes. As highlighted in Chapter 5, the workings of the political

---

[4] The political organizations that formed the EPRDF coalition have continuously controlled the four major constituent regions and the two autonomous city governments of the Ethiopian federation since 1991. The same is true of the remaining five developing regions (Afar, Benishangul-Gumuz, Gambella, Harari and Somali) where ethnic ruling parties are closely associated with EPRDF and designated as 'allied' organizations.

system under EPRDF gravely has constrained the roles of parliament and other state organs in terms of entrenching good governance and democratic transformation. As a result, the opposition seriously questions the credibility of the courts and the electoral body as impartial and non-partisan entities by citing that the prime minister, who is also the leader of the ruling party, nominates key officials of these organs. The fact that EPRDF's firm grip on parliament is used in ensuring the appointment of election officials and judges without facing hurdles of rigorous scrutiny reinforces the assertions made above. The unfolding of EPRDF's omnipotence is further reinforced by the promulgation and enforcement of prohibitive legislations[5] that are misused to impede legitimate democratic aspirations of society and political actors not privy to the mainstream locus of power.

The success of EPRDF in controlling political and socio-economic life in the country partly lies in its organizational prowess and relatively advanced experience in managing party politics as compared to other players. Given the many strands of diversity characterizing the polity and its constituent parts, Ethiopian political culture can be understood in view of mainstream values and beliefs that took effect following the making of the 'modern' Ethiopian state-society. According to Hagmann (2005), the co-existence of neo-patrimonialism and legal-rational domination that undermine institutional stability by reinforcing patron-client relations stands out as a key feature of the political system in post-1991 Ethiopia. Abbink (2006: 193) claims that authoritarianism, elite rule, and patron-client relations that disallow the present from extricating itself from the past underpin the major historical manifestations of Ethiopian political culture understood in this context.

Non-state actors

Considerable increase in the numerical size of both foreign and local civil society organizations (CSOs) that operate in Ethiopia was witnessed following EPRDF's ascent to power. This was expressed in the formation of several professional associations, non-governmental organizations (NGOs), trade unions, and mutual self-help and welfare societies. In this manner, the operational landscape of CSOs was transformed in several respects such as widening geographical outreach and diversification of activities. These notwithstanding, however, the dependence of Ethiopian CSOs on external support persisted unabated due to the absence of a culture of modern philanthropy in the country. In the mid-1990s, the EPRDF-led government introduced a directive governing the programmatic interventions of NGOs by urging them to

---

[5] These include the Media and Information Law (FDRE 2008a), the Anti-Terrorism Law (FDRE 2008b), and the Charities and Societies Law (FDRE 2009), among others.

demonstrate relevance and effectiveness that are in line with priority areas enshrined in national development plans (Clark 2000: 6). Once the euphoria of liberalization subsided, the legal-administrative environment within which CSOs operate experienced increased hurdles that eventually culminated in the promulgation of the Charities and Societies legislation (FDRE 2009). The new legislation stipulated that local CSOs drawing 10 per cent or less of their resources and other forms of support from external sources shall be eligible to engage in political advocacy and rights-based issues. On the other hand, both local and foreign CSOs receiving more than 10 per cent of their support from non-domestic sources – constituting the bulk of those currently operating in Ethiopia – are legally prohibited from dealing with issues related to democracy, rule of law, peace-building and conflict prevention, and human rights protection, among others.

The coming into force of the new CSO legislation entailed both opportunities and challenges. Regulatory regimes governing the formation and mode of operation of CSOs/NGOs in Ethiopia prior to 2009 were largely fragmented, haphazard and unresponsive to the legitimate demands of non-state actors and their constituencies. In view of this, the initiative taken by the government to bridge such gaps and address prevalent shortcomings by enacting a standalone law could be commended as a move in the right direction (Rahmato et al. 2010: 104). The opportunities that the new legislation brought about could lead to the development of the voluntary sector in various ways. First, enacting a comprehensive law governing the operations of the voluntary sector is indicative of CSOs' recognition in government policy. Second, classifying charities and societies by origin, type, mandate, and jurisdiction and competence avails choices for citizens to organize themselves in line with their preferences and interests. Third, the law makes it incumbent on federal and regional line departments and local sector offices to coordinate and facilitate CSO operations in their respective jurisdictions as a result of which government-CSO relations could be strengthened.

On the other hand, a number of challenges unfolded, resulting from the coming into force of the law. The typology and activity-based classification of CSOs as stipulated in the legislation entailed changes in the already established missions of several local organizations required to adhere to the legal provision dealing with proscribed activities. This in particular relates to Foreign and Ethiopian Residents' Charities constituting the bulk of CSOs that draw more than 10 per cent of their resources from non-domestic resources (Bekele 2009). Consequently, foreign funds and other forms of support earmarked for advocacy and rights-based projects in Ethiopia are diverted to other countries where the legal regimes do not prevent CSOs from engaging in these issues and concerns. Moreover, problems that constrain institutional and operational autonomy have surfaced as a result of the coming into force of the legislation. These include periodic renewal of registration, and the involvement of many levels of government (federal and regional) in re/de-registration and monitoring of operations under a situation where procedures for doing so are not clearly spelled out. In addition, CSOs classified as Ethiopian Residents' Charities and Societies are deprived of the right of judicial redress in cases of disagreement with the decisions of the regulatory body, namely the Charities and Societies Agency (CSA). Besides, the grounds for the Agency's refusal to renew registration are so broad that it leaves ample room for discretion. One of these is the presumption that CSOs have been used for unlawful purposes that are prejudicial to public peace, welfare and morality, the interpretation of which could be widely subjective.

Concerns were raised by a wide range of rights and advocacy groups, which anticipated that some provisions of the law could have adverse effects on the contribution of CSOs to democratization and citizens' empowerment. Whereas the government claimed the new law would help citizens' associations in ensuring accountability and transparency by instilling a sense of ownership of governance and democracy-related programmes, organizations argue otherwise, claiming that the law imposes too many barriers and restrictions on CSO activities and unhindered access to resources. The Horn of Africa Division Head of the Human Rights Watch, Leslie Lefkow, stated that the legislation 'restricts and criminalizes the activities of non-governmental organizations and associations in ways that violate the right to freedom of expression and association' (Lefkow 2010). A report produced by the Centre for International Human Rights at Northwestern University also opined that the new law is driven by the Ethiopian Government's antipathy against CSOs often resulting in silencing advocates of human rights (Bekele 2009).

The media and freedom of expression
The role of the media in Ethiopia assumed unprecedented significance following the post-1991 reforms. Most importantly, the abolition of censorship led to the proliferation of private media firms and the relative lessening of the absolute monopoly of successive regimes on media outlets (Nega 2000: 21). This commendable move by EPRDF facilitated improved access to information on the operations of government and major non-state actors. As a result, the public was provided with the opportunity for following up and monitoring developments in the country and elsewhere on the one hand and transparency and accountability of office bearers and public service providers on the other.

The 1995 Constitution guaranteed citizens' right not only to air opinions and contrarian views but also to enjoy unhindered freedom of expression in the form of seeking, receiving and imparting information orally and/or in writing through any medium of choice. Cognizant that the electronic and print media were exclusively state-owned, the Constitution provided that these shall be operated in a manner that ensures diversity of expression of opinion. According to the Constitution, such rights can be proscribed only under certain conditions that are prejudicial to well-being of the youth, and the honour, dignity and reputation of individuals and the public at large.

The principles enunciated in the constitution regarding freedom of the press were later elaborated in the Mass Media and Access to Information Proclamation (FDRE 2008a). This notwithstanding, representatives and operators of the private media often complain that the law is too restrictive and intimidating to allow for exercising media freedom without fear or favour. The fledgling private press had suffered significant setbacks in the aftermath of the 2005 elections, and the EPRDF-led government administered legal sanctions against the private print media on several occasions as a consequence of which their vibrancy diminished. Credible reports by domestic and foreign advocacy groups abound, stating harassment, arrest and firing of journalists thereby resulting in the labelling of the government as among those that are hostile to freedom of expression in the developing world.

The economic landscape

Although it could be argued that EPRDF's economic policy is largely a negation of that of the military regime, the previous state of affairs that put the economic commanding heights including all land as public property under the custody of the state remains. The post-1991 liberal economic reforms ushered in a market-based orientation by introducing deregulation and privatization of public enterprises and measures for annulling price control and production quota as mechanisms for determining demand and supply. This was in anticipation that the new direction could revitalize the war-devastated economy through adopting the normative principles of international financial institutions that advocated denationalization, currency devaluation, and reduction and/or elimination of subsidies for social programmes. In the mid-1990s, the Agricultural Development-Led Industrialization (ADLI) strategy was introduced as an overarching economic policy presumably aimed at bringing about economic recovery and fast growth by enhancing the performance of smallholder producers. Official justification in introducing the strategy emphasized that improvements in the performance of smallholder agriculture could lead to increase in the volume of production, farmers' income, and industrial raw materials including exportable surplus (Rahmato 2008). The imperative of transforming the performance of smallholder farmers is premised on the rationale that the overwhelming majority of the country's population are producers of primary commodities inhabiting the rural areas where comparative advantages in abundant land and labour are available (FDRE 2002: 4).

According to Berhanu and Poulton (2014), the rationales that underlie EPRDF's support for smallholder producers are propelled by the urge for attaining the twin objectives of ensuring economic growth on the one hand and building legitimacy and securing support for its programmatic drives on the other. In regard to economic growth, the role of smallholder producers is rightly acknowledged as a major source of food supply, employment for the bulk of the population, export trade, and foreign exchange earnings. In politico-administrative terms, smallholder communities are duly recognized as constituting a sizeable electoral constituency, source of human power supply for ensuring regime security and survival, and bulwark against internal and external threats poised against the political establishment. Besides, it is believed that EPRDF seeks to retain its support base rooted in smallholder farming communities that took shape during the heydays of its armed insurgency against military rule. Moreover, it appears that EPRDF has drawn lessons from experience signified by the downfall its predecessors that was partly precipitated by the alienation and disaffection of smallholders, which it strove to avoid at all cost.

Changes in the direction of stimulating agricultural development unfolded as of 2006 by enacting a policy of land allocation to local and foreign investors seeking to engage in medium and large-scale commercial agriculture. This took place with a view to boosting production of agricultural commodities for both domestic use and export trade. The taking effect of this policy made Ethiopia one of the major hubs of transnational land investment that grew by leaps and bounds following the 2007/08 hike in global food prices (Anseeuw et al. 2012). The argument in favour of large-scale land investments is also premised on the assumption that land resources earmarked for investment are 'unutilized' and 'underutilized', and hence could supplement smallholder production rather than replacing it. These views advanced by the government are supported by multilateral agencies like the World Bank as a move in the right direction that could lead to agricultural transformation and production efficiency (World Bank 2010). On the other hand, CSOs, researchers, academics and rights groups have expressed their misgivings on the ongoing large-scale land deals underpinned by a plethora of shortcomings. According to Rahmato (2011: 5–6), the magnitude and intensity of allocating large tracts of land to profit-seeking local and foreign private operators tends to alienate smallholders from their customary rights and ways of life. Moreover, commercialization of land on such a grand scale has the potential of boosting the powers of the bureaucratic and economic elite at the expense of smallholders whose voices are muted due to paucity of consultations and participation in decision-making (Berhanu 2013).

Although still at a nascent stage, positive trends were recorded as regards the contribution of the industrial sector to the economy. The share of industry in Gross Domestic Product (GDP) was between 13 and 14 per cent while that of the manufacturing sub-sector remained at around 4 per cent in 2014 (Giger and Moller 2015). On the other hand, the service sector registered considerable growth in terms of its contribution to GDP. By and large, Ethiopia experienced remarkable annual growth rate amounting to double-digits per annum on average during the last decade (*ibid.*). However, the distribution of proceeds resulting from economic growth is indicated by growing inequality. On a more serious note, the distribution of proceeds from accrued growth remained lopsided, raising doubts on the inclusiveness of the development process (UNDP 2015). Although the economic policies of the post-1991 years were largely antithetical to the excessively centralized schemes of the military regime, EPRDF also can be viewed as a force that strives to control the economic commanding heights by limiting private sector initiatives in several respects. In spite of improvements in the overall socio-economic and political landscape that accompanied the fall of the military dictatorship, the dominant position of the state over the important aspects of the economic milieu largely remained intact. Government monopoly over land, road and air transport, major financial sectors, power and energy, and telecommunications, among others, is indicative of this. In addition to its direct control of the major economic sectors, EPRDF commands significant leverage through monopolistic syndicates dubbed as 'endowments'[6] that are affiliated to its constituent members (Abegaz 2011). These 'endowments' stand out as the biggest 'private' investment schemes that enjoy preferential treatment by virtue of their close association with and proximity to the locus of power. It could thus be argued that constraining private initiatives for the sake of extending preferential treatment to selected economic actors would impair the emergence of a robust middle class that could spearhead efforts towards entrenching the democratization project in the country.

Overcoming bottlenecks in Ethiopia's democratization drive

Overview
Several positive developments expressed in the relative broadening of the public space that led to betterments in socio-economic and political

---

[6] These include the Endowment Fund for the Rehabilitation of Tigray (EFFORT), Tiret, Dinsho and Wondo that are controlled by EPRDF-affiliated ruling regional parties in Amhara, Oromiya and the Southern Regions respectively.

spheres of life in Ethiopia took place following the 1991 regime change. These notwithstanding, however, alarming signs reminiscent of past mishaps that call for taking remedial measures in good time are also observed. As admitted by the ruling Front at its 10th Congress held in August 2015, several challenges persist unabated. These include unmitigated authoritarian dispositions of public officials and service providers, shrinking of the public space constraining civic engagement and proactive participation of citizens, derailment of the rule of law, and prevalence of neo-patrimonial behaviours and petty and grand corruption, and governance deficits. The identified deficits are attributed to factors like lack of accountability and transparency in transacting government business, escalation of intra- and inter-group conflicts spearheaded by the mandarins of ethnic politics, paucity of a robust system of checks and balances in public institutions mediated by the blending of party and state structures, among others. It is widely recognized that the cumulative effects of all these could pose serious risks to the viability of the political system and durability of the gains made so far in terms of realizing socio-economic developmental goals. EPRDF's policy reforms that pledged to extricate society from the shackles of poverty and lack of development are neutralized by unbridled state dominance in the economy under the guise of enhancing the public good and addressing consequences resulting from market failure. Although this seems plausible under certain conditions, the real driver behind disproportionate state interventionism could be attributed to the urge for controlling the economic and political commanding heights. As a result, the viability of individual and organized private sector operators located outside mainstream power is in the process of being threatened.

Structuring the Ethiopian federal system along ethnic lines ushered in the pervasive influence of those claiming to represent majority groups in the constituent regional states. Under the current administrative arrangements that are at work in Ethiopia, prospects for effective management of diversity and minority rights by overhauling the already entrenched institutional design cannot be envisioned (Kefale 2013). However, the more recent creation of special zones and districts inhabited by minority groups within majority regions could be viewed as a proper move in the right direction. Democratic processes that are in tune with effective management of diversity by ensuring equitable representation of different groups should, therefore, be based on proactive participation of the public in elections and other governance processes. This cannot be expected to occur in the absence of an independent judiciary and an impartial election management body whose modes of operation are solely premised on the rule of law. It should thus be noted that the opposition and other sections of society continue to persistently claim that the appointment of election officials, judges and others occupying positions where crucial decisions are made is done by considering political loyalty rather than merit. Pausewang et al. (2002) argue that the problem in Ethiopia's transition to democracy is not the absence of laws that enhance democracy but lack of commitment in enforcing them even-handedly. Similarly, Tronvoll (2010) claims that the problem in this regard is that legislations dealing with elections and managing diversity in Ethiopia are either ignored at will or fail to be strictly enforced. Following the recent change in the top-leadership of government caused by popular upheavals, several promising measures are being taken to deal with the underlying factors that led to widespread mass discontent.

In search of alternative arrangements
Taking note of the aforementioned pitfalls militating against efforts aimed at democratizing the Ethiopian state-society, the following remedial measures for addressing the experienced shortfalls are proposed.

First, events and occurrences resulting from ethnic-based exclusivist trends that transpired during the last two decades have wreaked havoc on prospects for ensuring multiculturalism, accommodating differences and managing diversity in several instances. It is widely believed that such deficits mainly emanate from according primacy to ethnicity as a sacrosanct organizing principle in structuring the federal system of government and shaping inter-group and state-society relations. While recognizing that inalienable ethnic rights and ensuring citizens' participation in self-rule and shared-rule is worthwhile, disregard for other factors like geographic contiguity, mutually beneficial economic interaction, administrative expedience, and commonalities in livelihood systems has prompted tendencies towards exclusiveness through the deliberate misreading of well-intended policies by spoilers and self-serving ethnic political entrepreneurs. These have often resulted in inter-group rivalries and polarizations resulting in far-reaching adverse consequences that have negatively impacted on social cohesion, unity of purpose and common belonging that are vital for democratization. The frequent territorial claims and counterclaims involving violent conflicts, displacement of people from places of their original domicile, and discriminatory practices in accessing employment opportunities and public services and amenities are evidences of the emerging disconcerting trends.

Cognizant of the unhealthy state of affairs along these lines, it is incumbent on the government and all others concerned to revisit the principle and practice of ethnic-based federalism and replace it with some kind of feasible arrangement that could neutralize the negative effects resulting therefrom. However, changes along these lines may not be practical in the short run. The fact that this has been portrayed as a sacrosanct principle and the cornerstone of the federal arrangement since the 1991 regime change renders the urge for ameliorating this difficult. Nevertheless, in so long as the principles and attendant practices pertaining to self-rule and shared-rule as bastions of Ethiopian federalism are not compromised, there is little problem that would be encountered in relegating the primacy of ethnicity to the background. The recently announced measures by the government to terminate the Addis Ababa City Master Plan Project that caused the ire of people in the Oromiya Region, the plan for effecting changes in the electoral system, the promise for amending some constitutional provisions that could result in undesirable outcomes, among others, could be taken as indications of the possibility of revisiting the centrality of ethnicity in governance arrangements. In light of this, it could be envisaged that recent developments along this line might serve as impetus for embarking on the task of dealing with inadequacies experienced.

Second, the current centrally managed decentralization scheme in Ethiopia is in the process of rendering the highly cherished project of self-rule and shared-rule futile. The erosion of the principle of federalism that can serve as a basis for democratizing the Ethiopian state and society has the potential of ushering in contradictions in the systems that currently underpin state-society relations. Unless addressed in good time, these could eventually reverse the progress made so far in terms of entrenching the initiated democratization project. In light of this, adherence to the constitutional principles allowing for devolution of powers and functions by developing mechanisms for enforcement through establishing autonomous institutions would be in order.

Third, procedures for amending constitutional provisions are so rigid and cumbersome to allow for revision and adjustment even when these are found to be useful in promoting democratization. Hence there is a need to develop mechanisms that provide for flexibility in amending constitutional provisions that are either out-dated or whose persistence could be inimical to democratization.

Fourth, the policy formulation process in Ethiopia is characterized by top-down approaches in a manner that inhibits meaningful participation of stakeholders and the public at large, and contrary to what is stipulated in the constitution and other laws. In the absence of promotion of participatory processes in policy formulation, possibilities for entrenching democracy as a way of managing public affairs are highly unlikely. It is, therefore, necessary to put in place mechanisms for open and unconstrained dialogue that limits the discretionary power of leaders so as to ensure that the voice and preferences of citizens in decision-making are heeded.

Fifth, the Constitution recognizes that the existence of a multi-party system is essential for the attainment and sustenance of a vibrant democracy. As things stand now, however, the Ethiopian Government is controlled virtually by one party in a manner that undermines prospects for the development of democracy in the country. Although it appears that the workings of the political system pretend to support and strengthen opposition political parties, these are far from adequate and the situation in this regard manifests a progressive deterioration of the state of affairs. This is evidenced by the fact that there was only one opposition party member in the House of Peoples' Representatives following the 2010 Elections, which was followed by EPRDF's total control of federal and sub-national legislative assemblies in the May 2015 Elections. In view of this, the reality on the ground demands that the government should seek means and ways of supporting and encouraging thriving opposition parties so that they can actively and effectively participate in the political process. Hence the government should unfailingly address legitimate concerns and complaints that relate to the freedom to hold meetings and rally supporters without undue restraint. To this end, rules governing the financing of political parties and conducting election campaigns should be periodically reviewed so as to enable the opposition to contest elections without facing undue extra-legal perils and pressures.

Sixth, there is a need to revisit the first-past-the-post (FPTP) electoral system that is currently at work in Ethiopia given that it has negative implications for the country's democratization. This electoral system produces 'winner-takes-all' outcomes, despite winners failing to secure majority votes in elections. It is, therefore, suggested that the FPTP electoral system be replaced by either the proportional representation or a mixed system more in line with the principle of exercising meaningful democratic rights by the electorate. It is hoped that introducing changes in the existing electoral system could address some of the underlying causes leading to persistent controversies that often accompany election outcomes by addressing the diverse interests of societal groups and enhancing prospects for peace and harmony by ensuring equitable representation in elected governance bodies. One of the problems surrounding election-related controversies in Ethiopia is the absence of a secure digital voter register as an essential safeguard against perceived and actual inaccuracies relating to votes cast. Such a system for registering voters and counting votes could reduce election-related disputes as well as enhance the credibility of elections by allowing for greater transparency of involved processes. It is to be recalled that the integrity and credibility of the election management body in Ethiopia is seriously questioned by many who rightly lament its partisanship and subservience to officialdom by citing the mode and manner of its formation and its negative record in adjudicating election-related litigations. Given this, it is recommended that this body should be constituted of members comprising those with proven records of integrity, impartiality, respect for the rule of law, and professional competence in electoral politics, law and human rights. In as much as possible, these should be drawn from the ranks of those representing a wide spectrum of stakeholders: the ruling and opposition parties, CSOs, women and youth groups, professional associations, legal professionals, trade unions, and religious groups. The profile and track record of short-listed nominees should thus be subjected to rigorous public scrutiny in an open and transparent manner on platforms organized by federal or state councils, as appropriate, prior to their assumption of office.

Seventh, opposition groups and several observers of events in society are of the view that the organization of the judiciary and the appointment and performance of judges in Ethiopia leaves a lot to be desired in several respects. Although the constitution has clearly stipulated that the courts operate on the basis of nothing other than the law, the reality on the ground depicts this is not actually the case. It is beyond contention that respect for the rule of law is an overarching principle that impacts on a wide array of governance issues. The perception that human rights are not respected in Ethiopia as demonstrated in several instances prompting concerns of several internal and external advocacy and human rights groups is caused by nothing other than lack of independence, of integrity and of capacity characterizing the judicial branch. Moreover, the judiciary is not empowered to exercise the power of judicial review that is made the preserve of the EPRDF-dominated House of Federation. This arrangement disallowed the Ethiopian Supreme Court from adjudicating on cases that relate to violation of constitutional provisions by individuals, government officials and executive agencies, among others. In light of this, it is suggested that there is a need to strengthen the independence of the judiciary and enhance its commitment to serious law adjudication and enforcement. To this end, the principle of judicial independence enshrined in the constitution should be enforced with greater vigour and determination by ensuring merit-based appointment of highly qualified, committed and independent-minded judges who discharge their duties without fear or favour.

Eighth, the blending and fusion of ruling party and government structures underpinned by the absence of institutional checks and balances and separation of powers characterize the workings of the current Ethiopian political system. Official declarations and rhetoric aside, this is expressed in: overarching executive dominance in a manner that has decreased the role and influence of other branches; the prevalence of party discipline and loyalty in the EPRDF-dominated legislatures resulting in the erosion of parliamentary oversight; and the absence of a protected civil service that enjoys autonomy from undue political influence. These trends have undermined governance structures resulting in failure to adhere to constitutional provisions by limiting discretionary powers of the executive branch. Conversely, good governance and democracy are products of viable and purposive policies that allow for the proper functioning of governance institutions in accordance with the rule of law and due process. Hence an arrangement for clearly demarcating the boundaries of authority exercised by the ruling party and the different branches of government is indispensable so as to prevent undue concentration of powers and functions.

Ninth, unduly constrained operation and non-autonomous existence of CSOs is detrimental for smooth interplay between diverse and legitimate interests of citizens. It should be noted that the multi-faceted positive ramifications of autonomous CSOs include: facilitating unfettered exercise of democratic freedoms and liberties sanctioned by the constitution; exposing abuse of power; reinforcing accountability and transparency of government; enhancing freedom of expression; and contributing to realization of socio-economic developmental goals. Instead of this, the government has disempowered CSOs by introducing legislation in 2009 that imperilled proactive engagement of the voluntary sector in advocacy, democracy and other rights-based activities. Given that the existence of a vibrant civil society enhances the prospects of entrenching democratization, it is recommended that there is a need to repeal the aforementioned prohibitive legislation and replace it with another that allows CSOs to operate responsibly without facing undue hurdles.

Last but not least, one of the post-1991 reform initiatives for introducing changes in the country's economic policy and attendant practice relates to replacing the centrally planned model by the free market variant. This notwithstanding, however, the role of the government in economic activities expressed in the control of the economic commanding heights persists unabated. This has unfolded in a manner that diminishes the role of the private sector and individual entrepreneurial motivations needed for the emergence of a vibrant middle class that could shoulder the onus of consolidating democracy. Cognizant of the adverse implications of existing state of affairs for democratization, it is recommended that there is a need to limit government interventions to strategic areas of market failure that cannot be tackled by individual operators and private firms. Moreover, party and government-affiliated monopolistic syndicates and endowments enjoying preferential treatments should be abolished in so far as their activities can be easily undertaken by private sector entities and individual entrepreneurs. No doubt the role of government in transforming the subsistence sector is critical, particularly in strategic areas where the thriving market forces lack the resources and other capacities to ameliorate existing shortfalls and bridge entrenched gaps. The argument is rather that the dominance of party-owned and affiliated monopolistic syndicates in activities that can be handled by the market tends to stifle legitimate private initiatives and the emergence of a thriving middle class that can shoulder the task of unfurling the democratization agenda. Hence the need for limiting government intervention to enacting regulatory policies and participating in strategic areas that are beyond the prowess and capacity of the market is suggested.

Conclusion

It had been hoped that the reform measures of the post-1991 years would bring about changes in the workings of the major institutions of governance and state-society relations that could lay a solid foundation for democratization. In spite of several improvements in the different aspects of socio-economic and political life resulting therefrom, trends of reversal of the democratization projects initiated are being witnessed in a gradual and piecemeal manner. These are driven by political exigencies anchored in the lust for control and self-perpetuation of power holders who failed to deliver on what they promised through series of official pledges and solemn declarations. The recourse to administrative fiat that limits the urge for democratic transformation to formal posturing that is devoid of practical commitment is an alarming trend. As the saying goes, confining projects associated with democratization to pretensions and formal posturing alone cannot beget substance unless these are reinforced by the vigour of practice. As highlighted in the preceding sections of this chapter, several shortcomings that militate against efforts for entrenching democracy in Ethiopia are being experienced. There are justifiable concerns that the failure to address the identified pitfalls could result in dire consequences reminiscent of past mishaps expressed in conflict, shrinking of the public space, prevalence of authoritarian dispositions, and popular protests leading to divergence in state-society relations. In light of this, means and ways of ameliorating the identified shortfalls by resorting to alternatives that could entrench the taking root of a democratic dispensation in the country are suggested.

In the drive aimed at ensuring the taking effect of broad-based democratization, there is a need to ensure that the Ethiopian peasantry constituting the bulk of the productive population is not left out of the process of democratization by focusing on urban elite groups alone. The task of bringing this section of the population on board calls for embarking on a wide range of measures that positively impinge on the fabric of the current political system.

The transformation of the country's political economy and attendant practices is characterized by top-down approaches marked by exclusionary dispositions that are detrimental to proactive participation of the peasantry. In order to tap the energy and other potentials of farming communities that could boost efforts towards rooting

Ethiopia's democratization on a solid foundation, a series of measures are needed. These include: understanding local conditions and involving the concerned stakeholders in the different processes and phases of decision-making; facilitating provision of physical and social infrastructural services so as to enable rural populations to benefit from outcomes of democratization by precluding possibilities for resistance and conflict caused by alienation and marginalization; unleashing participatory processes in institutions charged with the responsibility of facilitating rural development; and ensuring unhindered mobility of labour, capital and agricultural products by avoiding the confinement of these factors to localities of origin, as often is the practice, shaped by ethnic regionalization.

Bibliography

Aalen, L. 2002, *Ethnic Federalism in a Dominant Party State: The Ethiopian Experience 1991–2000*. Bergen: Christian Michelsen Institute.

Abbink, J. 2006, 'Discomfiture of Democracy? The 2005 Election Crisis in Ethiopia and its Aftermath'. *African Affairs* 195(419): 173–99.

Abegaz, B. 2011, 'Political Parties in Business', Department of Economics Working Paper 113. Williamsburg, VA: College of William and Mary.

Adebo, T. 1996, 'Democratic Political Development in Reference to Ethiopia'. *North East African Studies* 3(2) 53–96.

Anseeuw, W., Boche, M., Breu, T., Giger, M., Lay, J., Messerli, P. and Nolte, K. 2012, 'Transitional Land Deals for Agriculture in the Global South', Analytical Report based on Land Matrix Data Base. Bern/Montpellier/Hamburg, CDE/CIRAD/GIGA.

Bekele, Y. November. (2009). 'Sounding the Horn: Ethiopia's Civil Society Law Threatens Human Rights Defenders'. Evanston, IL, Center for International Human Rights, Northwestern University School of Law.

Berhanu, K. 1995, 'Ethiopia Elects a Constituent Assembly', *Review of African Political Economy* 22(63) 129–35.

—— 1998, 'Democracy, State-Building, and "Nations" in Ethiopia: 1974–1995', in J.-G. Gros (ed.), *Democratization in Late Twentieth-Century Africa: Coping with Uncertainty*. Westport, CT and London: Greenwood Press.

—— 2003, 'Party Politics and Political Culture in Ethiopia', in M. A. Salih (ed.), *African Political Parties: Evolution, Institutionalization and Governance*. London: Pluto Press.

—— 2013, 'CAADP Ethiopia: A New Start?' Working Paper 60, Brighton, UK, Future Agricultures Consortium.

Berhanu, K. and Poulton, C. 2014, 'The Political Economy of Agricultural Extension Policy in Ethiopia: Economic Growth and Political Control'. *Development Policy Review* 32(S20): 199–216.

Clapham, C. 2002, 'Controlling Space in Ethiopia', in W. James, D. Donham, E. Kurimoto and A. Triulzi (eds), *Remapping Ethiopia: Socialism and After*. Oxford: James Currey.

Clark, J. 2000, 'Civil Society, NGOs and Development in Ethiopia: A Snapshot View', Washington, DC, World Bank.

EPRDF – Ethiopian Peoples' Revolutionary Democratic Front. 2006, *Development, Democracy and Revolutionary Democracy*. Addis Ababa: Mega Printing Enterprise (Amharic).

FDRE – Federal Democratic Republic of Ethiopia. 1995, *The Constitution of the Federal Democratic Republic of Ethiopia*. Addis Ababa: Berhanena Selam Printing Press.

—— 2002, *Rural Development Policies and Strategies*. Addis Ababa: Mega Printing Enterprise (Amharic).

—— 2008a, 'Proclamation to Provide for Freedom of the Mass Media and Access to Information'. Addis Ababa: Berhanena Selam Printing Press.

—— 2008b, 'Anti-Terrorism Proclamation'. Addis Ababa: Berhanena Selam Printing Press.

—— 2009, 'Charities and Societies Proclamation'. Addis Ababa: Berhanena Selam Printing Press.

Giger, M. and Moller, L. C. 2015, 'Fourth Ethiopia Economic Update: Overcoming Constraints in the Manufacturing Sector'. Washington, DC: World Bank Group.

Hagmann, T. 2005, 'Beyond Clannishness and Colonialism: Understanding Political Disorder in Ethiopia's Somali Region, 1991–2004'. *Journal of Modern African Studies* 43(4): 509–36.

ICG – International Crisis Group, 2009, 'Ethiopia: Ethnic Federalism and its Discontents', Africa Report 153. Brussels, International Crisis Group.

Kefale, A. 2013, *Federalism and Ethnic Conflict in Ethiopia: A Comparative Regional Study*. London and New York: Routledge.

Lefkow, L. 2010, 'Testimony of Leslie Lefkow, Horn of Africa Division Head of Human Rights Watch, to the U.S. House Committee on Foreign Affairs, Africa Subcommittee, 17 June 2010', www.hrw.org/news/2010/06/17/statement-us-house-representatives-horn-africa, accessed 25 September 2019.

Lijphart, A. 1994, 'Introduction', in A. Lijphart (ed.), *Electoral Systems and Party Systems: A Study of Twenty Seven Democracies, 1945–1990*. Oxford: Oxford University Press.

Nega, B. 2000, 'The Media and Its Consumers in Ethiopia: Results from an Audience Survey' (unpublished mimeo).

Pausewang, S. and Tronvoll, K. 2000, 'The Elections in Context', in S. Pausewang and K. Tronvoll (eds), 'The Ethiopian 2000 Elections:

Democracy Advanced or Restricted?' Human Rights Report 3/2000. Norwegian Institute of Human Rights, Oslo.

Pausewang, S., Tronvoll, K. and Aalen. L. 2002, 'Introduction', in S. Pausewang, K. Tronvoll and A. Aalen (eds), *Ethiopia since the Derg: A Decade of Democratic Pretension and Performance*. London: Zed Books.

Rahmato, D. 2008, 'Ethiopia: Agricultural Policy Review', in Taye Assefa (ed.), *Digest of Ethiopia's National Policies, Strategies and Programs*. Addis Ababa: Eclipse Printers.

——2011, *Land to the Investor: Large-Scale Land Transfers in Ethiopia*. Addis Ababa: Forum for Social Studies.

Rahmato, D., Bantyirgu, A. and Endeshaw, Y. 2010, *Ethiopia: Partners in Development and Good Governance*. Addis Ababa: Flamingo Printing Press.

Ta'a, T. and Kenea, Z. 2007, 'Constitutional Development in Ethiopia', in K. Berhanu, O. Tafesse, K. Asnake and E. Jalele (eds), *Electoral Politics, Decentralized Governance and Constitutionalism in Ethiopia*. Addis Ababa: Addis Ababa University Press.

TGE – Transitional Government of Ethiopia. 1991, *Transitional Period Charter of Ethiopia*. Addis Ababa: Berhanena Selam Printing Press.

—— 1992, *Proclamation to Provide for the Establishment of National/ Regional Self-Governments*. Addis Ababa: Berhanena Selam Printing Press.

Tronvoll, K. 2010, 'The Ethiopian 2010 Federal and National Elections: Re-Establishing the One-Party State'. *African Affairs* 110(438): 121–36.

Tronvoll, K. and Aadland, O. 1995, 'The Process of Democratization in Ethiopia: An Expression of Popular Participation or Political Resistance?' Human Rights Report 5. Norwegian Institute of Human Rights, Oslo.

UNDP. 2015, 'National Human Development Report 2014: Ethiopia'. United Nations Development Programme, Addis Ababa.

World Bank. 2010, 'Rising Global Interest in Farm Land: Can it Yield Sustainable and Equitable Benefits?' World Bank, Washington, DC.

5

Parliament-Public Engagement in Ethiopia: A Weak Link in Democratic Transformation[1]

MEHERET AYENEW

Introduction

In a democracy, parliaments are important institutions with three key functions – making laws, exercising oversight over the executive, and serving as representatives of the people (Johnson 2005). The extent to which parliaments effectively perform these functions has a bearing on the institutionalization of democracy and good governance in a particular country. Throughout much of Africa, there is the dearth of effective and strong parliaments that can be pillars of democracy and representational rule (UNECA n.d.).This is a major democratic deficit that has resulted in the perpetuation of authoritarian regimes, and has held back opportunities for multi-party politics and accountable governance in many parts of the continent, including among member states of the Intergovernmental Authority on Development (IGAD).

Strong parliamentary institutions that represent wide cross-sections of the population can empower citizens to have a say in how they are governed through their legitimately elected representatives. Given the diversity of African Nations, there is a need for a broad-based and all-inclusive parliamentary representation to mitigate political instability and avoid alienating significant segments of the population. When people gain political representation, they develop a sense of belongingness and will have a stake in the system. This in turn reduces the proclivity to subvert the system, because there is some degree of

[1] This chapter is based on research funded by the Economic and Social Research Council and Department for International Development (ESRC-DfID) titled 'Parliament, Public Engagement and Poverty Reduction in Bangladesh and Ethiopia'. The project is a comparative study of the Bangladeshi and Ethiopian experiences in parliamentary democracy, and is intended to assess parliamentarians' engagement with their constituencies and how this has contributed to public participation and poverty reduction in the two countries. Summary of key findings of the Ethiopian experience is presented in this piece.

satisfaction with the status quo (UNECA n.d.; Veit et al. 2008; Power 2012). The attempts by African states to institutionalize democracy and stable governance can therefore bear fruit through the instrumentality of strong parliaments that represent the interests and concerns of the broad sections of the citizenry.

Parliament and public engagement with it are important aspects of the democratic process that can help attain three important goals, viz. strengthening the representational role of parliament, availing opportunities for the electorate to provide inputs that can influence public policy, and making it imperative for elected officials to consult regularly with their constituencies. All these are important yardsticks of accountable and responsive governance that allow for public needs and concerns of diverse constituencies to be considered in the law/public policy-making process. Effective parliament-constituency interactions deliver good governance and promote accountability, which are instrumental in effective poverty reduction for a country (Merilee 2007; Aribisala n.d.).

Apart from broadening the democratic space, effective interactions between parliamentarians and constituencies can further economic growth and reduce poverty and inequality (Aribisala n.d.). Regular contacts with constituencies can help politicians to be responsive to the needs and concerns of the groups who elected them and, therefore, can play an important role in enacting good laws that can lead to poverty reduction and the attainment of sustainable democracy. In addition, strengthening the oversight functions of parliaments can ensure good governance and effective implementation of development plans, and this can have the effect of reducing poverty and promoting the welfare of the people (Parliamentary Centre 2009; UNECA n.d.). Simply put, when citizens regularly engage their representatives, public voices can be better heard in laws and policies made by the government. Public input into the legislative process promotes accountable governance, enhances legitimacy and garners support for governments' anti-poverty plans and programmes. It can be argued that these roles assume particular significance in a poor country like Ethiopia because an effective parliament can contribute not only to strengthening democracy but also should play a pivotal role in the government's efforts to reduce poverty.

Formal representation is a hallmark of Ethiopia's parliament but the institution is a weak link in the country's democratic transformation because it is dominated by a single ruling party. For many reasons, multi-party or competitive politics has not taken root in the governance set up. Single-party dominance has meant that parliament has a less than desirable record in its oversight function over the executive branch of government, and all laws and policies easily get endorsed by parliament with little or no public discussion and consideration of alternative options that could have provided better prospects for democratic governance and the development of a stable society and economy. In addition, the absence of a viable opposition that can harness the people's energy for organized political action and offer a coherent political and economic alternative has perpetuated a monolithic one-party rule. The ruling party maintains unrivalled control over the executive and legislature, and this has hindered efforts at institutionalizing multi-party politics and a participatory and competitive governance system that can offer alternative economic and political programmes.

Another important and more positive feature of the Ethiopian parliament is the high representation of women members in its ranks. According to the findings of an ongoing study titled 'Parliament, Public Engagement and Poverty Reduction in Bangladesh and Ethiopia' jointly being undertaken by researchers from Bangladesh, Britain and Ethiopia, there has been a progressive increase in the number of women members of parliament (MPs) during the country's past five elections. Examples of other African countries with a similarly high representation of women MPs in the national parliaments include Rwanda (63.8 per cent), Senegal (42.7 per cent), South Africa (41.7 per cent) and Namibia (41.3 per cent) (IPU, 2016). According to the views of the Ethiopian women parliamentary caucus interviewed for this study, the Ethiopian study suggests that if the right conditions, such as government commitment and constitutional guarantees for equality, are in place, the presence of a high number of women MPs in parliament can be an important boost for women empowerment and advancement of their rights.

In recent years, Ethiopia has scored good economic success. The gains have contributed to significant reductions in poverty levels in both rural and urban areas. For example, according to the World Bank Group's latest poverty assessment, poverty in Ethiopia fell from 44 per cent in 2000 to 30 per cent in 2011, which translated to a 33 per cent reduction in the share of people living in poverty (World Bank, 2015). However, this economic success has not been accompanied by an equal measure of democratization and widening of the political space for non-state actors, and this has generated widespread political discontent and apathy towards the system. Indeed, it appears that despite the country's relative economic success and poverty mitigation efforts, political and social volatility seems to be on the ascendency. As the political space continues to shrink, there has been widespread unrest and upheaval. Indeed, the Ethiopian experience suggests that development conceived in the narrow sense without a corresponding measure of political democratization may not be sustainable in the long run (Fisseha, 2014; Ayenew, 2014). One of the objectives of this chapter is to identify possible explanations for this mismatch and suggest ways and means on the way forwards.

The overall objective of this chapter is to assess the challenges and constraints of the Ethiopian parliament in strengthening democracy and representative governance. It will examine critical aspects of the engagement of parliamentarians with the electorate and other political actors, such as civil society organizations, as a vehicle for accountable governance and active citizen participation in politics. Despite the country's relative economic success, it will be argued that the shrinking of the political space as epitomized by the dominance of one-party rule and the absence of competitive politics have become the order of the day. Therefore, the authoritarian political order has to give way to the institutionalization of a participatory and all-inclusive governance arrangement to mitigate social and political unrest as well as to render the country's current economic growth sustainable and equitable.

Methodology and approach

This study was based on extensive field work involving interviews with about thirty participants consisting of parliamentarians, academics, civil society leaders and activists as well as donor representatives and five focus group discussions (FGDs) with constituency groups in three regions and two major urban centres, viz. Addis Ababa and Dire Dawa. The aim is to gather the perspectives of different stakeholders on the role of parliament and the extent of interaction of parliamentarians with their constituencies, and how this can strengthen democracy and reduce poverty and inequality.

Care was taken to keep the gender and socio-economic balance in the sampling frame in conducting the interviews and FGDs. For example, FGD participants were selected by civil society organizations working with the poor and other vulnerable groups to ensure that different socio-economic groups were represented in the discussions. In addition, FGDs were held with the women caucus of parliament and individual women parliamentarians, some of whom are chairs and members of important parliamentary standing committees. This was intended to find out the extent to which their lobbying and advocacy work has helped women's causes and rights, and how this group interacts and behaves with their male counterparts. Since Ethiopia is formally a federal state, regional council members and constituencies in major regions of the country – Amhara, Southern Nations, Nationalities, and Peoples' Region (SNNP) and Tigray – were also consulted in this study.

The research programme, 'Parliament, Public Engagement and Poverty Reduction in Bangladesh and Ethiopia' has brought together academics with varied backgrounds, including social anthropologists, political scientists/experts in Public Administration and Policy. It has drawn together a multi-disciplinary team of researchers so as to better understand from multiple perspectives how the role of parliament, and parliamentarians' interaction with their constituencies can help in strengthening democracy and poverty reduction efforts. The findings will stimulate further academic discourse into the work of parliaments as representative institutions, and will influence governments and donors engaged in strengthening parliamentary programmes. In this regard, the efforts of the Hansard Society, which works to strengthen parliamentary democracy and encourage greater public involvement in politics, can be cited as an example (www.hansardsociety.org.uk/ projects/parliaments-public-engagement-and-poverty-reduction).

Parliament as agent of democratic transformation: a theoretical overview

Parliament is a potent symbol of the sovereignty of the people, which holds that it has absolute authority, and is supreme over all other government institutions, including executive and legislative bodies (Oliver 2014). Historically as well as in the contemporary world, no institution can be more important than parliaments in the democratic transformation of a nation. One of the best lessons that can be drawn from the world's longest and strongest democracies, mainly those of the United Kingdom and USA, is that democracy and human freedom are inconceivable without strong representative institutions that serve as levers on absolute power, and safeguard the rights and freedoms of the population who elected them.

In a divided government or a government characterized by checks and balances, the supremacy of parliament is a sacrosanct fact of life. As such, it performs the following cardinal functions:

- To check and challenge the work of the Government (scrutiny), for example, through questioning ministers;
- To make and change laws (legislation);
- To debate the important issues of the day (debating);
- To check and approve Government spending – budget/taxes.

It is equally important to recognize that parliaments are not static institutions, and there are several causes of change contributing to their increasing functions and roles as pillars of representation and accountable governance. According to a Green Paper prepared for the European Commission, the main causes of change affecting the work of parliaments include *increasing scientification of politics*, particularly the use of expertise in law/policy-making; *expanding the role of organizations as vehicles of collective decision-making because of the diffusion of governance beyond parliament and its government; and the changing international environment*, which is characterized by globalization, transnationalism, and regionalization (European Commission 2000). The Inter-Parliamentary Union (2007: xi) in its 'Guide to Good Practice' for twenty-first century parliaments, affirmed in the points replicated below that these are becoming more responsive, and working hard:

- to be more inclusive in their composition and manner of working, especially in relation to women and minority and marginal communities;
- to be more effective public communicators, through opening more of their work to the media, and through the development of their own websites and broadcasting channels;
- to experiment with new ways of engaging with the public, including civil society, and enabling them to contribute to the legislative process;
- to recover public confidence in the integrity of parliamentarians, through enforceable codes of conduct and reforms in party funding;
- to streamline the legislative process without limiting the proper scrutiny of bills;
- to exercise more effective oversight of the executive, including in the increasingly important field of international policy;
- to be more active in transnational collaboration, so as to provide a more effective parliamentary component in regional and international organisations, and in the resolution of violent conflicts.

There is no doubt that the preceding coping strategies will go a long way in making parliaments indispensable tools of representation as well as inclusive and accountable governance.

While the afore-stated principles and values are self-evident in well-functioning parliaments in many parts of the world, this is not always observable in the parliaments of many African states. The absence of effective and well-functioning representative institutions that effectively play the crucial roles of law-making, scrutinizing the executive and representing the people is the scarcest of political commodities throughout much of the continent. This dim reality of parliamentary politics has given rise to the perpetuation of authoritarian rule that has bred inefficiency, corruption and lack of accountability and responsiveness to the needs and demands of the citizens. The main contributing factor to this political malaise has been the fact that parliament has been 'the most underdeveloped amongst the three arms of government as it suffered from long years of authoritarian and military dictatorships in which the parliament was either outlawed or completely muzzled out in governance' (UNECA n.d.). It is against this background that this chapter examines the prospects and challenges of parliament acting as a genuinely representative institution in Ethiopia, carrying out the core representational, oversight and law and budget making functions.

Recent political history: parliament and democracy in Ethiopia?

Since the Second World War, Ethiopia has had three regimes of different persuasions and ideologies, viz. a traditional absolute monarchy (1931–1973), a repressive leftist military dictatorship (1974–1990) and a left-leaning-cum-capitalist government (1991-to the present). None of these governments had what could be considered strong, freely and democratically elected parliaments that served as genuine representative institutions. Parliament was often dominated by a ruling clique with vested interests or a single party, with multi-party and competitive politics the exception rather than the rule. The political order was authoritarian and top down. Simply put, all the three post-Second World War governments commonly shared an unenviable historical legacy of failure to institutionalize a truly parliamentary and democratic form of rule.

In the caricature of Ethiopian politics, the legislature has often been dominated by the executive branch of government, and this has impacted its oversight function as well as propensity to represent the interests and needs of the electorate. When it comes to law-making, the legislature has also been a weak institution serving only to rubber-stamp government policies and programmes without sufficient public scrutiny. Unless there are changes in these fundamental tenets of Ethiopia's political praxis that are commonly shared by successive regimes, aspirations for parliamentary democracy and participatory governance will remain unfulfilled dreams for many years to come.

As noted above, an elected parliament acting as a genuinely representative body is a rare political success in contemporary Ethiopia. The country has a long history of independent statehood, but a formal parliament as an institution was first established under the long-reigning monarch Emperor Haile Selassie I in 1931. At the time, it was not a genuinely representative body but popularly accepted as a benevolent act of imperial reform and a progressive measure to build a centralized and modern state. There were no political parties and candidates for parliament were either largely drawn from the feudal aristocracy or selected for their support of the status quo. It was also around this period that the first written constitution was promulgated to lend modernity to a traditional monarchy whose legitimacy was largely derived from tradition and culture (Clapham 1969; Perham 1948).

The Imperial Ethiopian parliament could hardly be characterized as democratic or representative because it was not a freely elected body, and the members, almost all of whom belonged to the feudal gentry, were appointed by the monarch as a dispensation of imperial favour. The building of a modern administrative and political infrastructure was at its infancy, and politics was the business of the narrow feudal elite as the mass of the people were passive agents who did not dare to question the power of the rulers. According to many observers of feudal Ethiopia, the Emperor appointed members of what he considered to be rebellious aristocracy to parliament as a means to undercut their regional support bases and place them under the watchful eyes of the central government (Perham 1948; Beyene & Markakis 1974; Koehn & Hayes 1978).

Starting in the mid-1950s, the imperial regime instituted some reforms aimed at modernizing parliament and the constitution. A harbinger of this initiative was the introduction of the revised 1955 Constitution, which saw a slight improvement over the original 1931 Constitution. There was some degree of universal suffrage, and some rudiments of a functioning parliament were sown, such as a more assertive legislature over the executive and more open and critical parliamentary debates on social and economic issues. Ostensibly, all these measures were intended to pave the way for a constitutional monarchy, and also institutionalize some form of parliamentary democracy, however embryonic it might be.

Despite its feudal and decidedly traditionalist credentials, the imperial regime (1931–1974) had introduced significant administrative reforms, such as the creation of a modern professional standing army and a civil service bureaucracy, and expanded modern education and health services (Zewde 2002). At the international level, the country became a respected member of the club of nations, and was very much active in pan-African politics, including playing an important role in the establishment of the Organization of the African Unity (OAU) in the early 1960s – now the African Union (AU). Equally important, the regime also enjoyed a great deal of legitimacy and public support that neither of its two successors had been able to attain since its departure in the early 1970s (Perham 1948; Clapham 1969).

The preceding steps aimed at opening up the traditional Ethiopian state did not bring about substantial change in the composition and workings of parliament, and the imperial regime continued with business as usual until it was swept away by a popular revolt in 1974. An oppressive left-wing military dictatorship popularly known as the *Derg*, which plunged the country into unprecedented turmoil for the next seventeen years, replaced one of the world's oldest monarchies (Halliday & Molyneux 1981; Markakis 1974). Subsequently, the First Ethiopian Republic was set up, with the military disguising itself as a civilian government. The military regime has a notorious record with no bounds for its egregious human rights record, including ruthless suppression of individual freedoms, brutal crackdown on dissent, arbitrary and unlawful arrests, killings en masse, etc.

The military-led government had a highly repressive governance system that was devoid of any semblance of participatory democracy.

Economic management was modelled after the then-Soviet prototype and largely controlled by the government. There was extensive nationalization of land and other forms of private property. A one-party state masquerading as representing the working class and rural farmers was crafted, slamming the door on any competitive and participatory politics. The parliament, or the *Shengo* as it was then called, was extremely weak, an institution with no authority at all but to rubberstamp the decisions of a ruling military clique (Ayenew, 1997; Tiruneh, 1993; Halliday & Molyneux, 1981).

The *Derg*'s (1974–91) misrule generated widespread discontent and resistance among the people. As a result, a number of ethnic-based opposition movements proliferated throughout the country and waged an armed struggle to topple the regime. This became a recipe for instability and destruction of the country's economy and infrastructure. The economy was left in ruins, living standards reached an all-time low level, and the country's infrastructure was in total disrepair. Much of the country's meagre resources were invested in fighting internal wars. The mismanagement of the state and society inevitably brought about the violent downfall of the regime in 1991. It was replaced by the Ethiopian Peoples' Revolutionary Democratic Front (EPRDF), which is a coalition of ethnic-based organizations that continues to rule the country to this day (Harbeson 1988).

As a movement, the EPRDF espoused a leftist economic and political ideology. Upon coming to power in 1991, however, the group appeared to abandon much of the left-leaning economic and political posture adopted during many years of armed struggle, and opted for a market-driven economy and a participatory political process, including free and multi-party elections. Because of the historic changes in the world scene with the Soviet Union gone and the rest of the world dominated by the USA and the West, the EPRDF did not have much option but to reaffirm its commitment to a form of democracy and elected government, and an economic development model that would recognize the private sector as an important player. Many critics of the current government took this as a gimmick to consolidate power rather than a solemn pledge to institutionalize meaningful democratic rule, because after nearly twenty-five years of EPRDF rule Ethiopia still remains a one-party authoritarian state. This was no wonder for many observers of the Ethiopian political scene given the pro-Chinese-Marxist-Leninist credentials of the Tigray People's Liberation Front (TPLF)-EPRDF as a guerrilla movement that fought and replaced the military regime (Pausewang et al. 2002).

Upon assuming power, the EPRDF Government expressed commitment to an elected popular government and a sovereign parliament that would be a vehicle for democracy and good governance. It also expressed respect for fundamental human rights, including freedom of expression, assembly and organization. The right of the diverse ethnic and nationality groups to self-rule was recognized as a possible remedy to end many years of ethnic-based strife and instability. In the first few years of its rule, there were also some prospects that encouraged the emergence of an independent and free private media functioning competitively alongside a government-owned counterpart, and there was a permissive environment for unfettered and free activity by civil society. All this was, however, short lived.

To be more specific, on the political front, unwarranted and gross violations of human rights that characterized the *Derg* era were capped, and there was increased respect for citizen rights and freedoms. Formal elections were also conducted from time to time to institutionalize a democratic parliament. On the whole, the EPRDF offered Ethiopian society better prospects for a more accountable, humane and participatory rule than its predecessor – the military-dominated *Derg*. It needs to be observed, though, that these commitments in many instances were easier said than fulfilled, and the Ethiopian people still yearn for the full realization of these rights and the institutionalization of a truly democratic political order after over 25 years of EPRDF rule (Rahmato & Meheret 2004; Fisseha 2014).

Elections and parliamentary democracy under the EPRDF?

Despite repeated formal elections, the electoral landscape in post-*Derg* Ethiopia is characterized by single-party dominance. As has been argued in the preceding paragraphs, upon coming to power in the early 1990s, the EPRDF currently ruling the country had committed itself to parliamentary democracy, including free and competitive elections and a pluralist political order. As a result, it has conducted five national elections, viz. 1995, 2002, 2005, 2010 and 2015. Despite this fact, little or no headway has been achieved in instituting multi-party competitive politics because the ruling party has always been the dominant winner in all the elections, often with a landslide. Over the years, this has resulted in the entrenchment of one-party rule, and the absence of any alternative opposition worthy of the name.

As can be observed in Table 5.1, the ruling party and its allies have always been the big winner since the advent of multi-party politics in the country. In the last two elections the outcome has eroded the legitimacy of parliament as a representative institution, and dimmed any hopes of introducing multi-party competitive politics in Africa's second-largest country (by population) any time in the near future. As can be observed in the table, what is unprecedented is the fact that the governing party won all parliamentary seats in the 2015 national elections, which gave rise to questions about the credibility of the outcome.

Table 5.1 Results of National Elections in Ethiopia under the EPRDF, 1995–2015

	Election year	Parliamentary seats won by the ruling party and coalition partners	Parliamentary seats won by the opposition and independent candidates	Percentage of seats won by the ruling party
1.	1995	496	50	89.0
2.	2000	481	66	87.9
3.	2005	367	172	66.9
4.	2010	545	2	99.6
5.	2015	546	–	100.0

Source National Electoral Board of Ethiopia, 'National Election Results' 1995, 2000, 2005, 2010 and 2015, and *The Guardian* June 2015.

From among Ethiopia's elections, that in 2005 was the most democratic, free and competitive in the country's history, most importantly because the, opposition parties and independents won a dramatic 34 per cent of all parliamentary seats (Table 5.1) at the national level. They also won nearly all the city council seats in the capital Addis Ababa, which, being the capital city, is a highly significant political jurisdiction. This was a fact of history considered extraordinary given the country's relatively short experience in democratic political practice. The secret of the 2005 success was the fact that there was an even playing field and a conducive environment that allowed genuine political competition, considerable public interest and a free and fair electoral process. In addition, non-state actors, including civil society organizations, trade unions, professional associations and the media, all played active roles in the election, and there were lively debates and discussions by all contestants on important national issues (EU Election Observation Mission 2005; Carter Center 2009).

Although Ethiopia's 2005 elections were hailed as a success in democratic experiment, the results were short lived in creating a genuinely competitive political process. The opposition alleged voting irregularities and cheating by the ruling party/government, and as elsewhere in Africa, the latter accused their competitors of refusing to behave according to rules. Subsequently, both parties contested the outcome, and turmoil and violence ensued, leading to the unwarranted killing of innocent civilians. This was a serious setback and an unfortunate episode in terms of turning back irreversibly the wheels of democracy in Ethiopia, and also a harbinger for the institutionalization of one-party rule. Equally important, what could be considered a promising start by the opposition to scrutinize government and hold public officials accountable for decisions and actions were all gone thus paving the way for an authoritarian political order.

In relative terms, the 2010 elections were less violent but not as free and competitive. According to election observers from within and outside of the country, there was little by way of an even playing field for all parties contesting the country's politics. In addition, non-state actors and other democratic forces showed little interest in the election process, the media was muted, and there was very little of the debate and discussion characterizing competitive elections. As a result, the final outcome was overwhelmingly dominated by the ruling EPRDF claiming all but two (one opposition and one independent) out of the 546-seat parliament (NEBE 2010).

After the 2005 national elections, which, as indicated earlier, were marred by violence, the government took steps to clamp down on forces that would dare to challenge the party's hegemonic position. Parliament, in which the ruling party had an overwhelming majority controlling 544 of the 546 seats, passed the civil society (2009), media (2008) and anti-terrorism (2009) laws that dealt a severe blow to the potential involvement of independent organizations in political activity. They were indeed meant to cement the political authority of a single ruling party. The measures were widely criticized by human rights organizations and independent observers as being restrictions on civil and political rights of citizens. The criticisms have been justified because the cumulative effect of the measures has been the progressive narrowing of the political space, the weakening of the opposition, a restricted media, and the entrenchment of an authoritarian single-party rule that controls the executive and the legislature (U.S. Department of State 2013; Human Rights Watch 2014, 2015). For its part, the government claims that these measures are necessary to contain foreign interference in the country's internal affairs, keep law and order, and also fight terrorism.

In May 2015, Ethiopia held the third important national and regional elections under the EPRDF, and the results were a foregone conclusion. The ruling party won in a landslide victory claiming all the seats in the 546-seat national parliament, and all the seats in the regional councils. This hundred per cent victory marked a major turn of events in Ethiopia's political evolution with no opposition in parliament since the EPRDF came to power more than twenty-five years ago. Many observers and critics of the government characterized the election as flawed and not up to international standards for a free and fair election because the opposition was marginalized, and the political space was very much skewed in favour of the ruling party, which employed formal elections only to seek a cloak of legitimacy (Lyons 2015). In addition, there were restrictions on the voices of civil society, the media and the opposition to be involved in the election processes. No external election observers from the European Union and the USA were invited, with only observers from the African Union allowed to oversee the elections (African Union 2015; U.S. Department of State, 2015).

From the preceding, it can be observed that, despite repeated elections, multi-party and competitive politics have not taken root in Ethiopia, and the system remains dominated by a single ruling party. In other words, parliament has remained a one-party institution because there has not been a viable opposition that has made much headway in contesting the ruling party. This will no doubt negatively impact parliament as a genuinely representative institution reflecting different views and perspectives. Although the country has attained significant economic progress in recent years, this victory has not been repeated in the political democratic realm. Simply put, Ethiopia is effectively a one-party state today as it was when the EPRDF came to power in the early 1990s. For a country as diverse and complex as Ethiopia, democratic politics is as critical as economic progress to guarantee its stability and continuity as a state.

Ethiopia: political background

With an estimated population of more than 100 million, Ethiopia is Africa's second-most populous nation after Nigeria. With a population growth rate currently exceeding 3 per cent per annum, the numbers are projected to reach 175 million by 2050, which will make it one of the most densely inhabited countries in the world.[2] The country is a demographic power house accounting for more than 35 per cent of the total population of the IGAD countries comprising ten nation states in the north-eastern and Horn of Africa region. The population is largely young with a significant 40 per cent aged under 24 years (CIA 2016; U.S. Census Bureau 2014).

The Ethiopian state is a land of great diversity comprising numerous ethnic and religious groups. Most Ethiopians are followers of two major religions – Christianity and Islam.[3] A significant majority of Ethiopians are Christians accounting for nearly 63 per cent of the total population. Among these, Orthodox Christians constitute 43.5 per cent; Protestants 18.6 per cent; Catholics 0.7 per cent, and about 3 per cent belong to different religions. Muslim Ethiopians constitute about 33.9 per cent of the total. While all beliefs can be found in almost every community, Islam is most prevalent among the Somali (98.4 per cent), Afar (95.3 per cent) and Oromia (47.5 per cent) Regions (CSA 2007).

Ethiopia is unique in very many respects. It is Africa's oldest inde-

---

[2] Some sources project a higher figure, depending upon varying assumptions.
[3] The number of Ethiopian Jews otherwise known as 'Bete Israel' has diminished since their exodus to Israel beginning in the mid-1980s.

pendent country that has enjoyed an uninterrupted tradition of state-hood, and has never been colonized by the Europeans except for the brief five-year occupation by Fascist Italy during the Second World War. It has a distinctly indigenous alphabet and calendar system that set it apart from other nations. The rich heritage and diversified value systems and traditions of Christians and Muslims point to the possi-bility that Ethiopia might have for centuries been a meeting centre of African, Arab and Asiatic cultures.

In 1991, Ethiopia's geographic political boundary was redrawn following a referendum that resulted in Eritrea, with the two vital ports of Assab and Massawa, becoming a separate state, having previ-ously been a constituent part – albeit a problematic co-existence. This rendered the country land-locked with no outlet to the sea. As a result, it resorted to using the port of Djibouti and to some extent other ports in East Africa, such as Mombasa in Kenya, Port Sudan and Berbera in Somaliland, for trade and other links with the outside world.

From 1998 to 2000, Ethiopia and Eritrea, to the dismay of friends far and near, fought a bitter border war that cost the lives of about 100,000 people in total; and relations did not heal for a long time (Abbink 2003; Banks et al. 2005). A no-peace-no-war, but tense, situation existed along their common border for more than two decades. Hence, relations between the two nations that share a great deal of common historical, linguistic and religio-cultural ties had remained on edge. Unnecessary and costly clashes again erupted in 2016 resulting in considerable loss of lives and property damage on both sides. This situation was dramati-cally reversed in 2018 with the coming to power of Ethiopia's new Prime Minister Dr Abiy Ahmed who courageously restored normal relations between the two countries thus ushering a new era of peace and oppor-tunities for collaboration between the two peoples.

Ethnicity and language are important features shaping national politics in Ethiopia; and in recent years have been important factors in restructuring the state and political representation at national and regional levels. The current government led by the ruling Ethi-opian Revolutionary Democratic Front (EPRDF) is the torch bearer of this political agenda. Upon assuming power in 1991, the EPRDF Government reorganized the country along ethnic and linguistic lines, and established a federal state structure that consisted of nine autonomous ethnic regions and two administrative areas. These are Gambella, Harari, Oromiya, Somali, Southern Nations, Nationalities, and Peoples (SNNP) and Tigray regional states with Addis Ababa and Dire Dawa city administrations designated as self-governing adminis-trative areas. Most of these regions have their own constitutions and enjoy formal self-rule, including the right to develop their cultures and history as well as the right to use regional languages in public admin-istration, service delivery and the school system. As much as these political rights are important in a genuinely federal system, critics of the government have argued that these policies have been used to entrench ethnic divisions and sow mistrust among the country's disparate groups to achieve short-term goals of divide and rule.

Ethiopia: economic background

On the economic front, Ethiopia's economy is predominantly agriculture based, which accounts for 46 per cent of GDP and more than 80 per cent of total employment. For much of the 1970s and 1980s, the country suffered from recurrent famines and food shortages that affected millions of people. In recent years, the Ethiopian economy has been showing signs of improvement resulting in reductions in national poverty levels. The government has been spearheading development by undertaking major infrastructural projects in the power and communication sectors, and significant investments in developing large-scale sugar industries and allied activities. The government's role is also preponderant in other areas. For example, land is held by the state, and the banking and insurance industry is restricted to domestic investors, with telecoms services off limits to foreign investment. Through the relatively successful implementation of the country's Growth and Transformation Plan I (GTP I), 2011/12–2014/15, good progress has been attained in the provision of education, low-cost housing and health services, and also in infrastructure expansion (MoFED 2014).

The economy is also showing signs of structural transformation with industry and the services sector contributing 13.4 per cent and 45.6 per cent to GDP respectively (MoFED 2010, 2014; Rahmato et al. 2014). Despite recent economic gains, however, there is widespread public perception that development has not been inclusive and participatory, and the benefits have not been equitably shared among the different ethnic and social groups, and this has been the primary cause of the recent social upheaval in the country.

Another area of concern that increasingly attracts bad publicity is the government's less than desirable record on democracy, human rights and media freedom. Despite the praiseworthy performance in economic growth, criticisms continue to be labelled against the government for stifling dissent and independent opinion, as well as its heavy-handed restrictions on opposition parties, the media and civil society organizations (Amnesty International 2016; Human Rights Watch 2008, 2009; U.S. Department of State 2013). These undemocratic credentials have hurt the country's image and diverted the spotlight from its economic success. In addition, the long-term consequences of these confines on the political and societal stability of the nation remain unpredictable.

Parliamentary democracy in Ethiopia: limitations and challenges

Structure of parliament

According to Article 53 of the Ethiopian constitution, the Ethiopian parliament has two houses: (i) the House of Federation (HoF), and (ii) the House of Peoples' Representatives. The former is a 153-member assembly, which can be considered the upper house, and consists of members designated by regional governments representing the different ethnic or nationality groups. It has formal powers only to deal with constitutional issues and ethnic or nationality matters. In other words, it does not deal with substantive legislation. The House of Peoples' Representatives (HoPR), which can be considered the lower house and is elected by public vote, constitutes the 546-seat parliament of the nation, and is the main law-making or legislative body of the country. Members are elected for a five-year term.

Since Ethiopia has formally a cabinet form of government, both houses of parliament are controlled by the ruling party, which also leads the executive branch of government. This raises questions about the efficacy of the checks and balances arrangement, the more so in the Ethiopian situation where one-party monopoly of state and government is an important feature of the political system. This only helps the ruling party to ride roughshod over laws and policies without sufficient debate and often with unanimous consensus. No doubt the absence of a viable opposition thanks to the restrictions on political activity and civil society as well as lack of unity within the opposition side have contributed to one-party rule and absence of competitive governance and political process.

Parliament's roles, features and limitations

As modern politics dictates, the formal functions of the Ethiopian parliament include representing the people in one of the most important institutions of government, scrutinizing the work of the executive, and making laws and policies that promote the development of the country and society. In fulfilling their representational duties, parliamentarians are expected to interact with their constituencies regularly so that they can consider voter concerns and preferences in the law and policy-making process. This will help them to be responsive and accountable to the electorate, which in turn can lend legitimacy and popularity to the government of the day.

As elsewhere in Africa, formal elections of one type or another have been standard features of Ethiopian politics under the three post-Second World War regimes. But, these elections cannot qualify or be considered as expressions of the democratic aspirations of the people because they have always been short of being free, fair and competitive by international standards (except perhaps the 2005 national elections). It needs to be pointed out, though, that the situation can be even more complex because, in a diverse and vastly rural country such as Ethiopia, it may not always be possible to capture the true needs and concerns of the disparate population. Even with this caveat, free and fair elections lend legitimacy to the political process, and there should not be any compromise on their conduct according to internationally accepted practices. Modern Ethiopia has never experienced peaceful transfer of power nor has there been change of government through the electoral system. As a result, post-Second World War Ethiopia has been for the most part effectively a one-party state with serious shortcomings in critical fundamentals of democratic governance and political plurality.

In Ethiopia, the dominance of the executive for a long time has meant that parliament has been an instrument in the hands of the ruling party rather than an autonomous representative institution reflecting the democratic aspirations of the people. Over the years, the weakness of parliament has given rise to fundamental problems in the political system, including lack of respect for the rule of law; absence of due process; impunity in government and lack of accountability by public officials; excessive dominance of public life by the executive; and absence of an independent judiciary that can uphold the basic rights of citizens. These dysfunctions of the political system were repeatedly mentioned as the most serious obstacles to Ethiopia's democratic transformation by organizers and leaders of civil society organizations, academics and researchers and participants in the FGDs, all of which were important sources of information for this study on the Ethiopian parliament.

Despite the preceding challenges, however, it is not all doom and gloom for the Ethiopian parliament. Worth mentioning in this regard is the fact that the national parliament has a very influential and active women's caucus consisting of seventeen women parliamentarians in the executive leadership. The sizeable female membership in parliament's composition has been a critical factor contributing to the success in giving prominence to women rights and concerns. For example, the important role women MPs played in the adoption of the family law and the strong advocacy work that they staged to promote girls' education in the nation's colleges and universities as well as their vigorous efforts to build the capacity of female members of parliament through further education and training can be cited as cases in point. The caucus' hard work has helped to elevate the status of women as leaders and members of important parliamentary standing committees. In the current parliament, there are 212 women MPs (38.76 per cent) out of the 547-members' assembly, who vigorously work to have enough representation of women in the six permanent standing committees, and actively participate in the budget debates to ensure that gender is

mainstreamed in key pro-poor and growth sectors, including education, health and infrastructure budget allocations.

In field discussions, it was also learnt that the women's caucus is very
active in many areas. For example, it had prepared a checklist to guide
discussions with constituencies by women parliamentarians. The aim
is to ensure that women's issues and concerns are given sufficient focus,
particularly in national poverty mitigation efforts. In its campaign
work, the caucus also solicits the support of male parliamentarians to
earn votes for legislation and policies that support the cause of women,
such as the national women's policy and the law on rural land registration and certification. The checklist has been particularly useful in
scrutinizing the performance reports of executive departments and
bureaus against plans and targets that are intended to bring about the
fulfilment of the economic, political and social rights of women. Be it
at the regional or federal levels, it was revealed in the interviews with
women MPs that the implementing bodies will be required to provide
explanations for discrepancies between plan and performance, or offer
commitments to follow through the accomplishments of planned objectives targeting women. For example, it was also learnt that the checklist is shared with and popularized among other male parliamentary
peers supporting the cause of women rights to help them in constituency engagements.

In addition, the caucus has been very active in championing and
targeting pressing needs of women and girls. For example, monitoring
the activities of public health service providers and other interested
parties to mitigate the adverse effects of harmful traditional practices,
such as early marriage, on women and young girls has been one of the
priority areas of concern. Despite mixed success, working to reduce the
attrition rate of female students in colleges and universities has also
been yet another of caucus's preoccupations. An equally important
success story that deserves mention has been the admirable work of
lobbying and campaigning that the caucus carried out that resulted
in a significant increase in the number of female councillors in the
emerging and historically marginalized regional states of the country,
such as the Somali and Afar regions of Ethiopia, where there are more
potent cultural norms and attitudes that discourage the participation
of women in politics than in the highland areas. This observation came
out during discussions with parliamentarians from these regions and
some members of the women caucus. It has also been confirmed by data
from the National Electoral Board of Ethiopia (NEBE), which indicated
that there had been a substantial increase in the number of women
representatives in parliament. For example, in the Somali region, while
the twenty-three-member regional representation was an all-male
club during the 2010–14 parliamentary sessions, women occupied
fourteen seats in the 2015 national elections. By the same token, out

of the nine-seat regional representation in Benshangul-Gumuz, two were women between 2010 and 2014, and this number increased to four women out of the nine representatives in the 2015 national elections (NEBE 2015).

The preceding discussion is intended to provide a proper context for assessing the strengths and weaknesses of parliament in Ethiopia, including why it has not developed into a potent vehicle for the democratic transformation of the post-Second World War state, the more so over the past twenty-five years of rule. In particular, it has to be noted that the country has achieved relative economic improvement and poverty reduction but there has also been increased political and social instability because of a shrinking political space and authoritarian rule. Democracy rooted in a strong and a genuinely representative parliament may be one answer to unlock the impasse, and the provision of a stable political and social environment. Here below, are presented some of the observations.

Ethiopian parliamentarians face conflicting roles that have impacted responsiveness to constituency needs and concerns
Based on field data and FGDs with the electorate and interviews with selected parliamentarians, Ethiopian parliamentarians' perception of their role is dual, i.e. they view themselves as representatives of both the electorate and the party. Since most candidates are nominated for election by the party in power, they see themselves as playing an intermediary role between the electorate and the government. On the other hand, this conflicting role is not well received by the electorate because it has engendered a widespread perception that parliamentarians are representatives of the party/government and not of the people, and thus cannot be purveyors of genuine concerns and needs of their constituencies in government decisions and policies. In the long run, this can erode public trust in parliament as a representative institution, while at the same time reinforcing the perception that party loyalty is more important than constituency interests, the more so in a political landscape monopolized by a single political party. Also, given the preponderant nature of single ruling parties and their monopoly grip on power, this can also affect the accountability of politicians for their decisions and actions.

For their part, politicians see their engagements as exercises in democracy and accountability but also as fulfilling party requirements to meet the citizens who elected them twice a year, which is a characteristic of a highly organized and ideological party, such as the EPRDF. Simply put, parliamentarians perceive dual roles in dealing with their constituencies: as representatives of the ruling party and as conveyors of the interests and concerns of those who elected them. In FGDs, this was a subject of much criticism by the electoral public, who continue to demand more accountability and responsiveness from their parliamentary representatives. On the other hand, politicians have accepted it as a legitimate form of engagement with citizens with no potential conflict of interest.

Need for more intensive and frequent engagement of parliamentarians
with constituencies for accountable governance
In Ethiopia, there is the need for more frequent and regular interaction between parliamentarians and their constituencies to strengthen accountability and responsiveness to voter concerns and needs in law/policy-making. At present, Ethiopian parliamentarians' interaction with their constituencies leaves much to be desired because of its formal and structured style, conducted according to party rules and guidelines, such that it provides very little opportunity for free and unfettered interaction. Constituency visits were arranged in consultation with regional/local governments or party offices who determined who they were to meet and what were the issues to be discussed, and these included discussions with some members of the electorate and local administration sector offices/bureaus about the state of public services and development being provided to the community. Simply put, to be expressions of democratic engagement and accountable governance, consultations that parliamentarians hold with constituencies have to be arranged in such a way that they will be free from party or local government influence. In addition, they should be organized according to times and places convenient to the community as this will make parliamentarians more accessible and easily reachable. This is very important because one of the complaints aired by the communities in FGDs was that they were often called upon to meet parliamentarians during times when they are fully or actively engaged in important social and economic activities, such as the harvest season or during important community or social chores.

Moreover, current party rules stipulate that Ethiopian parliamentarians should visit their constituencies twice a year. The experiences of some other countries suggest that frequent interactions between constituency groups and parliamentarians strengthen democracy and responsiveness (Mtanda 2014; Veit et al. 2008). In this regard, the Ethiopian experience was found to be inadequate to capture the voices of the electorate and ensure that the same is considered in development policies and programmes. Ethiopia is a big country and the poor infrastructure on the one hand and shortage of resources available to parliamentarians on the other can be possible explanations for not conducting frequent interactions. Since representing the views and concerns of the electorate is an extremely important duty of a parliamentarian, it is strongly suggested that means and ways be found to overcome the current constraints for enhanced parliamentarian-constituency interaction for greater accountability and responsiveness.

These preliminary observations of this study suggest a situation where citizens cannot discuss or debate community concerns freely and openly as they will be constrained to express their views about politics or economics because of the risks of being accused critics of the government. The Ethiopian experience of limited and formal engagement of parliamentarians with constituencies may sound a contradistinction in many parts of the world where parliamentarians or politicians are often criticized for spending too much time with their constituencies (to retain their seats) and are left with little time to fulfil their parliamentary duties. This may lead to the argument that it is not the amount of time that parliamentarians spend with their constituencies that is important but the quality of the interaction, i.e. whether citizens' voices and concerns are listened to by politicians.

Limited political space for non-state actors in the policy/law-making process by parliament
According to research findings of the research programme 'Parliament, Public Engagement and Poverty Reduction in Ethiopia and Bangladesh', there is limited public involvement in law/policy-making by parliament in Ethiopia. Hence, there is the need particularly for parliamentary standing committees to reach out to more stakeholders to provide inputs and recommendations for policy action. It can be argued that this has been an attendant consequence of single-party rule and a progressively narrowing political space for non-state stakeholders and opposition parties. In interviews with civil society leaders and activists, it was revealed that government policy or law-making was a largely ruling party affair. Be it at the federal or regional levels, legislators do not often consult or approach representatives of independent civil society organizations or other actors to listen to their views or seek inputs. Bypassing this important sector in government decisions can reduce policy responsiveness to community needs and demands. In addition, it is vitally important that policy or law-making be as participative as possible to enhance the democratic credentials of parliament as a representative institution.

In 2009, the Government of Ethiopia enacted a law that restricted the activities of civil society organizations and all forms of voluntary associations. Among other things, the law prohibited these organizations from engaging in advocacy or promotion of human and democratic rights if more than 10 per cent of funding for such activities comes from external/foreign sources (Assefa & Bahru 2010). In addition, the legislation put in place a strict legal and regulatory framework, and this has not helped the growth of the civil society organizations in the country. One indicator of this has been the fact that the number of civil society organizations in Ethiopia has been low compared with many other countries. For example, there were about 3,200 registered civil society organizations in Ethiopia in 2014 while in neighbouring Kenya – with less than half Ethiopia's population – there were more than 6,500 civil society organizations operating in the country (ICNL 2019a). The reality on the ground points to the need for the Ethiopian Government to recognize that a vibrant civil society culture with a conducive environment for unfettered public participation and engagement in the policy process is an important component of democratic governance.

High representation of women members in the Ethiopian parliament
That the Ethiopian parliament has a high membership of women among its ranks can be recognized as a noteworthy strength for a representative institution. Articles 14 and 35 of the Ethiopian Constitution provide for equal rights of men and women. One of the ways by which this can find practical expression is through the active involvement and recognition of women in policy and law-making as well as through leadership roles in the government's high offices. In this regard, Ethiopia has attained relative success by encouraging women to serve as politicians/parliamentarians and occupying important leadership positions (Gebre-Sellassie 2005; Ashenafi 2008). In this regard, the strong representation of women MPs in the eighteen different standing sub-committees can be cited as an example. Also, the fact that women MPs serve as chairs or deputy chairs in eleven of them lends credence to this observation (HoPR 2016).

As a country with more than 50 per cent female population, Ethiopia cannot afford to ignore the cause of women, and one of the ways of enhancing their status is fair representation in parliament and different levels of government. In this regard, there has been some headway in recent years. As can be seen in Table 5.2, the proportion of elected women representatives of parliament in the country's national elections over the past many years has shown significant increases in the federal legislature as well as in big regional councils. This increasing number of women MPs has been particularly evident during the past five elections conducted under the EPRDF.

In interviews and FGDs with women parliamentarians, it was revealed that the high female representation has contributed to the advancement of certain rights of women, who often are not treated equal as men when it comes to important social and economic benefits. Although it is difficult to draw a cause-and-effect relationship, it can be argued that the increasing number has helped to give prominence to women's issues and to make legislation and policies supportive of their causes. For this, some women MPs cited their advocacy and lobbying work in the enactment of the family law, which was enacted to recog-

Table 5.2 Distribution of Male and Female Members of the Ethiopian Parliament, 1995–2015

	Election year	Total number of candidates	Distribution of parliamentary seats		Percentage of women members
			Male	Female	
1.	1995	2,871	526	11	2.01
2.	2000	–	505	42	7.68
3.	2005	1,594	410	116	21.21
4.	2010	2,188	395	152	27.79
5.	2015	1,828	335	212	38.76

Source House of Peoples' Representatives (HoPR), Addis Ababa, Ethiopia, 2016

nize the right of women to paid leave from work before, during and after giving birth. Another success story has been the right of women in rural Ethiopia to secure land registrations certificates in their own names, reversing a long-standing practice of recognizing rights to farm land in the name of husbands or male-headed households. Thanks to the efforts of women parliamentarians, this has been dubbed as an important gain for women in rural areas all over the country. In discussions conducted with independent women groups, however, it was pointed out that some of these successes were not attained without the active support and participation of independent civil society organizations, such as the Ethiopian Women Lawyers Association and other civic groups – a claim also shared by women MPs.

Need to overcome constraints to effective parliamentary oversight of the executive
The degree of success that parliaments as representative institutions attain in exercising oversight over the executive is a litmus test of their effectiveness. Indeed, this is a strong element in representational politics because it is instrumental in holding government officials accountable and responsive to public demands and concerns. The voters through their parliamentary representatives want politicians to be held accountable for their decisions and actions. This will compel them to be more transparent and responsive to public needs and concerns, and the Ethiopian parliament cannot be an exception.

In Ethiopia, the performance of parliament in exercising its oversight function leaves much to be desired. This is partly explained by executive dominance over the legislature and the omnipresence of the single ruling party, which controls both branches of government. In addition, the absence of a viable and strong opposition has also contributed to limited legislative scrutiny over government programmes and plans. Simply put, in many one-party African states including Ethiopia, parliament's control over the executive is ceremonial, and is intended to provide legitimacy to the ruling party rather than an exercise in checks and balances

On the surface, there are some degrees of checks and balances in the Ethiopian parliament. For example, the prime minister is by law required to report on his/her government's performance every six months to the full house. In addition, all ministers and heads of federal agencies and commissions have also to report to parliament and selected standing sub-committees on their departments' performance and plans during formal question and answer sessions. However, these exercises remain largely formal and are subdued affairs because there is very little debate on alternative policies and laws due to the ruling party's overwhelming control of parliament, and in such a system, as the Ethiopian experience suggests, it is not easy for parliamentary representatives to offer options or to question plans and programmes presented by the executive.

As a way out, the Ethiopian Government needs to open up the political space to competitive electoral politics and encourage the growth of a vibrant media to strengthen public scrutiny over government. At a minimum, easing restrictions on civil society and the media, allowing freedom of action and a level playing field for opposition political parties, letting opposition political parties have equal access to the media, and, most important of all, amending the laws on civil society, media and the anti-terrorism bill, which are increasingly used to stifle dissent and freedoms of expression and organization, would be important first steps. The current government decision-making process, which is top down and authoritarian and carried out with little input from the public, should give way to a more transparent and participative model. In this regard, recognizing the supremacy of a parliament composed of freely and fairly elected representatives of the people as the final decision-maker in the land is of paramount importance. In addition, there needs to be a conducive political environment that permits the free flow of ideas and participation by different stakeholders to enhance accountability and legislative oversight over the executive.

Limited public participation in the policy process has been a brake on parliamentary democracy
An additional yardstick to assess the effectiveness of the Ethiopian parliament as a democratic institution is the extent of public participation in the law-making process. In particular, inviting inputs from experts and listening to the voices of the different societal and economic groups can make the laws responsive to the needs and demands of different constituencies. Wide public participation in the policy process can strengthen democracy, and enhance trust in parliament as a representative body working for the equality and fair treatment of all segments of society.

As has been argued elsewhere in this chapter, due to executive dominance and single-party rule, the Ethiopian legislature is known for hurriedly passing through laws and policies without sufficient critical public debate and input. This has rendered the political system authoritarian and much less inclusive, whereby alternative inputs into policies and laws by important societal actors, viz. opposition political parties, civil society, the private sector, the media, etc. are hardly entertained. The recent promulgation of controversial legislations, viz. the civil society law and the anti-terrorism and media bills, which, according to critics and observers of the Ethiopian Government, have been used to restrict democratic freedoms of speech, organization and independent political activity, can be cited as examples. Needless to say, a political system that is bent upon progressively narrowing the space, be it for all segments of society or a special section of the population, can hardly purport to be stable, sustainable and healthy, and the wave of unrest in many parts of Ethiopia in 2018 and 2019 lends credence to this observation.

Conclusion

Parliament can be an important institution in Ethiopia's democratic transformation, but there are huge challenges to overcome. Its effectiveness as a representative institution is compromised by single-party rule and executive dominance of many aspects of government. This has been a fertile ground for the perpetuation of an authoritarian system of rule with little accountability and responsiveness to the demands and interests of the people. In Africa as a whole, weak parliaments are a strong sign of the democratic deficit afflicting much of the continent. The Ethiopian parliament cannot be immune from this because it has manifested a mixed record in fulfilling its law-making function and representational role as well as exercising effective oversight authority over the executive branch of government.

In Ethiopia, the extent of public participation in the law/policy-making process by parliament leaves much to be desired. Often, laws are passed by fiat with insufficient public participation, and this has reinforced the perception that parliament is an appendage of the government. Its failure to consider the interests and needs of the different sectors of society has generated the perception that the legislature is subordinated to the executive. This has been a result of the progressive narrowing of the space for political activity by different stakeholders, including opposition parties, the civil society sector and the media. There is no alternative to a participative and inclusive policy-making and implementation process for a stable society and economy in Ethiopia and elsewhere in Africa.

Parliamentarian-electorate engagement is an important aspect of the democratic process because it is an effective means by which politicians can be held accountable and be responsive to the needs and concerns of the people. In this regard, the record of the Ethiopian parliament is far from desirable because constituency interactions with their representatives need to be conducted more often for meaningful democratic engagement. In addition, it is necessary to make these engagements less formal and free from party influence so that people can express their views and concerns freely and without any restraint.

One of the strong features of the Ethiopian parliament as a democratic and representative institution is the consistently high representation of women members among its ranks. Because of the strong leadership of the women's caucus in parliament, this has been an important factor in gender empowerment and the protection of rights and privileges of Ethiopian women. Although it is difficult to show a cause-and-effect relationship, the causes and concerns of women, more than 50 per cent of the population, have been better heard and considered in economic and social plans as well as laws thanks to the energetic efforts of elected women in parliament.

Finally, Ethiopia has registered success in economic growth and poverty reduction efforts in recent years. Despite the economic progress, however, there has been a rising level of social and political tension between the government and groups with different visions for the future of the Ethiopian state and society. A shrinking political space and the increasingly authoritarian style of rule are to blame for this. Over the past few years, the government has been following a heavy-handed policy of restricting the activities of different stakeholders, including the media, civil society and opposition parties, and this has raised the level of public discontent. The precarious political situation and instability have raised questions as to whether the country can continue on an economic growth trajectory in the long run. Hence, the lesson from the Ethiopian experience is that economic growth must go hand in hand with sufficient set of political and democratic freedoms and an acceptable level of public consensus to be sustainable and to have a lasting impact on the lives of the people.

Bibliography

Abbink, John. 2003, 'Ethiopia-Eritrea: Proxy Wars and Prospects of Peace in the Horn of Africa'. *Journal of Contemporary African Studies* 21(3): 407–26.

African Union. 2015, 'Ethiopian Election: Text of African Union Observer Mission' Report, https://hornaffairs.com/2015/05/28/preliminary-statement-african-union-election-observation-mission-ethiopia, accessed 27 September 2019.

Amnesty International. 2016, 'Ethiopia, 2015/2016', www.refworld. org/docid/56d05b59c.html, accessed 27 September 2019.

Aribisala, Wale. n.d., 'The Role of Parliament in Poverty Reduction', https://sarpn.org/documents/d0002909/Parliament_Poverty_ Reduction_Aribisala.pdf, accessed 26 September 2019.

Ashenafi, Meaza. 2008, *Participation of Women in Politics and Public Decision Making in Ethiopia*, Monograph 5, Addis Ababa: Forum for Social Studies.

Assefa, Taye and Bahru Zewde. 2010, 'Civil Society at the Crossroads: Challenges and Prospects in Ethiopia', UNDP Human Development Report, 2010/11, Forum for Social Studies, Addis Ababa.

Ayenew, Meheret. 1997, *Public Administration in Ethiopia, 1974–1991: Administrative and Policy Responses to Turbulence.* New York: State University of New York-Albany.

—— 2014, 'Ethiopia's Growth and Transformation Plan (GTP): Opportunities, Challenges and Lessons', in Dessalegn Rahmato, Meheret Ayenew, Asnake Kefale, and Birgit Habermann (eds), *Reflections on Development in Ethiopia: Trends, Sustainability and Challenges*, Addis Ababa: Forum for Social Studies.

Banks, Arthur, Muller, Thomas and Overstreet, William (eds). 2005, *Political Handbook of the World 2005–6.* A Division of Congressional Quarterly, Inc., Washington, DC.

Beyene, Asmelash and Markakis, John. 1974, 'Representative Institutions in Ethiopia', in *Studies in Ethiopian Government and Administration*, Asmelash Beyene (ed.), Addis Ababa: Haile Selassie I / Addis Ababa University Press.

Carter Center. 2009, 'Observing the 2005 Ethiopia National Elections, Final Report', December, The Carter Center, Atlanta, GA.

Clapham, Christopher. 1969, *Haile Selassie's Government.* New York: Praeger.

CIA. 2016, 'Ethiopia: People and Society', in *The World Fact Book*. Washington, DC: CIA.

CSA – Central Statistical Authority. 2007, '2007 Population and Housing Census of Ethiopia, Administrative Report'. Addis Ababa.

European Commission. 2000, 'The Future of Parliamentary Democracy: Transition and Challenge in European Governance'. Green Paper prepared for the Conference of the European Union, Speakers of Parliament, Brussels.

EU – European Union. Election Observation Mission 2005, 'Ethiopia Legislative Elections, 2005, Final Report', 1 December, http://eeas.europa. eu/archives/eueom/pdf/missions/finalreport-ethiopia-2005.pdf, accessed 27 September 2019.

Fisseha, Assefa. 2014, 'Development With or Without Freedom', in Dessalegn Rahmato, Meheret Ayenew, Asnake Kefale and Birgit

Habermann (eds), *Reflections on Development in Ethiopia: Trends, Sustainability and Challenges*. Addis Ababa: Forum for Social Studies.

Gebre-Sellassie, Roman. 2005, *Women and Leadership in Ethiopia: The Case of Tigray*. MBA Thesis, Amsterdam Graduate Business School.

Grindle, Merilee S. 2007, 'Good Enough Governance Revisited', ODA. *Development Policy Review* 25(5): 553–74.

Halliday, Fred and Molyneux, M. 1981, *The Ethiopian Revolution*. Woking: Unwin Brothers.

Harbeson, John. 1988, The *Ethiopian Transformation: The Quest for the Post-Imperial State*. Boulder, CO: Westview Press.

HoPR – House of Peoples' Representatives. 2016, 'Ethiopian Parliament' / 'Yetopia Parliament'. Addis Ababa.

Human Rights Watch (HRW). 2004, 2014, 2015, Country Reports on Human Rights Practices: Ethiopia.

ICNL – International Center for Non-Profit Law. 2019a, 'Civic Freedom Monitor: Ethiopia'. Washington, DC.

—— 2019b, 'Civic Freedom Monitor: Kenya'. Washington, DC.

IPU – Inter-Parliamentary Union. 2007, 'Parliament and Democracy in the Twenty-First Century: A Guide to Good Practice', www.ipu.org/ file/859/download accessed 27 September 2019.

—— 2016, 'Women in Parliament: World Classification', September. IPU, Geneva.

Johnson, John K. 2005, *The Role of Parliament in Government*. World Bank, Washington, DC.

Koehn, Peter, and Hayes, Louis D. 1978, 'Student Politics in Traditional Monarchies: A Comparative Analysis of Ethiopia and Nepal'. *Journal of Asian and African Studies* XIII(1–2): 33–49.

Lyons, Terrence. 2015, 'As Ethiopia Votes, What's "Free and Fair" Got To Do With It?' *Horn Affairs*, 18 May, https://hornaffairs.com/ 2015/05/18/ethiopia-votes-free-and-fair-terrence-lyons, accessed 27 September 2019.

Markakis, John. 1974, *Ethiopia: Anatomy of a Traditional Polity*. Oxford University Press.

MoFED – Ministry of Finance and Economic Development FDRE. 2006, *Plan for Accelerated and Sustained Development to End Poverty (PASDEP)(2005/06–2009/10)* September. Addis Ababa.

—— 2010, *Growth and Transformation Plan (GTP) 2010/11–2014/15*. Addis Ababa.

—— 2014, *Growth and Transformation Plan, Annual Progress Report, for FY 2012/13*, February. Addis Ababa.

Mtanda, Said Mohamed. 2014, *To Assess the Extent to Which Legislators Involve Constituencies, Voters Opinion Towards Law Making and Development Process: A case of Lindi Constituencies*. Master's thesis, University of Bradford.

NEBE – National Electoral Board of Ethiopia. 1995, 2000, 2005, 2010, and 2015, 'Election Results', www.electionethiopia.org.

Oliver, Dawn, 2013. 'Parliamentary Sovereignty in Comparative Perspective', UK Constitutional Law Association Blog, 2 April, https://ukconstitutionallaw.org/2013/04/02/dawn-oliver-parliame ntary-sovereignty-in-comparative-perspective, accessed 17 August 2014.

Parliamentary Centre. 2009, *Parliaments, Poverty Reduction and the Budget Process in Africa*. Ontario: Parliamentary Centre; Legon-Accra: Pro Writing (Ghana).

Pausewang, Siefgried, Tronvoll, Kjetil and Aalen, Lovise (eds). 2002, 'Ethiopia Since the Derg: A Decade of Democratic Pretension and Performance'. London: Zed Books

Perham, Margery. 1948, *The Government of Ethiopia*. New York: Oxford University Press.

Power, Greg. 2012, 'Global Parliamentary Report: The Changing Nature of Parliamentary Representation'. Inter-Parliamentary Union, Geneva; United Nations Development Programme, New York.

Rahmato, Dessalegn and Meheret Ayenew. 2004, *Democratic Assistance to Post-Conflict thiopia: Impact and Limitations*. Forum for Social Studies (FSS), Addis Ababa.

Rahmato, D., Meheret Ayenew, Asnake Kefale, and Habermann, Birgit (eds). 2014, *Reflections on Development in Ethiopia: Trends, Sustainability and Challenges*. Forum for Social Studies, Addis Ababa.

Tiruneh, Andargatchew. 1993, *The Ethiopian Revolution, 1974–1991*. New York: Cambridge University Press.

UNECA – United Nations Economic Commission for Africa n.d., 'The Role of Parliament in Promoting Good Governance'. Governance and Public Administration Division, www.uneca.org/sites/default/files/ PublicationFiles/role-of-parliament-in-promoting-good-govern-ance.pdf, accessed 26 September 2019.

U.S. Census Bureau. 2014, 'U.S. and World Population Projects'. Washington, DC.

U.S. Department of State, Bureau of Democracy, Human Rights and Labor. 2013, 'Ethiopia After Meles: Hearing before the Subcommittee on Africa, Global Health, Global Human Rights, and International Organizations of the Committee on Foreign Affairs', House of Representatives, One Hundred Thirteenth Congress, First Session, April.

—— 2015, 'Ethiopia's May 24 Parliamentary and Regional Elections', 27 May. Washington, DC.

Veit, P., Banda, G. Z., Brownell, A., Galega, P., Kanja, G.M., Nshala, R., Mtisi, S., Ochieng, B. O., Salomao. A. and Tumushabe, G. 2008, 'On Whose Behalf? Legislative Representation and the Environment in Africa'. World Resources Institute, Washington, DC.

Wikipedia. 2005, 2010, 2015, 'Ethiopian General Election', https:// en.wikipedia.org.

World Food Programme 2016, 'Productive Safety Net Programme in Ethiopia'. WFP, Addis Ababa.

Zewde, Bahru. 2002, *A History of Modern Ethiopia (1855–1991)* 2nd ed. Oxford: James Currey; Athens: Ohio University Press; Addis Ababa: Addis Ababa University Press.

6

Challenges and Prospects of Democratization in Sudan

AMR M. A. MAHGOUB

Introduction

Democracy as a concept and practice is rather new to Sudan. The norms of governance in the tribally based kingdoms and the Islamic Sultanates that existed in the country prior to the Anglo-Egyptian colonization of the country in 1898 were based on different levels of participation through 'Islamic Shura', which is a non-binding consultation process. The concept of democracy was introduced in the late 1930s by the British colonial authorities and, by the mid-1940s, was only practised in organizations such as students' unions and trade unions.

The first notable modern political organization in Sudan was the Graduate Congress (1939–52), which included all modern school graduates of the country. The Graduate Congress was formed by a conglomeration of two cultural groups, which had emerged in the 1930s in the capital and other major cities. One was the Abu Rouf group, which largely embodied Egyptian inclinations towards Arabization and Fabian ideas. The other was the Mourada group, which by contrast, was characterized more by a Sudanese nationalist identity within an Arabized context. Parts of the country with inhabitants of mostly African origin, such as the Nuba Mountains and Southern Sudan were outside the agenda and scope of the Graduate Congress, while Darfur and Blue Nile were given peripheral attention. All political parties in the country emerged from this broad organization in the years from 1946 to 1952 and were characterized by exclusionist platforms.

Influenced by the ideas of the Indian Congress, the Graduate Congress adopted peaceful methods of struggle for independence, projecting itself as having an Arabized and Islamized identity, but with the ideology of democracy according to the Westminster pattern. The 1955/1956 census indicated, however, that only 39 per cent were of Arabic origin and about 70 per cent Muslim (CBS 1956).

The colonial policies of Arabization and economic and social development also privileged the North and middle parts of the country, while marginalizing other parts, including the Nuba Mountains, Southern Sudan, Darfur and Blue Nile. Since they were all denied representation in the Graduate Congress, the populations of these peripheral regions often resorted to armed resistance in attempts to change their predicament. Such resistance gradually led to the eruption of civil wars, which continue to ravage much of present-day Sudan. The North-South civil wars (1955–2011) have resulted in the secession of South Sudan. The Nuba, Darfur and Blue Nile civil wars, which erupted in 2003, remain active. Under such a context of instability, Sudan was governed by electoral politics for only eleven years, while it has been ruled by military junta for forty-seven of its post-colonial years.

Challenges of democratization in Sudan are many and deeply rooted. This chapter discusses the challenges at the conceptual and practical levels, although the two levels remain highly intertwined. At the conceptual level, democracy in Sudan is affected negatively by three major community systems. These are religious heritage, family and tribal organizations, and educational systems. At the practical level, democracy is severely affected by lack of vision and failure to manage diversity and problems of social inequality. The remaining sections of the chapter discuss each of these challenges.

Religious heritage

Ahmed Al Katib's book *Towards a Succession Democracy: The Evolution of the Sunni Political Thought* (2008) asserts that the political system in Islam is a civic regime, not based on any religious or other specific text, nor with any indication of a detailed framework on issues related to succession. The author's analyses start from the Prophet's (PBUH) first Islamic state in the city of Madina. In contrast to the custom of kings and heads of tribes of passing power to their children or other kin, the Prophet neither appointed his successor nor left a religious text on succession. The first Khalifa was elected, the second, Caliph Omar ibn al-Khattab, also refused to bequeath power to his son, and the same applies to the third and fourth Caliphs.

Unfortunately, the dialogue that took place in choosing successors to the Prophet did not evolve into a constitutional institution. Only thirty years after the Prophet's death the Umayyad dynasty seized power by force and enacted a hereditary system of succession. This amounted to a coup against the most important principles of the Caliphate that the Caliph should base his governance on justice, consultation and national satisfaction (Al Katib 2008).

The Arabized and Islamized ideology in Sudan was built on a very solid historical and religious foundations, including the God-Kings of the Napata and Merowe dynasties (4th to 8th centuries BCE), the monarchical rule of the Christian Nubian kingdoms (300–1405 CE), the Feudal Islamic Sultanates of Fung (1405–1821 CE), and the Darfur (ended in 1874 CE), Tegali and Mussabaat sultanates. The Turco-Egyptian rule (1821–85) and the Prophet-mandated Mahdia (1885–89) and at last the autocratic central rule of the British Condominium (1989–56) were other sources of influence.

The long centuries of monarchical rule in Sudan together with the enactment of religious laws transformed the societal values and beliefs to acceptance of the (hard-line Islamic) Salafi ideology that demanded absolute obedience to rulers, and forbade resistance against oppressors. This was heavily supported by scholars of Islam who, over the centuries, justified the monarchy and gave it legality and legitimacy. This historical and religious heritage has heavily influenced thinking in Sudanese society, complicating its acceptance of democratic values. In contrast to the Salafist perspective, however, is the fact that democracy is practised in some large Islamic countries, such as Indonesia and Malaysia, as well as among the Muslims of India (Mahgoub 2013).

Family and tribal systems

Alongside the religious heritage, family, clan and tribal organizations also negatively affect cultural and behavioural attitudes towards democratic governance. Tribal rule has been dominant in Sudanese history since ancient times, although the Turkish and Mahdist rules notably weakened its role. The colonial authorities created and introduced the indirect rule, or 'civil administration', of the tribal notables to easily and cheaply control the country. Despite some modifications, much of post-colonial Sudan still largely adheres to the same pattern with all its values and anti-democratic perspectives.

Household affairs can represent a first experience of democracy. In Sudan, however, household management hardly nurtures democracy. Often absent are full equality between men and women and open debate between the couple, which would give the children a lesson and practice to engage in dialogue with respect to the views of others. Mostly, therefore, children in Sudanese families assume obedience and conviction without any real dialogue or serious negotiations. This norm disables growth of the freedom of individuals, and cripples creative abilities.

Educational systems

Schools can play an important role in nurturing values of democracy first by promoting knowledge compatible with democracy and second by practising it in their student unions. The modern educational system, established in 1902, was along the lines of elite British public schools with the view of training future bureaucrats and administrators. British educational policy in Sudan was based on patronage and the creation of hierarchies essential to colonial rule.

The educational curricula and extra-curricular activities in colonial Sudan changed with time, adjusting to the needs of both the colonial system, and emerging Sudanese nationalism. The crucial changes, encouraging critical thinking and creativity, emerged in the mid-1940s, resulting in a gradual democratization of the school environment. The post-independent Sudan educational system would follow suit until the 1970s. During the early part of this period, the pan-Arab curricula were adopted, essentially borrowed from Egypt and largely based on Arab nationalism with approaches of remembrance and indoctrination. To make matters even worse, the new Islamic state (from 1989), declared its intention to remould the identity of the Sudanese people. In education, which experienced the most significant change in aims and direction, this proved to be devastating. A new educational structure was imposed upon the country with little, if any, consultation or preparation. The new system emphasized the fundamentals of a faction of Islamic thought characterized by opposition to democracy and diversity, and by directed minds (Dafa'Alla 2015).

The country's dominant political parties also did not enhance the cause of democracy. Abdul Aziz Alsaawi (2012), a Sudanese intellectual interested in areas of democracy and enlightenment, contends that the major electoral parties (Umma and Unionist) were not a suitable environment for maturing enlightenment, due to the predominance of sectarian forces in their composition. The smaller parties, which represented modern social forces (Communists, the Muslim Brotherhood, and Arabic nationalists [Baathist]), were also largely incompatible with the ideology of liberal democracy. Both sub-types were pivotal impediments in entrenching democracy as a culture. For a number of reasons, Alsaawi (2012) believes that the highest priority is to focus on the educational system since democracy is not a set rule of system components, but a way of life and a way of thinking and behaviour.

Democracy in practice

Democracy as a concept was the most questioned topic through the years since independence. It was the single topic most researched and wrote about from all aspects and by a great variety of writers. Nevertheless, the 'Arab Spring' of the early 2010s brought with it additional questions about the relevance of democracy.

The catastrophic outcomes of the Arab Spring in countries such as

Iraq, Libya, Syria and Yemen have undermined the positive effects of democracy. Nevertheless, the prospects for democracy in the longer term are largely dominated by lack of vision, failure to manage diversity, and neglect of social justice (Mahgoub 2013).

As manifested in the successive military coups, Sudan is characterized by a failure of institutional democracy. Political parties in the country are known to call for democracy without themselves practising internal democracy. All party leaders in Sudan since independence died in office, until 2019 when Omar al-Bashir was deposed after being in power for thirty years. Moreover, the country, after six decades of independence, still has only a temporary constitution.

Lack of vision

Discussion on vision was rather rare in the political and cultural circles in post-independence Sudan. The first time attention was drawn to strategic vision was in articles written by the late Jaffar Mohammed Ali Bakhit, which appeared in *Khartoum Journal* between December 1968 and June 1969, under the title 'Power and Conflict of Loyalty in Sudan', and further illustrated in Ahmed Ibrahim Abu Shouk's (2008) article 'The Dialectical Relationship between the Intellectuals and Power'.

The idea of 'national vision', which took the form of a 'national plan', was first addressed in the ten-year national plan (1960–70) formulated by the first dictatorial military regime (1958–64). The plan was, however, abolished during the following democratic period (1965–69). The second attempt at delineating a national vision was instituted in the five-year plan by the second dictatorial military regime (1969–85). This too was abolished by the third democratic period (1985–89). The third military regime (1989 to 2019) developed a national vision (2000–2025), which was largely a strategy for regime survival, had plans and programmes with an Islamic hue and excluded the views of all other forces in the country. However, the vision was not implemented and, in any case, both the government and the opposition lacked a clear vision for Sudan's direction, and were overthrown in 2019. The country, devastated by civil wars in Darfur, Nuba Mountains and Blue Nile, needs to prioritize solving the questions of diversity and identity.

Democracy and failure to manage diversity

Democracy and diversity are two faces of the same coin. Diversity is about differences and respect. President Obama made the link very clearly:

> For progress to happen, we have to listen to each other and see
> ourselves in each other, and fight for our principles, but also fight to
> find common ground, no matter how elusive that may sometimes seem
> ... getting things done requires compromise ... democracy doesn't work
> if we constantly demonize each other. (2016)

Diversity is defined to include acceptance and respect of difference in ethnicity, language, culture, sex, religion, body image, and
socio-economic status, among others. Respect for differences means
celebrating diversity (Washington 2008). Constitutionally and legally,
diversity has been addressed in much of the world. In practice, however,
diversity remains poorly managed with dangerous effects even in countries generally regarded to be democratic. The Trump phenomenon in
the USA, with hate policies against everybody not white, clearly indicates that diversity management is at stake.

The colonial rule in Sudan relied on religious sects, tribal organization, and intellectuals with Arab-Islamic ideology, which excluded and
disrespected differences. It is to these groups that the British handed
over Sudan (Basheir 1974).

Sudan's modern history is a history of failure to manage diversity.
Although the country is home to more than 600 ethnic and language
groups, the Arabized elites adopted exclusionary policies ignoring the
federal arrangement agreed upon in the 1947 Juba conference, instead
concentrating wealth and public services in central Sudan. The elite
adhered to the colonial-era civil administration, which led to the waging
of a holy war in the name of Islam against the Sudan People's Liberation Movement (SPLM) in Southern Sudan. A similar approach has
continued at high intensity in Darfur since 2003, and South Kordofan
and south Blue Nile since 2011. The three military coups Sudan experienced were largely due to the North-South civil war which contributed
also to the fall of two juntas.

Social justice and prospects of democratization

Social justice in Sudan presents different faces to different people. The
colonial authorities made the necessary economic changes to integrate
northern and central Sudan into the world capitalist market. However, in
these regions, colonial efficiency and adequate pay started to decline over
the years, and in these marginalized areas the economic degradation was
exacerbated with a whole array of social, cultural and ethnic inequalities.

Post-colonial Sudan, like most other post-colonial African countries,
was characterized by deepening marginalization of certain ethnic
identities and geographical regions, widespread corruption, tyranny,
military coups and civil wars. As a result of all these conditions, the
country presently finds itself in total chaos.

While there is no one-fits-all governance system, historical experience shows that the essentials of effective governance in cases such as Sudan include nurturing a democratic culture, secularism, federalism and social justice. Developing a democratic culture is a far-reaching goal, which entails radical changes in the educational system. Political parties also play a critical role in developing democratic culture by rallying citizens around a set of political programmes, disseminating democratic practices, mobilizing citizens around political platforms to gain access to power through peaceful elections, influencing the decisions of the ruling authority and cultivating experienced political leaders.

Democratic parties are open to all citizens, while the religious parties, sectarian, tribal or factional organizations have a problem because they are based on the isolation and exclusion of some citizens. The nature of exclusive organizations challenges the fundamental principle of democracy, equal citizenship rights for all without any discrimination. Financing of democratic parties is also very influential in shaping polices of the state. All democratic countries have complex regulations and rules governing this practice. Most important is a clear transparent and integral funding process through public financing or through state funding.

Secularism

Secularism is defined as 'the separation of state institutions and persons mandated to represent the state from religious institutions and religious dignitaries'. Secularism was the product of ideas of a growing number of individuals, groups, and leaders against the once-dominant influence of the Catholic Church in Europe. It was a paradigm shift that favoured the localities and nations over the supreme rule of the Divine as expressed through the Popes (Smith 2012).

Sudan's political crisis in the post-independence era largely revolves around identities and diversities. The two versions of politicized Islamic rule – the Sunni religious state in Sudan and the Shia Welayat-e Faqih in Iran – have failed to provide good governance. Both are widely viewed to be among the most corrupt and oppressive states in the world. With the help and support of these two countries, the Islamic world has slid into trends of increasing militancy. This can be easily witnessed by the immense divisions in Islam, including Sunni and Shia: Sunni includes Wahhabi, Isis, Qaida, Muslim Brotherhood, Salafist and Sufi; while Shia includes the Twelvist Imamiya, Zayidya and Ismailia.

Secularism was often viewed by the Islamic movements as heresy, moral degradation and even sexual decadence. This led liberal forces in the Arab World, through the years, to replace the appellation 'secular state' with 'democratic civil state'. The largest Islamic countries, including Indonesia (with a population of 205 million), Turkey

(75 million), Malaysia (17 million), and India (where Muslims are the largest minority – 200 million or 11.1 per cent in 2018) all adopted secular systems. The Tunisian constitution of 2014 also adopted secularism without naming it; its 'Nahada' movement also transformed itself into a political party, abandoning its religious role.

Federalism

There are many definitions of federalism, but they all agree that it is a constitutionally based sharing of power between the central government (federal) and smaller geographic units (regions, states). Perhaps one of the best examples of a federal system is Belgium. Since the amendment of 1993, the first article of the Belgian Constitution states that Belgium is a federal state composed of communities (based on ethnicity) and regions (based on geographical boundaries). The interesting feature is the federalization of languages. The Belgian Constitution allows each group of population groups the freedom to use their language within their territory. Each ethnic group has its own language council, to develop and solve cultural and linguistic diversity problems. The country has three overlapping linguistic regions: French, Dutch and German (1 per cent). In Brussels Dutch and French are predominant. The principles derived from the above are good lessons for Sudan to consider as an approach for recognizing diversity and developing the country's languages.

Federalism was an important topic in Sudan's political discourse in the aftermath of the 1947 Juba Conference, when southerners demanded a federal arrangement. This demand was arrogantly rejected by the government leading to seventeen years of civil war (1955–1972). The 1972 Addis Ababa agreement granted regional autonomy to the South. The abrogation of that agreement in 1983 led to another twenty-three years of the most brutal civil war in the country's modern history. In the mid-1990s the right to self-determination of Southern Sudan was agreed by the political parties, paving the way for the eventual formation of the new country of South Sudan on 9 July 2011. However, as noted above, civil wars continue in Darfur, South Kordofan and Blue Nile.

Decentralization as a concept has a long history in Sudan. It was supposed to bring about the expansion of choices at the local level, and lead to improved efficiency, equity and financial soundness, and to improve accountability and democracy. In practice, however, it has led to inflated administrative apparatus without any improvements in governance. Decentralization and a form of federalism were imposed by two military dictatorships as tools to control the people and at the same time to delegate responsibilities without resources.

The military regime of 1989–2019 adopted what it called a federal system. The structure of regional administration (six regions) was replaced by the creation of twenty-six states, with their executives, cabinets and senior-level state officials appointed by the president, and their limited budgets determined by and dispensed from Khartoum. The states, as a result, have been economically dependent upon the central government.

Opposition parties in 2013 issued the Democratic Alternative Charter document, which proposed 'to cancel the current federal system of government, restructure the state system in order to achieve real democracy, and provide guarantees for all regions' rights to power, wealth and equitable distribution of development opportunities and services, and expression of cultural components' (*Sudan Tribune* 2013).

Social Justice
When people march on the streets in any revolution to fight a corrupt, authoritarian regime, the issue of social justice is either unclear, as in the case of Sudan in its October 1964 Revolution, or it is presented as a specific objective, as the Egyptians did in the January 2011 Revolution.

The social justice concept is often equated with creating economic solutions or perhaps equality at the social level by raising the income of the poor. Social justice was widely debated in Egypt as part of the national dialogue after January 2011 and three schools of thought emerged from the debates – the liberal, socialist and human rights perspectives. First, the liberals see social justice occurring in a democratic and pluralistic society within the major principles of freedom, equal opportunity and the rule of law.

A socialist concept stems from the view that the main societal contradiction is between the social mode of production and the private ownership of the means of production. From this point of view some aspects of social justice can be achieved through legislation to improve labour relations and working conditions, and the formation of strong independent trade unions. Social justice in Islam, by contrast, is based on the principles of equality and social solidarity. It includes practical affirmative action in the form of material assistance to the needy to secure their needs, through *zakat* and other forms of charity.

Social justice is, however, inseparable from the idea of human rights. Creation of meaningful linkage between social justice, human rights and the satisfaction of human needs requires a role for the state in regulating the economy rather than dependence on market forces alone to meet the requirements of a just society. The link between justice and human rights needs to be accompanied by equal opportunities for all. This, in turn, is largely governed by three conditions: absence of discrimination between citizens; empowerment of individuals to take advantage of opportunities; and competition on equal terms for gaining access to opportunities.

Democratizing Sudan: the road ahead

Present-day Sudan is characterized by skyrocketing inflation, and the people's agriculture in apparent terminal decline, with the selling off or leasing of huge tracts of arable land and urban real estate. Until 2019, the country was under the grip of a tyrant government, with freedom of speech and expression under siege. A transitional government was agreed upon in September: a transitional Council of State of six civilians and five army members, and a Council of Ministers, with the legislative council to be formed after not less than six months.

Following this, European countries normalized relations with the country, with funding to encourage the regime to stop the flow of emigrants. China had expanded its influence on the regime to advance its interests in the country and it is now difficult to speculate how relations will proceed. The long-standing United States sanctions (economic and terrorism related) are slowly coming under discussion.

Eric Reeves (Senior Fellow at Harvard University's François-Xavier Bagnoud Center for Health and Human Rights) had rightly predicted that the collapse of the Sudanese economy, and hence the regime, was inevitable, even if the tipping point was unclear at that time (Reeves 2016).

The long-standing establishment, based on Arabization and Islamization ideologies, has practised exclusion and marginalization of various identities, also using religion as a ladder to power. Tyranny and corruption also characterized all regimes since independence. Indeed, as the late Dr John Garang used to say, 'Khartoum is too deformed to be reformed' (PaanLuel Wël 2015). It is too early to predict the progress of the new government on these matters.

Based on the foregoing discussion of the various challenges confronting Sudan, the author of this chapter would like to suggest some principles that would be needed to transform the country into the path of meaningful democracy. To do so, the discussion will focus on three principal areas: diversity management, governance and social justice.

Comprehensive approach versus domain approach

Analyses of success stories of countries, such as South Korea, Malaysia, Brazil, China, Indonesia and South Africa suggests that each country first identified the main challenge it faces and devised visionary solutions around the core challenge. While the approaches that these successful developing countries took are not uni-dimensional, nevertheless, each country's approach seems to be anchored on addressing the core challenges. South Korea's approach was centred around developing the educational system, while Malaysia concentrated on enhancing economic growth rather than merely redistributing wealth. Brazil pursued a policy of zero poverty under the leadership of Lula Da Silva. China enhanced the participation of small business's share in the economy. Indonesia anchored its development on a diversity-oriented constitution, while South Africa's development was rooted on the promotion of national unity and reconciliation. In other words, based on their identification of the core challenges they faced, all these countries developed measures that tackled them.

In the case of Sudan, management of diversity is the core challenge, as evident from the chronic problems of exclusion and marginalization of various identities, which have condemned the country to endless civil wars. Given this challenge, it is proposed here that the diversity lens is the best telescope to be used to describe, analyse, and build consensuses on a set of principles for good governance, democracy and prosperity.

Diversity aspects in Sudan are multidimensional, and include:

- Ethnic – Arabs and black Africans and their sub-groups;
- Social – haves and have-nots, with a poverty rate of 46 percent of the population in 2009 and 70 per cent in 2014 (CBS 2010, 2015); this large difference is due to a discrepancy between the real results and faked government results;
- Gender;
- Territorial (central, semi-marginalized and marginalized);
- Skin colour (semi-white, brown, dark and black); and
- Cultural (languages, education, traditions and the whole cultural heritage of the country's communities).

These different aspects of diversity were meticulously studied through field surveys and well documented in the journal '*Sudan Notes and Records*' 1918–1997 (Volumes 1 to 65), which deeply explored various facets of Sudanese life. It was researched by renowned scholars and scientists from disciplines including anthropology, history, geology, architecture, geography, languages, social behaviours and traditions, epidemiological profiles, fauna and environment, as a short list. They collected data from the field, described, analysed and elegantly documented the findings.

This wealth of information was the main database for colonial authorities to transform a primitive medieval country, into a modern, stable country with working institutions, railways, airlines, huge agricultural schemes, an efficient civil service, health and education systems, and a national security force. The fathers of independence had this wealth of information under their noses, but rather than looking at it critically to move away from colonial policies, they, unfortunately, just copied the colonial policies (*Sudan Notes and Records*).

The failure of learning from the past, denial of diversity and imposition of a one-dimensional policy of unity through conformity led Sudan to a nation-building crisis that culminated with the separation of South Sudan and the long-term raging civil wars in Darfur, South Kordofan and Blue Nile provinces. The country's agricultural system is also failing, and finds itself on the verge of decay and total collapse.

Using a diversity lens

To approach diversity in an inclusive way requires profiling of all aspects of the lives of the people and their communities: ethnic composition, religions and belief systems, languages, social patterns, social and employment opportunities. territorial marginalizations, cultural modes and patterns (music, folk tales, celebrations and other traditions), skin colour, and gender attitudes and equality, as well as the ways in which bio- and environmental diversities affect their lives.

Diversity profiling delivers a database that can be analysed using the best scientific and statistical methodologies. The resulting data can be used to reflect and develop policies targeting each of the above-mentioned aspects. This can then form the basis for developing the constitution of the country and shaping the governance system. The profiles will point very clearly to the maldistribution of wealth and poverty, development programmes required, and the direction of economic reforms. The resulting proposed policies should be included in the curricula of the educational system, and become a basis for dialogue among political parties and for reconfiguring the media.

Recognition of and appropriate action on cultural diversity form the most powerful armamentarium for managing diversity at community level, and should include polices resulting in the sharing of cultural heritages (music, folk tales, celebration traditions, etc.), with equal space for different languages and dialects in school curricula and media outlets. Women's issues are extremely important and should be incorporated in all domains to enable their presence in the public space, their voices to be heard, and equality generally. Appropriate action on cultural diversity should be disseminated through friendly health, education, civil service and other public systems.

Although there exist many international declarations (human rights charters, declarations on cultural diversity, biodiversity, environmental agreements, etc.), they mostly have minimal range, and often reflect the interests of the most powerful countries. These declarations, therefore, are essentially useful as broad guidelines and as knowledge resources.

Inclusive approaches to diversity management

An inclusive approach to diversity management has never been put into action in Sudan, but putting it in place will not involve starting from scratch. In every aspect of diversity, there are huge national and international knowledge databases and local wisdom and practices. This approach involves a fully fledged democratic process with societal consensus on the basic concepts and definitions of diversity issues, followed by the achievement of positive policies to deal with them.

The consensus-building mechanisms in Sudan reside at three levels: the local level (mostly rural and nomadic communities), the provincial level (urban settings of towns and cities) and the federal level. These provide opportunities to open discussions and dialogues, starting from the grassroots level. If these are performed sincerely and with genuine good intentions of community participation, the products will be the first step for community enthusiasm and positivity when their help and support is needed. Dialogue will include the appropriate governance system issues and its determinants, and should be based on territorial and social justice as an objective basis for development. The inclusive approach will lay the grounds for agreements on developing the most needed tools, such as a permanent constitution, national vision, and measures of achieving social justice.

Permanent constitution
Failure to agree on a permanent constitution in Sudan has been the most clear and convincing evidence of the failure to deal with diversity. The experiences of two of the most diverse countries can provide useful lessons.

Indonesia is a highly diverse country with religious diversity, some 300 ethnic groups and 270 languages and dialects. When the country initiated the process of drafting its constitution, it chose as head of the constitutional committee a law professor, Mr Jacob Tobnj, a Christian – 9 per cent of the population identify with this religion – and also from an ethnic minority.

The process of creating a constitution for post-apartheid South Africa began in 1991 and ended in 1996, and was a true example of citizen participation. The representatives in the Constituent Assembly contacted the people to educate them and invite them to express their views. This included media campaigns, newspapers, radio and television stations, billboards on buses, as well as in the newsletter of the Constituent Assembly. The discussions on the new constitution took five years. An agreed constitution using a diversity lens is crucial for Sudan to go forward.

A national vision

Mahgoub's *Production of Failure: Where Are We Now?* (2013) was dedicated to exploration of the root causes of the glaring absence of thoughts on vision in the agenda of Sudanese intellectuals. This was done by analysing the eight visions dominating Sudan's political scene: the Mahdist rule, the 1924 revolution, the Graduate Congress, the mainstream parties (sectarian liberal parties), Arabic nationalism, communist ideology, Islamist ideology, and the New Sudan (conceived by SPLM). Each of the groups had its own version of democratic governance, often with anti-democratic concepts and practices.

Before embarking on vision development, the issues should be fully explored, using diversity lens analyses. These fall under two categories. First are governance-system-related issues: constitution, transitional justice, social justice, foreign policy, civil society. Second are economic and social-related issues: culture of democracy, women's empowerment, uprooting violence from political life, literacy, poverty, unemployment and debt.

When Sudan gained independence, there were in place four major core competencies (inherent strengths of sectors, more evident because of the existence of an enabling environment). These were: a democratic system of governance, with an interim constitution; a sufficiently efficient management system; disciplined and high-quality educational and health systems; successful and productive agricultural programmes. These competencies existed to serve the colonial interest to exploit the country at the lowest cost and with the greatest output.

Core competencies appropriate to the current situations in Sudan, and based on most objective and reliable information, from government, international and neutral sources, can pave the way for the future in Sudan, and the following are proposed. Natural resources, comprising land, water and livestock; human resources; technology acceptance; minerals and oil; biodiversity.

Conclusion

On 19 December 2018, widespread peaceful protests against the regime of al-Bashir broke out in many parts of the country. The protesters chanted slogans calling for the departure of the regime and the handover of power to the people. Leaders emerged from a crop of young people who had long rebelled against the patriarchal traditional authority and racist agenda of the regime. Their programme called for a democratic, civilian and pluralistic system, governed by the rule of law and preserving human rights, with balanced development and justice. The relentless protests forced the military to oust al-Bashir on 11 April

2019. The country is presently governed by a three-year transitional government led by a mix of military and civilian leaders.

Among the most promising undertakings of the uprising so far is its response to the issue of diversity. All opposition political forces and armed movements united in a coalition and, under the aegis of the Sudanese Professionals Association (2019) produced the 'Declaration of Freedom and Change'. Notably, the slogan 'you arrogant racist, the whole country is Darfur' has risen in the face of racism, Arabo-Islamism, and the anti-diversity policies of al-Bashir's ruling Islamist regime. Although it is too early to reach conclusions on the results of these issues due to their complexity and long span, the uprising and the declaration have laid the foundation for solutions.

Bibliography

Abu Shouk, Ahmed Ibrahim. 2008, 'The Dialectical Relationship between the Intellectuals and Power'. Abdel Karim Mirghani Centre, Omdurman, Sudan.

Al Katib, Ahmed. 2008, *Towards a Succession Democracy: The Evolution of the Sunni Political Thought.* Beirut: Arab Propagation Foundation.

Al Kid, Khalid. 2011, *The Effendia and Concepts of Nationalism in Sudan* (translated by M. O. Mekki). Omdurman: Abdel Karim Mirghani Cultural Centre.

Alsaawi, Abdel Aziz. 2012, 'In Sudan as Elsewhere, No Democracy Without Enlightenment', www.alsahafa.sd/details.php?articleid=49188&ispermanent=0, accessed 3 July 2017.

Bakhit, Jaffar Mohammed Ali. 1968/69, 'Power and Conflict of Loyalty in Sudan'. *Khartoum Journal*, December–June.

Basheir, M. Omer. 1974, *Revolution and Nationalism in Sudan.* New York: Barnes & Noble.

CBS (Central Bureau of Statistics) Sudan. 1956, 'First Population Census of Sudan 1955/1956 Final Report'. Khartoum.

—— 2010, 'Sudan National Baseline Household Survey (NBHS) 2009'. Central Bureau of Statistics, Khartoum.

—— 2015, 'Sudan National Baseline Household Survey (NBHS) 2014'. Central Bureau of Statistics, Khartoum.

Dafa'Alla, Adil A., Hussein, Elmouiz Siddeg and Adam, Marwan A. A. 2015, 'Critical Evaluation of the Education System in Sudan from Independence to Date', Sudanese Knowledge Society, London, www.sudanknowledge.org/download/critical-evaluation-of-the-education-System-in-sudan-from-independence-to-date-2, accessed 13 June 2017.

Democratic Alternative Charter. 2013, *Sudan Tribune*, www.sudantribune.net /ن‌ص‌و, ل‌ب‌د‌ي‌ل‌ا-ة‌ق‌ي‌ث‌و-ص‌ن/, 3286, accessed 2013.

Mahgoub, Amr Mohamed Abbas. 2013, *Sudan Vision*, Book 1, *Production of Failure: Where Are We Now?* (in Arabic), Khartoum: Azza House for Printing and Distribution.

—— 2013, *Sudan Vision*, book 2, *A Conceptual Framework: Where are We Going and How?* (in Arabic), Khartoum: Azza House for Printing and Distribution.

Obama, Barrack H. 2016, 'President Obama's Speech at the Democratic Convention', *The Washington Post*, 28 July, www.washingtonpost.com/news/the-fix/wp/2016/07/27/president-obamas-speech-at-the-democratic-convention, accessed 8 July 2017.

PaanLuel Wël Media (ed.) 2015, *The Genius of Dr. John Garang: Speeches on the War of Liberation*. Scotts Valley, CA: CreateSpace Independent Publishing Platform.

Reeves, Eric. 2016, 'Sudan in the Wake of a Trump Victory', *Huffpost Blog*, 15 November, www.huffpost.com/entry/sudan-in-the-wake-of-a-tr_b_12992814, accessed 8 July 2017.

Smith, Nicole. 2012, 'The Rise of Secularism in Medieval Europe', ArticleMyriad, 17 January, www.articlemyriad.com/rise-secularism-medieval-europe-historical-circumstances-advantages, accessed 8 July 2017.

Sudan Notes and Records. 1918–1997, vols 1–64, www.jstor.org/journal/sudanotereco, accessed 13 June 2018.

Sudanese Professionals Association. 2019, 'Declaration of Freedom and Change', www.sudaneseprofessionals.org/en/declaration-of-freedom-and-change, accessed 28 September 2019.

Washington, David. 2008, 'The Concept of Diversity'. Washington & Company, Durham, NC.

7

The Cultivation of a Caring Patronage System for the Sudanese Democratization Process: Compilation of Incompatibles?

ASMA HUSSEIN M. ADAM

Introduction

Throughout its post-independence history, Sudan has failed to develop any sustainable democratic system. There were three brief episodes in which the country experienced the Westminster type of electoral politics but all these failed to address the country's political instability, and to bring lasting change. It is also highly unlikely that re-adoption of the Westminster type of democratic model would produce different results. This chapter argues that one key factor for the failure of the past democratization experiments relates to the incompatibility between the Westminster model of democracy on one hand and the nature of the Sudanese political structure on the other. The Sudanese state has been dominated by powerful clientele patronage networks that caused a serious diversion of the state's resources to their own interests, contaminated democratic political competition, and converted the democratic political game to their own benefits. As a result, serious deficiency in the state's caring system becomes one of the most important characteristics of the post-independence politics.

Based on a gender-neutral analytical perspective of the feminist caring ethics, this chapter attempts to advance a new democratic approach based on new caring relations and caring patronage networks. The chapter approaches the problem through three major parts. The first part clarifies the nature of the current Sudanese clientele networks and how this pattern is responsible for producing a distorted version of democracy. The failure of the Westminster model of democracy and the current clientele networks and the types of Sudanese clients is discussed in detail in the first part. The second part of the chapter discusses the centrality of the concept of caring ethics to the Sudanese context and demonstrates how the Sudanese clientelistic nature of the state has created a serious state-based caring deficiency that ultimately promote poverty and political unrest. The third part discusses why a paradigm shift is required for the cultivation of a new caring democratic system capable of addressing the state's care deficiency and thereby introducing new social and economic realities.

The Sudanese clientele state: origin and impacts on democracy

Indigenous kingdoms, tribes and decentralized forms of political organizations, rather than a centralized state, characterized the pre-colonial history of Sudan. For several centuries, life was based on traditions, norms and customs. Political life as Abdel Ghaffar (1974, 1976) explained, was organized

> as a shifting structure of relations between core groups of <u>shaykhs</u> [chiefs] and variable numbers of followers. The shaykhs occupied power centers by virtue of their control over important resources, especially grazing areas, water sources, and trade routes. They were organized into solidary kin-based cores which justified their claims to rights over resources in a region on the basis of common descent from an ancestor reputed to have been the first in the area, or who was important for some ideologically significant reason. Such power centers attracted followers who sought access to its resources and protection against attack by others. The extent of this attraction depended on the resources base commanded by the shaykhs, their reputation for generosity to their followers, and their ability to defend the group's interests. (Quoted in O'Brien 1979: 137–8, original underlining)

On the basis of this kinship-based structure, an indigenous stratified social structure based on patron-client relationships was established. The relationship between the patron and his clients was hierarchical, based on exchange of benefits between the two sides. The clients were responsible for showing loyalty and offering services as demanded in exchange for protection and other caring services offered by the patron. Such patronage relations were largely regarded and accepted as legitimate socio-economic arrangements, as Beekers and van Gool illustrated:

> The clients who are the less resourceful individuals can make use of their relations with their patrons to secure access to a plot of land to cultivate, a steady job, material goods, wealth, physical protection or direct assistance in times of scarcity and illness. (2012: 6)

This indigenous patronage system was caring enough to bond poor people to rich patrons through strong social relational norms and traditions. It created a deeply rooted caring ethos, which is still practised, especially in rural areas and villages. These caring ethics have contributed to the protection of poor nomads, peasants and ordinary citizens against political, economic and environmental fluctuations, the preservation of shared morals and norms of social responsibilities as common social capital, and the maintenance of social ties among people descending from dissimilar economic strata. In fact, the reputation of a patron was largely depended on his ability to show good response to his clients' needs, and to hold the moral responsibility of protecting the weaker and never let a client down. It was a direct uncomplicated relationship based on informal societal ethics which can be easily recorded in the contexts of the extended family, neighbours, ethnic groups, tribes and friends.

Since the beginning of colonialism, this informal caring ethics has been increasingly threatened by the emergence of a complicated selfish ethics perpetuated after independence. The new ethos is based on a care in exchange for benefit attitude, where care in the form of money, goods, protection, jobs, education and other services is distributed by the patrons through the channels of the state's policies in exchange for clients' political support. Although this new ethos was embodied in the same patronage structure, it was based on 'processes of resources extraction and capital accumulation, in this sense, their [clients'] economic structures and paternalistic ethos strengthen and enhance the material and political power of the patrons' (Fatton 1990: 460); nevertheless, it holds no moral responsibility towards the clients even in times of great difficulty.

This new opportunistic clientele structure was first established during the Turku-Egyptian colonialism (1821–83), and continued as a major colonial strategy during the British colonialism (1889–1956). The successful subordination of Sudan under one centralized state during British colonial rule opened the country to the world market system. The transformation of local production from food crops into a cash crops mode of production caused radical destructive impacts on the indigenous population and its economic independence. This is mainly because the new economic policy, as O'Brien explained,

> controls their conditions of production in its role as the essential supplier of their chief means of production ... and through shaping the market for their products to the needs of the dominant export sector/ luxury consumption link; and, second enjoys a decisive competitive advantage as against petty branches of production'. (1979: 176, original underlining)

As a part of this transformation, several railway lines, trade routes and seaports were developed, and education and health services were initiated. Several irrigated and pumped agriculture schemes at different localities were launched, the most important of which was the Gezira Scheme in the centre of Sudan which started in 1925, as Bernal (1997) observed: 'In partnership with multinational capital, the British were turning millions of acres inhabited by farmers and pastoralists into a vast irrigation project dedicated to the production of cotton ... [to become] the largest centrally-managed irrigation project in the world' (447). Through this ambitious 'modernization' process, the British colonial state was able to expand the market base of the Sudanese economy, consolidate its control over the new state, and enrich its treasury.

To minimize popular resistance, a new form of political organization, namely, 'the indirect rule system' was established whereby many local chiefs were appointed on the basis of their willingness to cooperate with the colonizers in order 'to collect taxes, provide laborers of governmental projects, settle disputes, and in general, to keep the peace' (Frantz 1977: 187). According to Sanderson (1989) it was difficult for the government to establish the indirect rule until the late 1920s when it felt secure enough to 'embark on a program of long-term manipulation of Sudanese politics and society along lines which would (it was hoped) frustrate the effective development of nationalism and perpetuate British political control' (64). Although the native administration failed due to the 'widespread absence of discernible tribal organization [and hence] ... revealed a very unsatisfactory state of affairs' (*ibid.*:.72, 86), nevertheless, the only exception was found at the White Nile province where native administration was controlled by Abdel Rahman Al-Mahdi (*ibid.*: 87).

Abdel Rahman Al-Mahdi was the son of the most famous Sudanese national Sufi leader who was able to overthrow Turkish colonialism, Muhammad Ahmad Abd Allah. Unlike his father's history as a national hero, the son decided to adopt a cooperative policy with the British government. According to Ibrahim, Abdel Rahman conducted a cautious campaign among Sudanese people in order to consolidate his power. As an example,

> without explicit government approval, he initiated for himself a system of mandoubs [agents] and wakala [local or sub-agents] that gradually extended to cover most provinces including Kordofan and Darfur. This system, described by a tribal chief as 'multiplicity of hands', eventually became the chief means for the organization and spread of Mahdism. (1989: 173–4 original underlining)

Towards the end of the 1940s, Abdel Rahman became the richest Sudanese landowner. This was mainly due to the generous support offered to him by the British government. In addition, his status as a businessman Sufi leader offered him the chance to collect extra huge profits from his business, rituals imposed on his Ansar (followers), and 'work-for-free' activities provided voluntarily by his followers. To balance his unlimited political and economic ambition, the British colonial government decided to financially support his rival Ali el-Mirghani (the leader of the Khatmiyya Sufi Sect and the major opponent to the Mahdists). These two traditional patrons (Abdel Rahman Al-Mahdi and

Ali el-Mirghani) were able to create a solid economic and social status that enable them to form and sponsor the biggest two Sudanese political parties (the Umma Party supported by Al-Mahdi and the Unionist Party supported by el-Mirghani). The two parties entered the first electorate democratic race against each other at the eve of independence. Although both political parties were organized on a modern pattern with an elected council and executive as well as various committees and a secretariat, nevertheless, the final word was in the hands of the two patrons (Al-Mahdi and el-Mirghani) and their approval had to be sought on every matter (Mahjoub 1974: 44).

The three Sudanese post-independence democratic experiments have been dominated by these two traditional political parties. They played a zero-sum politics and entered into intense competition and manoeuvring over politics, which led to the emergence of highly unstable civilian governments and the frequent downfall of democracy through military coups d'état. Both political systems are unable to respond positively to people's needs. Both of them depend on bureaucratic clientele networks to penetrate the society and extract the state's resources for their own benefit.

The impact of clientelism on Sudanese democracy

The essence of democracy, as Dahl (1989) explains, is to provide 'an orderly and peaceful process by means of which a majority of citizens can induce the government to do what they most want it to do and to avoid doing what they most want it not to do' (95). Such a condition requires the prevalence of a reasonable degree of representativeness, awareness and equality among citizens that give the majority of them the power to select and monitor their government. However, within the context of the Sudanese clientele polity, 'the individual's ability to define her preferences free from politically relevant constraints' (Higgins 1997: 1664) turns out to be a myth or, as Gordon and Gordon (2001) put it, 'like a hand-me-down suit never fitted to its new wearer, Western multiparty political systems, hastily handed over to Africans experienced mainly in colonial despotism, did not "fit"' (3).

Since independence, the clientele political structure was responsible for the failure of democracy since it produced weak and unstable governments that proved to be insensitive to citizens' and regions' needs, distorted the freedom of citizens' political choice, helped in the misrepresentation of the majority will, and created stable norms of bad-governance. This clientele political structure is also blamed for the creation of clientele political parties. As Ali and Matthews noted:

> From their early formation these parties [the main two political parties] were more like business enterprises than organs of national liberation. After independence they remained preoccupied more with

political intrigues than with confronting the larger political, social and economic problems of the country. Never did these parties seem aware of any such urgent needs at all. (1999: 203)

The Sudanese case has several things in common with Englebert and Dunn's (2013: 146–9) basic features of African political parties. In general, Sudanese political parties revolved around one person, lack political programmes, are based on informal relations rather than organizational structure. In sum, they are 'characterized by important differences from the role and nature of political parties as typically taught in political science classes' (*ibid.*: 143).

In Sudan, one can count four main types of political clients, all of whom work within different, but interrelated, clientele networks that go against key democratic principles. The first type of client participates in need-based clientelism. The client enters the clientele networks and offers his vote, support and other political services in exchange for expected future basic benefits. Within this context, need-based clients are recruited from small officers, labourers, poor-to-middle classes, local peasants, pastoralists, and other similar strata. Those clients are often living their lives as vulnerable or potentially vulnerable groups. Wars, famine, low wages, liberalization of economy, are the main factors that make their lives insecure. They are often selected and recruited during electoral campaigns by local middlemen, who are tied to upper patrons through a complicated serial of patronage linkages. Those clients provide their votes and political support in exchange for either individual-based benefits (like money or jobs) or public-based expected benefits (roads, new water sources, clinics). The dilemma they often face is that they have no power but their voice to offer and thus they might always be cheated after the elections. Whether the winning patron fulfilled his promises or not, this type of clientele relations violates the free-choice democratic principle, since clients have no real choice but to vote for their patrons knowing that 'basic goods and services, which all citizens should have automatic access to, become commodities on which officials can collect rents' (Chandra 2007). Putting into consideration that both democratic and military rule systems are playing on clientelism to stay in power, the need-based clients might be considered as an important source of clientele networks. This fact can partially justify why it is in the elite's interests to keep as large a sector of the citizens as poor as possible. Gonzalez-Acosta observed:

Because of this 'symbiosis between clientelism and poverty,' clientelist parties have a vested interest in maintaining a high degree of poverty. Improvements in voters' socio-economic status erode the value of clientelist appeals ... As a result, clientelist parties may provide material benefits to clients that seem to be a form of welfare service, but the reality is that these parties are not interested in reducing poverty, but rather in maintaining clients as poor, dependent, and obliged to their political patrons'. (2009: 13)

The second type of client benefits from greed-based clientelism. This kind of network is highly selective and influential. Clients are often recruited from high-status officials in the state's bureaucracy, rich local patrons, merchants, high military ranks and those of other neo-military institutions, intellectuals, and landlords. Clients do not only offer their voices and other political services to their patrons, but most importantly, it is they who open the gates of the state's treasury to their clientele's benefits. In fact, As Hemmer (2009) rightfully illustrated, this type of relations distorts basic rules of good governance replacing them with 'various strategies – ranging from lying, and scapegoating a minority community, to bribery and miscounting votes – in order to ensure that the conduct of elections does not jeopardize their hold on power' (2).

Moreover, since these sorts of relations are so pragmatic and depend on pure opportunistic ethics, clients can shift their loyalty smoothly from one patron to another depending on who will pay better. This sort of pragmatism causes unstable politics. Furthermore, since those who have been elected represent their networks' interests rather than the majority's interests, the representative democratic principle is hereby violated. Worse still, this sort of politics deprives other people of their rights of enjoying equal access to state's opportunities and resources and hence perpetuates poverty and marginalization and other grievances, flaming sources of popular discontent and violence.

The third type of client comes from a very special stratum where political services are regarded as a duty. In Sudan, there are abundant numbers of clients, especially in far villages and remote areas, who are always ready to obey their patrons' orders blindly for no return. The two major political parties draw plentiful popularity from their background as Sufi Sects. Large numbers of followers place their political patrons in a semi-holy position because they are their Sufi leaders, rather than regarding them as political elites, and this stops them from opposing any of their masters' opinions and decisions. In such a structure, winning the majority of voices does not resemble the democratic majority-will principle and one cannot expect that the government that results from such voting process can commit itself to the needs of the masses or to respond effectively to their problems.

The last type of client involves non-hieratic clientele relations. These have friendship-like relations with their patrons and deal with them as equals. This sort of client tends to make clientele relations more individualized and such a structure allows for the state's budget and resources to be devoted to specific areas and persons on the bases of personal friendship ties. This situation does not only perpetuate unjust distribution of resources among citizens, but also destroys the principle of the rule of law, and encourages corruption. It also reduces democracy to a regularization tool through which competing interests of powerful patrons are structured and represented. This clientele typology is also held responsible as a cause of political instability and rivals' competition over power. The friend-like client is able to manipulate the patron, to siphon more resources for his own interest, and to hinder any agreements or policies that go against his interests. He can also shift his loyalty to the party of an opponent – one who presents himself as the best alternative patron – and pave the way for military intervention in the political scene if he disagrees with his friend-patron or is unhappy with the economic and political outcomes of their relationship.

Classifying and reviewing the prevalent types of clientelism illustrated above can help in explaining reasons behind the failure of the democratization process in Sudan. The democratic-military vicious circle that has characterized Sudanese politics since its independence cannot be attributed only to the strong hand of the authoritarian governments and the weak hand of the democratic ones. The weakness and segregation of the opponent political parties, along with their unrestricted struggle over the economic benefits generated by clientelism politics have increased the tendency towards authoritarianism in Sudan. One of the serious impacts of this scenario was the creation of the deep-seated phenomenon I call the 'state's caring deficiency'. This caring deficiency has meant that Sudanese economic resources are dedicated to the benefit of a few social strata, and hence deprived the masses of their just share of the state's social, economic and political outcomes and opportunities.

The clientele state's caring deficiency

This part of the chapter discusses a new approach for real changes to mitigate violent conflicts in the country and improve the lot of the population. At the same time, the new approach does not base itself on radical change of the social settings of Sudanese society. The approach is based on a feminist concept of caring ethics. In this context, 'care' is defined by Merriam-Webster's Learner's Dictionary as an 'effort made to do something correctly, safely, or without causing damage'. For the feminist caring ethicists, caring ethics is a core life value. Caring ethics takes the self to be relational, rather than discretely individualistic, simply because 'human beings are thoroughly embedded in a host of involuntary, as well as voluntary, supportive social relations through which we define ourselves' (Koehn 2001: 5). Accordingly, 'caring' has precisely been re-defined by Fisher and Tronto as follows:

> On the most general level, we suggest that caring be viewed as a species activity that includes everything that we do to maintain, continue, and repair our 'world' so that we can live in it as well as possible. That world includes our bodies, ourselves, and our environment, all of which we seek to interweave in a complex, life-sustaining web. (1990: 40)

Care as an applied social theory has always been undervalued by many philosophers and social researchers. At best, it has been regarded as a natural effort and narrative feeling that binds families and friends, or as a maternal value. Consequently, caring theory has often been excluded from 'genuine' socio-political and economic discussions, public debates and political affairs. This understated position was dramatically changed on the publishing of Carol Gilligan's (1982) book *In a Different Voice: Psychological Theory and Women's Development*, in which she states that women and men respond differently when facing moral problems. She claims that men often tend to solve problems from a justice point of view, approaching solutions through their justice-based conceptual framework that 'ties moral development to the understanding of rights and rules' (*ibid.*: 19). Conversely, according to Gilligan, women tend to view issues from a contextual framework that 'centers moral development around the understanding of responsibility and relationships' (*ibid.*). Understanding this difference is essential since it means that men see the world from an abstractive individualistic angle, while women see the world from a relational angle that focuses on needs.

Although Gilligan's book has been intensively criticized because it re-stressed the women/men differences stereotype, nevertheless it moved caring ethics from a narrow feminist spot of research to a leading distinguished socio-philosophical theory, opening the door for several intellectuals to re-think caring ethics and its relations to the several social phenomena.

Returning to the Sudanese case, as explained before, the informal societal-based caring ethics is now facing the threat of being replaced by an opportunistic caring ethics where care is controlled and distributed by the state and dominant patrons exclusively for the benefits of their clientele networks, pushing out at the same time those who are, for one political reason or another, excluded from the state-based care zone. As a consequence, many of the state's developmental projects were set on an inclusive/exclusive approach. In essence, since it is the state that formulates economic policies, and because this exclusionary state does not represent the ordinary citizen, it is not strange to discover that the entire area of public policies, the state's economic facilities and many economic projects 'depend less on economic criteria of growth or productivity than on the level and quality of inducements they place at the party's disposal' (Scott 1969: 1154), and that the triangular nexus of clientele network, clientele state and business has obstructed the pursuance of a just distribution of resources and state-based caring policies, thus creating an increasing rate of the 'state's caring deficiency', by which I mean a situation where the state fails to create the suitable political structures that help the government to respond effectively and efficiently to people's caring-needs. Caring-need is every material or non-material need and/or circumstance of life that, when satisfied, helps to constitute the possibility of living a reasonably dignified life.

In circumstances where a high level of poverty, illness, civil wars, and illiteracy rates prevail, many citizens – intellectuals, journalists, businessmen, state officials and many others – find themselves among those who are excluded from the state's care services, and hence, to balance their care sheet, some of them decide to resort to violence, corruption or migration.

Consequently, this clientele state's caring deficiency does not only allocate national resources in an unjust manner, but also perpetuates the Sudanese crisis. It creates a severe structural inequality that has been transmitted throughout several generations since it 'produce[s] measurable outcomes that affect people throughout their lives, maintaining the privilege of those with the greatest resources available to them' (Tronto 2006: 27–8). For example, those who are inside the state's care zone have better access to healthy food, clean water, good housing, sound health services and excellent educational opportunities, including better schools and universities. Consequently, the state itself becomes a major source of economic value around which competition, cleavages and conflicts revolve.

Since the mid-1990s, as the liberal economic programme was implemented, the caring deficiency became part and parcel of the clientele state's laws, rules, economic policies, social programmes, bureaucratic norms, private business activities, and mode of performance of public institutions; worse still, care was commoditized. The problem of the commoditization of care is well explained by Tronto:

> If we think about care as a commodity, we will think of it as a scarce value. If we think of care as a scarce thing then we are likely to imagine that care is best distributed by the market mechanism, and then we are likely to think of care as a zero-sum provision. (2010: 164)

In addition, the Sudanese state's caring deficiency has threatened the non-opportunistic, traditional societal-based caring ethics with being replaced by this uncaring selfish ethos, especially with the rising rates of poverty and unmet economic needs. Poverty may lead people to try to calculate their choices according to what they gain rather than whether their actions are ethically wrong or right. In this sense, as Barlow and Duncan (1999) put it:

> Values, moral attitudes or virtues like altruism, compassion or unconditional love are easily (dis)qualified as 'traditional' or as only pertaining to private life. This produces not only a limited view of ethics; it also prevents a deeper understanding of the moral motivations that people employ in their actual daily life practices. (Quoted in Sevenhuijsen 2004: 27)

As dominant political patrons identified their interests as being against those of the people, they continued siphoning the state's resources. Eventually, the Sudanese economy became weak, fragile and unable to bear the heavy burden of the clientele networks' endless greedy wants and demands. As Arriola concluded from his empirical research:

> Such a resource-intensive strategy produces diminishing returns once the number of ministers grows beyond a country-specific threshold. Leaders who overextend their coalitions appear to tempt rebellion, rather than minimize it, whenever they accommodate additional partners by allocating thinner slices of a relatively fixed pie. (2009: 1340–1)

A new democratic alternative: the need for a paradigm shift

This section discusses possible steps needed for establishing a caring democratic political system. It argues that a new paradigm shift in political caring ethics is essential for achieving sustainable democracy. The December 2018 uprising and its aftermath has profoundly reshaped and changed the Sudanese political scene. Within a complicated context where several opponents are now working to dismantle the new transitional (military-civilian) government that holds power after the collapse of al-Bashir regime, preparations should be made for the democratic elections scheduled to take place after three years. Within the existing clientele political structure, sowing the seeds for a new politics – caring rather than exploitative, and relational rather than individualistic – is expected to be challenging. There is a need to create a new democratic alternative that 'entails a commitment to be responsive to expressed needs that asks leaders to govern by more than popularity polls or special interest donations' (Hamington 2015: 9), and that unlocks all possible legal channels of for citizens to equally access resources, rights and needs. Such deep change needs an essential paradigm shift towards a political caring ethos emanating from the deeply seated indigenous Sudanese caring values.

The new paradigm should also enable a shift towards a re-definition of politics as an art of looking after human lives in the best possible way, rather than an art of enriching its participants. As Hamington (2015) rightfully observes, politics should not be viewed as a game that 'focuses more on winning elections and thus the race to accumulate and maintain power rather than on responsive governance, which facilitates the flourishing and growth of a populace' (5), but instead as a serious matter concerning the management of humans. The caring state 'affords a rule of living as well as a test of faith' (Anderson 2004: 6), and is conceived by its citizens as 'the container within which care is allocated' (Tronto 2013: 3). In other words, the new Sudanese caring state needs to be able

> to meet the most basic economic needs of their citizens – specifically the provision of employment, health care, education and basic services. This places an onus on government to shape its interventions into the economy in such a way that maximizes the benefit to the most needy sections of society. (Ramaphosa 1998: 77)

Accordingly, the Sudanese state, which has been built on the image of the colonial state and on the premises of the extensive extraction of the country's wealth and resources to the benefit of those who are at the top of power, needs to be seriously revised. The main end of the Sudanese state should be re-defined to 'have no ends but public ends; and in practice it [should have] none but what its organs conceive to be public ends' (Bosanquet 2001 [1899]: 198–200).

There is also an urgent need for the creation of a new caring economic foundation on new bases that prioritizes the fulfilling of the basic needs of ordinary citizens. As suggested by Ramaphosa:

> The power of the State as a source of investment should not be underrated. Through the strategic investment of its resources, government can serve as a catalyst for growth and development in particular areas. It can also act as a source of finance for sectors of the economy, such as small and medium-sized businesses, which require special encouragement. (1998: 77)

Is it necessary in order to attain a new caring democracy to eliminate the existing patron-client system? This is an essential question as this chapter is focusing on clientele relations seeing it as a core cause of the Sudanese crisis. As discussed already, the patronage system is deeply rooted in the Sudanese socio-political premises since pre-colonial history. Trying to uproot those premises in a hope that this will help creating a caring democracy would fuel the Sudanese socio-political complications rather than solving them. Additionally, any radical change towards the elimination of the patronage system would be considered as a serious signs of threat not only against the dominant patrons, but also against the other several layers of patronage networks. This is mainly because, 'political clientelism is not an ad hoc strategy adopted by parties to gain the upper hand, but rather a political approach that functions through a well-established political and social infrastructure' (Gonzalez-Acosta 2009: 11). Furthermore, in several stable democracies, political parties depend on their patronage networks to keep their parties running, to guarantee people's support, to mobilize more candidates, to reward followers, to help further the state's policy goals, and to fund their budgets. Consequently, a patronage system is needed and should be preserved, but this should be done on a new non-opportunistic caring basis.

The December 2018 uprising has successfully inflamed popular optimism; but it is a hope mixed with authentic warnings and fears. The transitional government is faced with the challenge of combating the widespread political, administrative and economic corruption accompanied by what I can call a 'political apathy situation', where civilians care so much and follow all steps and policies undertaken by the government, hoping a radical improvement would happen to their life. This is as dangerous as in any time; if they lose hope and patience, they may resort to either a peaceful or a violent popular movement to change their misery. Any such trend will be exploited by the previous politically broken patrons who wait for any opportunity to go away with all the positive results of the revolution.

The new transitional government is composed of two main groups – the civilian and the military factions. The former is a collection of several political parties, including the traditional Umma Party, professional unions, several civil society organizations, and some rebellion forces who took up arms against the previous government. On the other side, the military faction is composed of leading military officers in addition to the Rapid Support Forces militia – created by the previous regime to support President al-Bashir. For several reasons, many people look with a sceptical eye at the Umma party, the military and the militia as anti-revolutionary components of the new transitional government. In fact, this mosaic mixture was able to overthrow the dictatorship, but it is premature to predict whether they will also be able to rescue the Sudanese political future. In addition to its heterogeneous composition, the government is facing several serious political spoilers: the previously dominant Islamic patrons; emerging Jihadist movements; rebellion forces, especially in Darfur; and several international pressures that go against the majority will.

This complex political configuration holds contradictory interests that may ruin efforts for establishing a new democratic system. As a result, the new paradigm shift, badly needed, should lie on five main pillars: creating an effective legal system; empowering poor clients; popular pressure for change; strengthening Sudanese societal-based caring ethics; and the deep eradication of corruption.

Creating an effective legal system

There is a need for establishing clear-cut standards upon which the bureaucracy would be able to implement public policies on a more caring basis. These standards should also clearly shape state-society relations and allow individuals to obtain their rights without the need to resort to violence. However, re-establishing a strong and just Sudanese legal system will not be an easy task. How the lack of proper standards that has affected Sudan for decades is described by Chabal and Daloz (1999: 14):

> [T]he weakness of rational-legal bureaucracy and the prevalence of personalized rule are particularly profitable. These provide [the elites] with direct access to public resources, which they can use for self-enrichment or investment in clientelist networks. They have little reason to dismantle this system of 'political disorder', which serves them so well. (Quoted in Beekers & van Gool 2012: 16)

In a case where a transitional government is able to enforce law and re-establish professionalism rather than opportunistic clientelism on bureaucracy, while reforming the legal institutions on a new regular system, it is expected that rent-seeking behaviour will be controlled and the state will never again be seen as an arena for competing interests. Benczes and Szent-Iványi (2010: 4–7) throw some important lights on how these sorts of change are possible and how they have been behind the success story of development in some Asian countries. These states were able to shift the interests of several social forces, interest groups, institutions and customs to match more closely with public interests, modernization and economic growth. This institutional autonomy should create a new caring paradigm shift at the level of political parties' competition over power. Political parties will be obliged then to build their campaigns on detailed care-sensitive programmes. This should help in bringing to an end the opportunistic type of clientelism. Such a paradigm shift may also persuade militia and military leaders to compete over power by entering the democratic game rather than hijacking it.

Empowering poor clients

Although important, the institutional autonomy alone is not sufficient to create the required new paradigm shift. The existence of an economic space of autonomy between political patrons and their clients is another crucial condition for establishing a new caring democracy. Because the clientele system is based on exchanges of benefits and services, it is essential for the clients to recognize that patrons cannot continue in power without them. In other words, the patrons need the clients as much as the clients need their patrons. The logic behind economic autonomy, therefore, is to empower the poor to such an extent that they are no longer in fear of losing their essential livelihood because of their voting choices. A shift towards a caring democracy will educate clients on how to make their political choices without being economically exploited by selfish patrons. Conversely, the parties' patrons will be enforced to plan their campaign on true care programmes. This shift is not impossible although it is not an easy task.

> The achievement of popular access to economic power is by definition a process, rather than a single event, and quite a long process, at that ... Nevertheless, the progressive achievement for all citizens of economic power is vital to any democracy, and needs to be pursued with vigour as part of any democratization process. (Ramaphosa 1998: 77–8)

Popular pressure for change
The continuation of the current popular pressures in the form of peaceful movements and demonstrations is important for guaranteeing a minimum presence of the majority will and popular needs at the political scene. People should continue to show themselves as essential part and parcel of the current political change. They should learn how to do this so smartly without dismantling or disturbing government routine duties. Continuous popular pressure can also help in eradicating the opportunistic-individualistic ethos since it pressurizes the political bloc to match their private interests with those of the people.

Strengthening Sudanese societal-based caring ethics
Sudanese people have often repeated their intention that the December 2018 uprising is not only a political revolution; it is 'a revolution of awareness'. Consolidating the sort of collective relational caring ethics that appeared during the popular uprising period (December 2018 to September 2019) is key for any successful paradigm shift. Despite bullets, teargas, sieges, fear of the regime's brutality and distress, Sudanese people have been able to show themselves as caring, harmonized and warm people. Within the context of highly cruel and violent governmental reaction against the protesters, it was normal to see them protecting each other even if this might have cost them their lives. Such an ethos was typical of the secrets behind the success of the Sudanese uprising, and is deeply rooted in popular morality. Through the creation of many non-political media (traditional and digital) spaces, citizens can lobby for the re-establishment of a new caring democratic system. Citizens can also contribute to the strengthening of a level of caring ethics in society and the preservation of the positive side of patronage networks. Such a caring paradigm shift can help to create a new caring political system that 'embodies the value of care without limiting or subordinating the potential role of rights' (Spring 2011: 80).

Deep eradication of corruption
The new government should firmly combat corruption and corrupted persons. This is not only essential for local political and economic

considerations but, most importantly, for preventing the re-emergence of the serious Jihadist movements now trying to re-organize themselves against the government. Showing itself as a decisive, strong and just government is essential for dismantling corruption as well as terrorist networks.

* * *

Humans are so complicated and their agents of change depend on several non-linear interactions among several actors, factors, and circumstances. However, the Sudanese revolutionary forces who were able to uproot a thirty-year dictatorship can lead Sudan to a genuine caring democracy.

Conclusion

A caring democratic system is the only alternative democracy that can cure the Sudanese state's care deficiency crisis given the fact that 'not being able to get care means loss of life' (McCracken 2014: 6). In a caring democracy, the Sudanese patronage system should be the element that transfers citizens' needs, aspirations and demands to the government, and the channel through which the government can implement its public policies.

Additionally, the new caring system should be based on the generous traditional Sudanese caring ethics. It is the responsibility of the formal and the informal institutions and bodies to reform the constitution, laws, policies, education and mass media on a new cooperative caring basis. It is the responsibility of the society to positively encourage, lobby and respond to all caring trends. National elites, youth, educators, civil society, traditional leaders and wise elders should positively participate in the formulation of a peaceful paradigm shift towards a caring state-society relationship. The road towards a caring democracy is long and uneasy, but, as Abdul Azim Abubaker – a young Sudanese protester – said just before he was killed by government forces in April 2019: 'We are tired, my friend, but no one can lie down during the battle'.

Bibliography

Abdel Ghaffar, M. A. 1974, *Shayks and Followers: Political Struggle in the Rufa'a al-Hoi Nazirate in the Sudan*. Khartoum: Khartoum University Press.
—— 1976, '"Tribal" Elite: a Base for Social Stratification in Modern Sudan', Bulletin 40, 8 November. Economic and Social Research Council, Khartoum.

Ahrens, J. 1999, 'Toward a Post-Washington Consensus: The Importance of Governance Structures in Less Developed Countries and Economies in Transition', in N. Hermes, and W. Salverda (eds), 'State, Society and Development: Lessons for Africa?' CDS Research Report 7: 12–43, http://citeseerx.ist.psu.edu/viewdoc/download?-doi=10.1.1.201.1685&rep=rep1&type=pdf, accessed 14 June 2016.

Ali, T. and Matthews, R. 1999, 'Civil War and Failed Peace Efforts in Sudan', in T. Ali and R. Matthews (eds), *Civil War in Africa; Roots and Resolution.* Toronto: Mc-Gill Queen's University Press, 193–221.

Anderson, M. E. 2004, 'Jane Addams' Democracy and Social Ethics: Defending Care Ethics'. *Macalester Journal of Philosophy* 13(1): Article 2, http://digitalcommons.macalester.edu/philo/vol13/iss1/2, accessed 13 June 2016.

Arriola, L. R. 2009, 'Patronage and Political Instability in Africa'. *Comparative Political Studies* 42(10): 1339–62.

Barlow, A. and Duncan, S. 1999, 'New Labour's Communitarianism: Supporting Families and the "Rationality Mistake"'. Centre for Research on Family, Kinship and Divorce, University of Leeds.

Beekers, D. and van Gool, S. 2012, 'From Patronage to Neo-patrimonialism: Postcolonial Governance in Sub-Sahara Africa and Beyond', ASC Working Paper 101. African Studies Centre, Leiden, https://openaccess.leidenuniv.nl/bitstream/handle/1887/19547/WP101.pdf?sequence=4, accessed 16 June 2016.

Benczes, I. and Szent-Iványi, B. 2010, 'State-Society Relations in a Dynamic Framework: The Case of the Far East and Sub-Saharan Africa', MPRA Archive 23384. Munich, http://mpra.ub.uni-muenchen.de/23384, accessed 20 June 2016.

Bernal, V. 1997, 'Colonial Moral Economy and the Discipline of Development: The GeziraScheme and "Modern" Sudan'. *Cultural Anthropology* 4(12): 447–79.

Bosanquet, B. 2001 [1899], *The Philosophical Theory of the State.* Kitchener, ON: Batoche Books.

Chabal, P and Daloz, J.-P. 1999, *Africa Works: Disorder as Political Instrument.* Oxford: James Currey; Bloomington: Indiana University Press; in association with the International African Institute, London.

Chandra, K. 2007, 'Counting Heads: A Theory of Voter and Elite Behavior in Patronage Democracies', in H. Kitschelt and S. Wilkinson (eds), *Patrons, Clients and Policies: Patterns of Democratic Accountability and Political Competition.* Cambridge, UK: Cambridge University Press, 84–109.

Dahl, R. 1989, *Democracy and its Critics.* New Haven, CT, Yale University Press.

Englebert, P. and Dunn, K. 2013, *Inside African Politics.* Boulder, CO and London: Lynne Rienner.

Fatton, R. J. R. 1990, 'Liberal Democracy in Africa'. *Political Science*

Quarterly 105(3): 455–73.

Fisher, B. and Tronto, J. 1990, 'Toward a Feminist Theory of Caring', in E. Abel and M. Nelson (eds), *Circles of Care: Work and Identity in Women's Lives*. Albany, NY: State University of New York Press, 35–62.

Frantz, C. 1977, 'Shifts in Power from Nomads to Sedentaries in the Central Sudanic Zone', in Y. Hasan and P. Doornbos (eds), *The Central Bilad Al Sudan: Tradition and Adaptation*, Sudanese Library Series number 11. Khartoum: El Tamaddon Press, 171–92.

Gilligan, C. 1982, *In A Different Voice: Psychological Theory and Women's Development*. Cambridge, MA: Harvard University Press.

Gonzalez-Acosta, E. 2009, 'Political Parties and Policy Development: The Conditions which Lead Political Parties to Adopt Progressive Policies', Discussion Paper 15. IDEA and UNDP, Oslo, www.idea.int/resources/analysis/pp_policy_development.cfm, accessed 15 June 2016.

Gordon, A. and Gordon, D. 2001, 'Introduction', in A. Gordon and D. Gordon (eds), *Understanding Contemporary Africa*, 3rd edition. Boulder CO and London: Lynne Rienner, 1–6.

Hamington, M. 2015, 'Politics Is Not A Game: The Radical Potential of Care', in D. Engster and M. Hamington (eds), *Care Ethics and Political Theory*. New York: Oxford University Press, 272–92, https://wpsa.research.pdx.edu/papers/docs/hamington.pdf, accessed 20 June 2016.

Hemmer, J. 2009, 'Ticking The Box: Elections in Sudan', Netherlands Institute of International Relations (*Clingendael*), The Hague, 1–45, www.clingendael.nl/sites/default/files/20090900_paper_cru_hemmer_elections_sudan.pdf, accessed 20 June 2016.

Higgins, T. 1997, 'Democracy and Feminism'. *Harvard Law Review* 110(8): 1657–1703. Ibrahim, H. 1989, 'The Role of Sayyid 'Abd al Rahman al-Mahdi in the Sudanese National Movement 1908–1956', in M. Al Safi (ed.), *The Nationalist Movement in the Sudan*, Sudan Library Series 15. Khartoum: University of Khartoum Printing Press, 171–201.

Koehn, D. 2001, *Rethinking Feminist Ethics: Care, Trust and Empathy*. London: Routledge.

Mahjoub, M. 1974, *Democracy on Trial: Reflections on Arab and African Politics*. London: Andre Deutsch.

McCracken, D. 2014, Tracing Place to Care: Humanitarians and Migrants in World Politics. Ph.D. Thesis, University of Minnesota Digital Conservancy, http://hdl.handle.net/11299/168133, accessed 14 June 2016.

O'Brien, J. 1979, *The Political Economy of Development and Underdevelopment: An Introduction*, Development Studies Book Series 2. Khartoum: Khartoum University Press.

Ramaphosa, C. 1998, 'The Main Elements of Democracy: A South

African Experience', in Inter-Parliamentary Union (ed.), *Democracy: Its Principles and Achievement*. Geneva: Inter-Parliamentary Union, 73–9, www.ipu.org/PDF/publications/DEMOCRACY_PR_E.pdf, accessed 25 June 2016.

Sanderson, G. 1989, 'Indirect Rule in the Northern Sudan as an Anti-Nationalist Strategy 1920–1939', in M. Al Safi (ed.), *The Nationalist Movement in the Sudan*, Sudan Library Series 15. Khartoum: University of Khartoum Printing Press, 63–110.

Scott, J. 1969, 'Corruption, Machine Politics and Political Change'. *American Political Science Review* 63(4): 1142–58.

Sevenhuijsen, S. 2004, 'Trace: A Method for Normative Policy Analysis From the Ethic of Care', in S. Sevenhuijsen and A. Svab (eds), *The Heart of the Matter: The Contribution of the Ethic of Care to Social Policy in Some New EU Member States*. Ljubljana: Peace Institute for Contemporary Social and Political Studies, 13–46.

Spring, J. 2011, 'On the Rescuing of Rights in Feminist Ethics: A Critical Assessment of Virginia Held's Transformative Strategy'. *Praxis* 3(1) 66–83.

Tronto, J. 2006, 'Vicious Circles of Privatized Caring', in M. Hamington and D. Miller (eds), *Socializing Care: Feminist Ethics and Public Issues*. Lanham, MD: Rowman & Littlefield, 3–26.

—— 2010, 'Creating Caring Institutions: Politics, Plurality, and Purpose'. *Ethics and Social Welfare* 4(2) 158–71.

—— 2013, 'Democratic Caring and Global Responsibilities for Care', a paper prepared for presentation at the Annual Meeting of the Western Political Science Association, Hollywood, https://wpsa.research.pdx.edu/papers/docs/Tronto%20WPSA%20paper%20 2013.pdf, accessed 15 October 2019.

8

Contestation of Democracy in Kenya

MACHARIA MUNENE

Introduction

This chapter looks at the construction of democracy in Kenya, one of many African countries that, over time, has been subjected to all sorts of external pressures that have served extra-continental interests; pressure that produced their own counter-force which made democracy very contested as concept and practice.

The meaning of the term 'democracy' is also contested, partly because 'democracy' has become a tool for use in geo-political warfare. It has particular attributes and applications that end up making it relative. Among them is the fact that democracy is only one form of government in a state but it may not be the only one. It is, as Churchill claimed, 'insurance' for the people in the concerned state (Langworth 2009). Ideally, it is the involvement of citizens and interests, although not necessarily the people as individuals, in the governance of the state. It can be, as Kidane Mengisteab argues, a reconciliation of the interests of modern and traditional institutions in Africa (2011: 12–14).

In theory, democracy strives to give a stake to, and involves, as many people within the state as possible to ensure they have a direct interest in maintaining the well-being of that state. Those who believe that governments should be expressions of the will of the people emphasize the subordinate role of governors and governments to the collective will of the people, failure in which they can be replaced. These include Chinaman Confucius insisting in the sixth century BCE that rulers had to be virtuous, respectful of and considerate to people, or be overthrown. 'Without the trust of the people', he declared, 'no government can stand' (McArthur 2010: 24). Much later, this view of having respect for people, of non-subservience to existing government, and 'revolutions' found clarity in the arguments presented by American Thomas Jefferson (1968: 83–93), South African Nelson Mandela (1965: 178–9), and Kenya's Mwai Kibaki. The government, Kibaki asserted, 'is not supposed to be a burden on the people, it is not supposed to intrude on every aspect of life and it is not supposed to mount roadblocks in every direction we turn in life' (Kibaki 2002).

In reality, democracy varies in meaning and application. The attitude of the Western powers, and those who subscribe to Western European and North American views, tends to limit the application of democracy when it comes to Africans. When Winston Churchill, after the British people kicked him out of office following the end of the Second World War, reportedly paraphrased an unknown wit about democracy being the 'worst form of government except for all the rest' (Langworth 2009), he never meant that observation to apply to colonized peoples or what he considered the lesser breeds (Jones 2012). As defender of the British empire, Churchill had no desire to give votes to 'Hottentots' irrespective of the formula or how educated they were (Quinault 2004: 43). The Churchillian attitude on Africans as not fit to govern themselves still prevails among many Westerners.

It is in its application on two fronts that the concept of 'democracy' is abused, misused, and contested in Africa. First, many African leaders abuse office and subvert the practice of democracy out of ignorance, mischief, or subservience to external interests. They ignore the reason the state exists, try to turn constituted states into personal property for relatives and clansmen/women, engage in short-sighted vindictiveness, and lose the big picture. This happens whether the politicians are in government or in the opposition. The events in the Gambia illustrate this shortcoming. When Yahya Jammeh lost the election and conceded defeat, the winners, Adama Barrow and his people, made the mistake of displaying vicious vendetta thereby precipitating a crisis, with Jammeh retracting concession. The Economic Community of West African States (ECOWAS) successfully negotiated a settlement that sent the former president to Equatorial Guinea (Kersten 2017).

Second, internal weaknesses are often reinforced by Western extra-continental forces seeking to control Africa. Subsequently, the Western forces have turned democracy into a geo-political tool by implying that only the West can determine the validity of democracy. In orchestrating the discourse on democracy that they were the ones to apportion praises to the 'good' ones, who received 'badges of approval' on one side, and heaped blame on the 'bad' ones mainly because they disagreed with hypocritical Western interpretations of African interests and failed to follow European ideas of how business and trade should be conducted.

Kenya was one such African country to be at the receiving end of the geo-political shaft and slated for regime change, and is the focus of this chapter. There are three phases to look at in examining the practice of democracy in Kenya. These are the colonial phase, the post-colonial period, ending with the return to multi-partyism in the 1990s, and the twenty-first century. Each was a product of constructed realities to suit particular interests.

Democracy in Kenya under colonialism

In the colonial days, Britain treated Africans as property and at the same time allowed white settlers to establish their version of democracy. It started with a 1907 decision to create a legislative council, known as the LegCo, to represent settler interests in the territory. Initially, the representatives were appointive and then they became elective as of 1919. Indians and Arabs were allowed to elect a few, on a communal basis, in 1923 (His Majesty's Stationery Office 1931: 4; Maxon 1993: 46–52, 112–20, 276–9). No 'natives' allowed.

The best that 'natives' could have was a semi-elective 'Local Native Council', LNC, whose purpose was to contain African politics and to avoid a repeat of the 1921–22 events. (Berman 1990: 216–17), in which Harry Thuku challenged the colonial state and received colony-wide support in a seeming effort to undermine the colonially appointed chiefs (Maxon 1993: 210–13). The LNC was created in 1925 to contain 'any mischievous tendencies which might develop in native political societies'. It was to give 'natives' localized political venting space under the guidance of the white District Commissioner as the presiding officer to contain 'native' politics (Berman 1990: 216–17).

The impact of the Mau Mau War

The effort to contain 'native' politics, however, ultimately failed with the outbreak of the Mau Mau War in the 1950s which forced colonial authorities to allow limited democracy for 'loyal' Africans (Kyle 1999: 61–2; Matthews 1997: 106–22). Tom Mboya, one of colonial Kenya's leading trade unionists and politicians, noted that the idea was also to encourage members of 'loyal tribes' to take up African leadership. Since Jomo Kenyatta, leader of the banned anti-colonial party Kenya African Union (KAU) and a convict for supposedly leading the Mau Mau War, was slated by the colonial government to be a non-person in African history (Kyle 1999: 62–3), it was necessary for the colonial state to create and 'to assist the emergence of responsible African leaders' among whom were to be the 'home guard leaders' (Voice of Kenya Statement 1954).

The assistance involved giving some 'natives' the chance to elect a few selected Africans in March 1957, but the conduct was contestable. It involved rigging Eliud Mathu out (Roelker 1976: 132, 134–43; Kiano 1957: 3–6; Hunt 1957) while electing eight supposedly pliant men who then refused to cooperate, demanded parity with Europeans, and created the African Elected Members Organization (AEMO). They forced Colonial

Secretary Alan LennoxBoyd to find a solution to their demands (Blundell 1964: 242): he allowed Africans to elect six more representatives in March 1958. The achievement in forcing an increase in their numbers from eight to fourteen strengthened the anti-colonial momentum.

The Lancaster House Conferences and the 1961 and 1963 elections

The British strategy of favouring some politicians backfired in Kenya's two pre-independence elections. The first Lancaster House Conference in 1960 spelled doom for white rule in Kenya and the government lifted restrictions on African political activities (Bennett 1963: 147–50). In June 1960, African politicians created a new national party, the Kenya African National Union (KANU) and proceeded to distribute party positions in as balanced a way as possible among the principal African leaders (Kyle 1999 117–18; Bennett and Rosberg 1961: 39–41; Munene, n.d.). The settlers then changed tactics, rebaptized themselves as a small 'white tribe' and looked for other 'small tribes' to form the Kenya African Democratic Union, KADU, to oppose KANU. The thinking was that if all the 'small tribes', more than forty other communities, united against the two 'big bad tribes' in KANU – the Kikuyu (because of the Mau Mau War) and the Luo (because of Tom Mboya, KANU Secretary-General, and Jaramogi Oginga Odinga, LegCo member and KANU Vice-President), – KADU would have a tyranny of tribal numbers and would therefore win. In the February 1961 election, however, the voters chose KANU over KADU despite government support for KADU (Munene 2002: 41–2).

This defeat forced the British government to adopt a new strategy to block KANU, and Jomo Kenyatta in particular. Incensed with the possibility of Kenyatta's leadership of independent Kenya, and terming him 'an evil man', the British cabinet in London in November 1961 worked out a strategy to fragment governance in independent Kenya through 'delegation of substantial powers to the various tribal regions of Kenya' by creating virtual autonomous entities that came to be called *majimbo* (Kamau 2016). In July 1994, Wilfred Havelock explained what happened:

> We realised that 'white power' was at an end when Britain committed itself to granting independence to Kenyans. We realised then that whites would be a very small minority ... We also realised that other peoples would be in the same situation, and with them, we advocated a regional system to protect smaller tribes from domination and exploitation by larger, more powerful groups. (Havelock 1994: 7)

Derailing and weakening Kenyatta and KANU were Britain's pre-independence political objectives. In the Second Lancaster House Conference in 1962, Britain imposed a *majimbo* constitution. KANU accepted it as a matter of political expediency (Odinga 1967: 228–30), with a determination to dismantle the *majimbo* structure once it was in office. As expected, KANU won the general elections in May 1963 which Kenyatta considered to be a kind of referendum on the *majimbo* constitution. On taking power as prime minister, on 1 June 1963, therefore, Kenyatta and KANU started dismantling the *majimbo* structure with the concurrence of the same British who had imposed it. In September 1963, some powers previously reserved to the regions were removed and the ability of the central government to amend the constitution was enhanced. Independence on 12 December 1963 was therefore attained under a document that was substantially different from that of 1962 (Munene 2003: 45–7).

In the two pre-independence elections, in 1961 and 1963, the democracy contestation was over the intelligence of the voters and their ability to make good choices. Despite the supposed 'tyranny of numbers' of the combined small tribes, including the Mijikenda, the Luhya, the Kalenjin, the Maasai, the Somali, the Borana, the Asians and Arabs, the Kamba, the Kisii, the Pokot and Turkana, the colonial settlers, and even the Embu and Meru, KANU won overwhelmingly because ordinary voters agreed with it rather than with their supposed tribal leaders. For the government, 'tribe' was supposed to trounce reason but for the Kenyan voter, reason and nationalism trounced 'tribe'. African voters chose reason over tribal fears and national interests over colonial manipulations. This reality would be repeated in the post-Cold War times.

The post-colonial period to 2002

The imperial interests, before independence, in shaping the outcome of the votes in Kenya resurfaced in the post-colonial times. This time, still smarting over its loss in the Mau Mau War, Britain was not alone in trying to manipulate outcomes. It was joined by other players in the 'conceptual West', which refers to all countries that consider themselves European culturally and ideologically irrespective of their geographical location. They include Australia which is geographically in the East but culturally and ideologically is an extension of Western Europe and North America. There were two distinct phases in that post-colonial electoral manipulation: the presidencies of Jomo Kenyatta and Daniel arap Moi up to 2002, and then after.

The Jomo Kenyatta presidency
The first phase was associated with the period before the end of the Cold War towards the end of the twentieth century. In the transition from colonialism to republican status, largely under Jomo Kenyat-

ta's presidency, foreign interests were Cold War-related and initially hovered around the ideological and political leadership rivalry between Vice-President Odinga advancing the Soviet line and Planning Minister Tom Mboya advancing Western interests. The latter, through Mboya, prevailed by pushing Odinga out of government and vanquishing him in the 1966 'little general election'. With Odinga and the Soviet interests out of the way by 1969 (Goldsworthy 1982: 232–47; Branch 2011: 35–65), Kenya became a virtual single-party state. Subsequent elections in 1969, 1974 and 1979 were rituals for confirming the unopposed president while parliamentary seats remained highly competitive. During the 1960 and 1970s the West was largely supportive of Kenya because of the Cold War rivalry and because Kenya was rather firmly in the capitalist ideology of the West in its development orientation.

The Moi presidency
When Kenyatta died in 1978, Vice-President Daniel arap Moi stepped into the presidency with a lot of initial goodwill and support, which dissipated in the 1980s. Since the Western powers, despite standing for 'democracy' and 'freedom', had lost in Vietnam, Iran, and Nicaragua, it became necessary to re-assess their positions in the 'Third World', and they decided to abandon those rulers who seemed like ideological burdens, and to project the image of being concerned with the 'people' as opposed to the leaders. The creation of the bipartisan National Endowment for Democracy, NED, in the United States to promote American interests in the Third World through the 'people' rather than the 'leaders' was the result. It caught many African leaders off-guard and among them was Moi of Kenya (Munene 2018: 116–22; Kissinger 2001: 29; Diamond 1995: 206–09).

Moi was caught in the geo-political fury that clouded Western logic. At a time when the West was distancing itself from perceived African dictators, he imposed constitutional amendments that made him unquestionable. Among them was Section 2A in June 1982 that decreed that Kenya was officially a single-party state and that party was KANU. After declaring that all Kenyans had to sing his tune, he compounded the situation by imposing *Mlolongo* or queue voting in 1988 in which officials announced ridiculous results. This helped to usher in the agitation for multi-party politics which coincided with growing interests of the Western powers to abandon their former friends. With President George H. W. Bush appointing journalist Smith Hempstone as ambassador, the stage was set for open Western interference in Kenyan politics (Munene 2018: 13–15, 122–6; Branch 2011: 172–82).

The West supported campaigns against Moi in 1992 and 1997 but there was no serious attempt at 'regime change', in part because the West was divided on how to treat Moi. Although Moi survived, however, he could not survive his own machinations. He had, in 1992, when he thought he would lose the multi-party election, imposed the two-term presidential limit. Finding stiff resistance when he tried to repeal his own amendment, he left office in 2002. His successor in the presidency, Mwai Kibaki, found the West extremely hostile (see next section).

By the time that Kibaki assumed the Kenyan presidency, Johnnie Carson was US ambassador to Kenya. Officially appointed to Nairobi in August 1999, he kept a relatively low profile for three years and was, according to *Daily Nation* columnist Kwamchetsi Makokha, pessimistic and sceptical about his assignment in Kenya (Makokha 2003). He was still ambassador in 2000 when US democracy went into crisis as Al Gore and George W. Bush battled for the US presidency, enabling Kenyans to enjoy ridiculing American 'democracy'. Since vote counting became an issue in Florida where Jeb Bush, a brother of candidate Bush, was governor, some Kenyans believed that 'rigging' American style was taking place. As a result, *Sunday Nation* columnist Gitau Warigi quipped, they tended to respond to the fiasco in Florida with 'a knowing wink' (Warigi 2000). Cartoonist GADO of *Nation* mocked US democracy portraying 'Uncle Sam' without pants that had been torn off by two boxers, Bush and Gore. Each boxer had raised up his half of the pants as evidence of victory (GADO 2000). Kwendo Opanga of the *Sunday Standard*, with similar views, asserted that the Bush victory was decided not by judges but by nine partisan 'politicians in black robes' (Opanga 2000).

The twenty-first century

Kibaki's contestation

Two years after the Bush-Gore debacle, Kenyans elected Mwai Kibaki in December 2002 and set stage for confrontation with the conceptual West. He made it clear that Kenya wanted to make independent decisions on what its interests were and this put Kenya at loggerheads with the conceptual West who thereafter became openly hostile. He said that he wanted to make Kenya 'rich once again, earn respect in Africa, and earn respect in the world'. Noting that Kenya had been attacked twice by terrorists, he pledged to 'work closely to root out the causes of terrorism in the world' (Kibaki 2002).

Kibaki, however, collided with the conceptual West, or 'master states' on who should determine Kenya's interests thus incurring their wrath (Munene 2005 120–1) – and Kenya had to be punished. The Westerners had not displayed passion to effect regime change the way they did beginning 2003. They wanted 'democracy' to suit pre-determined outcomes that serve perceived Western interests. The level of their hostility at this time made the first phase that dealt with Moi's last days appear very mild.

Intrigues at Bomas

Led by the United Kingdom, the United States and Germany, the conceptual West mounted a campaign to dislodge a sitting president mainly because he did not agree with some of their policies. They then pressed the international panic buttons and, as *Nation* commentator Chege Mbitiru observed, 'all but declared Kenya a terrorist nation' (Mbitiru 2003) and left little doubt they were punishing Kenya for not openly endorsing the Anglo-American invasion of Iraq (Editorial, *Sunday Standard* 2003). They started using threatening language. Carson accused Kenya of 'not doing enough to stop' terrorists and then dictated steps that Kenya 'must take immediately in order to prevent terrorism from destroying its future' (Carson 2003). His British counterpart, Sir Edward Clay, warned that 'if it wants to be part of the modern world, it is necessary that it has relations with people like British and Americans ... and accept that terrorism will be directed at this world'. Clay argued that Britain had had a 'valuable and civilized relations' with Moi which, by implication, it did not have with Kibaki (Clay Interview 2003). Such threats were meant to create despondency and to manufacture hostile consensus against the Kibaki government. Kibaki appeared to be oblivious to political happenings, even as forces plotted his ouster (Kihuria 2003; Agina, 2003). The manufactured hostility manifested itself in Kenya's politics of the 2005 referendum that started with a political circus at the Bomas of Kenya, a large official cultural events and leisure centre in the Langata/Karen suburb of Nairobi.

Political intrigues at Bomas, best represented by the public bickering between Kiraitu Murungi, Minister for Justice and Constitutional Affairs, and Raila Odinga, Minister for Roads, made Bomas a political battle ground between President Kibaki and Raila Odinga (Abdullahi 2003). Raila had the upper hand from the start, given that the commissioners and the delegates were mostly picked during the KANU-National Development Party (NDP) political love affair when Raila was chairman of the Parliamentary Select Committee on the Constitutional Review (*Daily Nation* 2005). Several commissioners, claimed Constitution of Kenya Review Commission (CKRC) secretary PLO Lumumba, were not only intellectually disappointing, they were 'instruments' of political control and represented particular interests (Lumumba 2005). The CKRC Chairman, Yash Pal Ghai, was even more contemptuous and considered commissioners and delegates to be intellectually incompetent and corrupt, to have repeatedly received bribes and misused public money, and mainly irrelevant to the deliberations (Ghai 2004: 16–17).

Bomas gave Raila what he wanted, an executive prime ministership. He had the backing of Ghai and the conceptual West. Ghai, one of the 'experts' who drafted the new constitutions for Afghanistan and for Iraq under American supervision (Onyango 2005), was in Raila's camp and was, Law Society Chairman Ahmednasir M. Abdullahi, observed, 'an eccentric and self-serving chairman ... under a delusion that, without him, the review and the country will go under' (Abdullahi 2003). Raila, argued Makau Mutua (a professor of SUNY-Buffalo Law School), 'mobilized ... the Conference to pass the Bomas Draft Constitution in which the Prime Minister would be the Chief Executive with a directly elected, but largely ceremonious president' (Mutua 2005). It recommended what Mutava Musyimi, National Council of Churches of Kenya (NCCK) Secretary General, called 'a structured anarchy where there was a proliferation of the centres of power' (Mugumo Munene 2005). It divided executive office between a powerful unelected prime minister and a weak elected president. Seen as a victory for Raila and a defeat for Kibaki, there was a lot of one-sided dancing and jubilation at Bomas. Okoth Ogendo, the Conference rapporteur, demanded that the parliament implement the document immediately arguing, 'I've never seen a situation where parliament wants to make corrections in advance' (Majteny 2004).

The Orange and Banana Referendum

After the celebrations, however, came the hard part because the document could not be adopted by parliament as it was. It went through revisions in Naivasha and Kilifi to become the Wako Draft that was submitted for the referendum. Kibaki submitted it to the public declaring that the choice was between the existing constitution and a new one. Watching politicians misrepresent the draft, Kibaki dismissed them as *'pumbavu'* (lit. foolish or thoughtless), which entered Kenya's political and humour lexicon as referring to people who are 'experts' on what they had not bothered to read. 'The members of the "Upumbavu" team', commented humour columnist Benson in the *Sunday Standard*, 'are experts on the content of the proposed new constitution also known as the Wako Draft which they discuss passionately although none has ever seen it let alone read it' (Benson 2005). It became clear that the issue was not what the draft said; it was the politics of ousting the president (*Africa Confidential*, 21 October 2005) and Kibaki was watching those micro-politicians probably, as 'Palaver' of the *Standard* quipped, 'with a wish that *waji* – enjoy' (Palaver 2005), meaning the micro-politicians should enjoy themselves.

The politics of the referendum that followed were about ousting the president, not the content of the constitutional document (*Africa Confidential* 2005). Raila was furious that his draft from Bomas had been adjusted. He made what the draft said take a back seat to the evolving political contest between President Kibaki on one side and Raila Odinga and the master states on the other. This was despite the fact that the economy was growing at the rate of 5 per cent, up from the 1 per cent before Kibaki came to office (Iraki 2006). This political contest was symbolically represented by two fruits, a banana and an orange. The Banana symbolized a YES vote (ostensibly to the new constitution) and the Orange symbolized a NO vote. The fruit symbols then took a political momentum of their own, dividing the country between the Banana and the Orange camps (BBC 2005).

The Orange side was serious but the Banana was not. Assistant Minister Fred Gumo noted, 'Orange campaigners have almost gone to all parts of the country before the time of campaign' and warned against political hooligans and the selfishness of those who started premature campaigns (*The Standard* 2005a). Among those campaigning was Kalonzo Musyoka whom the American-inclined Steadman Group touted as a possible president, and indeed fancied himself a president and started claiming that the whole Wako Draft had been designed to stop him from becoming president and that he would have become the third president had he not stepped down for Kibaki (Nzengu and Kamau 2005; Mutua 2005; *The Leader* 2005b; Miguna 2005; 'Glint' 2005). Anyang Nyong'o got so excited that he asserted 'we are the government and are preparing for yet another victory' (*Sunday Standard* 2005). The Orange team felt so cocky that Musalia Mudavadi was loudly crude and reckless as he excitedly talked of his side having had the president and the Banana team by the 'balls' (Kamau 2005b). Uhuru Kenyatta wanted the media to cover Orange rallies his way and warned: 'We have been nice to newsmen today but if they don't show the world the truth about our rallies then you will decide to deal with them' (*Sunday Nation* 2005a).

The Orange and their supporters wanted Kibaki to quit government if the Banana side lost in the referendum. Raila compared the Kibaki government to a 'centipede which must be thrown away with the stick' (*Sunday Nation* 2005b). Ghai added:

> an election after the referendum may be politically desirable if a 'No' vote wins. For that result would mean a vote of no confidence in Kibaki and the people have a chance to elect a successor. A new election may also be useful as no particular group in Parliament has a clear mandate or capacity to rule. (Ghai 2005)

Ghai, as noted above, a drafter of American-supervised constitutions in Afghanistan and Iraq (Onyango 2005), was part of the scheme in which 'Wanjiku's opposite number in Iraq', as *Sunday Nation* columnist Warigi quipped, 'will be voting ... for a constitution that has been imposed by an occupying army and its client regime' (Warigi 2005b).

In contrast, the Banana side was disorganized and key players contradicted each other. Kibaki and Internal Security Minister John Michuki said that District Commissioners (DCs), District Officers (DOs), and Chiefs would be retained in the new constitutional dispensation but Justice Minister Kiraitu Murungi and Attorney General Amos Wako said the positions would be abolished. Young politicians complained of being restricted by the 'old guard', those they called the 'Wazee Hukum-buka Outfit' (old people fondly remembering the past), who did not want to field the 'Banana First Eleven' and tended, an MP said, to think that 'some us are worse enemies than the "No" team of Raila and Company'. After a group of 'Yes' supporters demanded a clear leadership structure that could match the Orange group (Kihuria and Onyango 2005) there was a rushed assemblage of a dysfunctional group of people representing assorted interests. There appeared to be little concern on the part of the president.

There were other signs that the Banana side probably did not want to win. Among those unhappy was Health Minister Charity Ngilu, who felt slighted by not being anointed leader of the Ukambani 'Yes' team (*Sunday Standard* 2005). There was also the inexplicable harassment of street kiosk owners by Mayor Dick Wathika's City Council at a time when he should have been wooing them (*The Leader* 2005a). There was also a security raid on the house of Maina Njenga, leader of the shadowy Mungiki group, that seemingly encouraged Mungiki to link up with Uhuru Kenyatta and Raila Odinga, both in the Orange team, with whom they cut a deal for Mungiki followers to oppose the draft (Wanjiku 2005). The Orange was supposed to win.

The master states, in their eagerness to make the Orange side win, displayed their partisanship in the campaigns. *The Leader* observed that 'self-appointed democracy watchdogs' funded the Orange camp 'under the name of civic education', and these included 'our colonial master, Britain ... of course with a helping hand from the Americans' (*The Leader* 2005b; Kamau 2005a). The watchdogs, Mutuma Mathiu of the *Sunday Standard*, noted, became 'factional warriors in the Narc wars ... taking sides in the power struggle' because the power struggle gave them 'an opportunity to project more influence through them' (Mathiu 2004).

The most prominent international factional 'warriors' in the Kenyan referendum campaign were the Germans, the British and the Americans. German Ambassador Bernd Braun accused the Kenya government of breaking the law and the spirit of the constitution (Nzioka 2005). British High Commissioner Andrew Woods received Raila, and announced that the EU was to give KES 80 million (about GBP £600,000 and US $1 million at the time) to be used by referendum agents (Njeru 2005). With US Ambassador William Bellamy pledging support for Kenyans to become 'courageous' (Mugonyi 2005) there appeared to be an upsurge of 'presumably well-funded civil societies types' (Editorial, *Daily Nation* 2005) who carefully orchestrated protest events. One of the 'protest' organizers was a globe-trotter and an 'experienced hand at mass protests ... a professional protester', as Oscar Obonyo of the *Sunday Nation* put it. He took advantage of TV cameras to plead with the police to shoot him but the police were not interested (Obonyo 2005).

The 'protest', British Labour MP Tony Colman reportedly claimed, was about demands that parliament accept the Bomas draft without any change because 'Bomas has come out with its contribution, very much about having a prime minister, being accountable and elected from parliament' (Mudhai 2005a).

The purpose of the created despondency was to lead to the regime change desired by the master states. Peter Mwaura of *Nation* observed that there was 'a rogue superpower seeking a regime change' and ready to back a coup (Mwaura 2005). In the process, manufactured riots were expected to produce a Ukraine-like American backed 'Orange Revolution' in Kenya. Britain-based *Sunday Standard* Columnist Fred Mudhai observed that 'Public opinion can be mobilized ... through the media and motivation of influential groups' in order to 'stir a revolution against the government'. He also noted that Britain had started spreading rumours that things 'could get really bad' and that the government did not seem to 'realize that people are fed up' (Mudhai 2005b).

In their efforts to 'mobilize opinion', the master states believed that 'their criticism should be treated as sacrosanct' (Warigi 2005b). The local media helped them to feel 'sacrosanct' by seemingly committing journalistic fraud to give the wrong impression (Barth 2005), distorting stories to make the government look weak and not acceptable (Branch and Cheeseman 2005: 332–5), and becoming tools of turning low-level diplomats into celebrities. Using NGOs and 'civil society' organs that front for selected politicians as well as raising the pitch in *diplomatic noise making*, both orally and in print, ambassadors became columnists and guests in electronic media talk shows to tell Kenyans how to act when relating to 'donors'. They occasionally hurled insults at the country in the belief that they had a natural right to do so and that, more than Kenyans, they knew best what was best for Kenyans (Warigi 2005b).

The coup talk appeared to have some support. Mudhai quoted Gene E. Bigler, a veteran of the United States Information Agency (USIA) and State Department operations, in a statement: 'the US and other Western governments, the OSCE [Organization for Security and Co-operation in Europe], and a variety of NGOs ... helped trigger the Orange Revolution' in Ukraine. He claimed that since 'traditional diplomacy targeting President Kibaki has failed ... bilateral donors have resorted to public diplomacy that ... could stir a revolution against the government' (Mudhai 2005b). Kalonzo Musyoka openly talked of a coup in the event of the draft passing, 'effectively inviting military takeover' (Mwaura 2005), and Raila argued that if the draft is defeated, the government should quit (*Sunday Nation* 2005a). Once the referendum results were out and the 'No' side won, Raila demanded a new election which he assumed he would win. He asserted: 'We are not interested in any negotiations. Kenyans have spoken on our behalf ... we want elections' (Mugonyi and Barasa 2005).

Although the draft was defeated and the government did not quit, the defeat liberated both Kibaki and Raila. Kibaki had led a campaign of organized ineptitude to lose the referendum which enabled him to get rid of insubordinate ministers. It also had a divisive effect on the 'No' side. A new political party, the Orange Democratic Movement, ODM, was created only for it to split over who should be its presidential candidate. Raila changed his mind about his electability or endorsing Kalonzo for president. He thereafter, commented *Sunday Nation*, became a serious presidential candidate to the disappointment of Kalonzo Musyoka (*Sunday Nation* 2006). The two men, by the end of 2005, looked at each other suspiciously. Saying he was tired of endorsing other people, Raila asserted at Kakwajuok village in East Karachuonyo, '*Nyocha awacho ni aol gi wacho ni ng'ane tosha omiyo nyaka ung'e ni ok an ngoro*' ('I said recently I am tired of saying other candidates are fit for the presidency. You must note I am not a coward!') (*The Standard* 2006).

Although Raila and the Western master states expected the government to fall and it did not, Kibaki did not think that there was crisis (Gaitho 2005). For him, the referendum was never about his government, it was about a document on how to govern and Kenyans had a choice either to accept or reject the suggested constitutional document. He had not been enthusiastic about the proposed constitutional changes. Comfortable with the existing governing structure, he hardly had either a campaign secretariat or a strategy for the Banana side, except probably to lose. This campaign to lose was manifested in the behaviour of such big players as Nairobi Mayor Dick Wathika and Internal Security Minister Michuki who, instead, were busy fixing potential Banana voters. Michuki was publicly quarrelling with Defence Minister Njenga Karume on how to deal with bad youth (Munene, 2006b: 215–36). Once people voted, Kibaki was quick to concede that the Banana side had lost and said: 'The people have made a choice and as I have always said, my Government would respect the choice of the people ... This referendum, whose aim was to adopt or reject the proposed constitution, has clearly shown that Kenyans have rejected it.' He then told Kenyans to concentrate on development work and 'live the way we have lived as Kenyans, which is envy to many'. Most importantly, he reminded Kenyans, there was no constitutional vacuum because the current document was still in force (*The Standard* 2005b).

The reaction among the Westerners and their Africanists was peculiar and displayed pre-set geo-political minds. They were happy that the Orange side won but were disappointed that Kibaki was not shaken. German Ambassador Braun told Kibaki 'to redeem his Government from the current political crisis' and dissolve 'Parliament so that all the MPs could seek fresh mandate from the electorate' (Okeya 2005). Richard Joseph of The Brookings Institution made comments on the 2005 referendum that showed that he either had not read the actual document or was acting out of mischief. Although the document reduced the powers of the president, compared to the existing constitution, and created a post of prime minister, Joseph authoritatively asserted that 'a November 2005 referendum meant to expand the government's powers was decisively defeated' (Joseph 2008: 99). Joseph ignored Kibaki's concluding remarks that there was no constitutional vacuum because Kenya had an existing constitution (*The Standard* 2005b).

The 2007 election
The controversies over the proposed constitution and the referendum set the stage for two electoral confrontations, in 2007 and 2013, involving struggles between domestic and international players as to whose wishes should prevail. The master states were clear on what Kenya should or should not do; they undertook to contain it (Kamau 2005; Kabukuru 2005: 32–4; Musila 2005; Oluoch 2005; Munene 2006a: 132–5). Having failed with the referendum, the master states concentrated on the 2007 elections and managed, after their candidate lost the election, to force power sharing on the country. Led by Britain calling the shots, they relied on statements by one of their tools, the European Observer Mission (EOM), which decreed that the election was not free and fair. British Prime Minister Gordon Brown, wanting to 'see the possibility explored where they can come together in government' (Human Rights House 2008), quickly offered to 'mediate' (*METRO 97M* 2008). David Miliband, British Foreign Secretary, then called for 'the sharing of political power' (BBC 2008). Influential Britons like those in the Royal African Society actively campaigned to discredit President Kibaki (Cherry 2008: 52–4; Dowden 2011; Blair 2008; Munene 2008b) or to make him the 'the bad guy' (WikiLeaks 2011). They seemingly promoted a new doctrine of encouraging favourite election losers to reject outcomes (Munene 2010: 282–6) even if through violence.

The Africanists, in their Western comforts, joined the British bandwagon and virtually repeated calls for power sharing. Joseph of The Brookings Institution accused the Kenya government of refusal to lose and claimed that 'a government that voters had rejected chose to nullify their decision' (Joseph 2008: 105). His intellectual soul mate, Larry Diamond, writing in the March/April 2008 issue of *Foreign Affairs* also jumped to conclusions, stating: 'In December 2007 electoral fraud in Kenya delivered another abrupt and violent setback' (Diamond 2008). Another 'expert', Joel Barkan, echoed the British call for power sharing in January 2008 (Barkan 2008a) and repeated the same a month later when he testified before the US Senate. He insisted that 'some form of power-sharing deal is imperative to resolve the current crisis' (Barkan 2008b).

The United States had initially recognized Kibaki's victory only to backtrack seemingly in the face of British hostility. *The Economist* of

London commented: 'Initially, America made the mistake of endorsing the President's re-election'. It asserted that 'most of the diplomatic pressure should be exerted on Mr Kibaki's supposed new government to annul the results and organize a recount – or a new vote' (quoted in Wolf 2015: 174). That Americans were under pressure was revealed in an exchange between Ethiopian Prime Minister Meles Zenawi and American Assistant Secretary of State Jendayi Frazer when they met in Addis Ababa. Kibaki, Zenawi told Frazer, had 'not incited violence' and yet the West was giving Raila 'a free ride' even though his side was 'responsible for most of the violence'. In defence, Frazer claimed that it was 'difficult to have leverage over the opposition, since the natural leverage of a government is over another government'. Besides, she said, 'Odinga is an excellent communicator and very good at playing victim and the media love the concept of the "good guy" versus the "bad guy"', and added that 'Odinga wants to internationalize the conflict and maintain a state of crisis' (WikiLeaks 2011).

With the United States whipped into the European fold, the master states were hyperbolic in condemning Kibaki for not losing an election to Raila. With their collective mind made up prior to evidence, they did not bother to investigate as they engaged in strange activities. Their diplomats, already with the bad manners of ignoring laws, including traffic rules, in the host countries (Gaitho 2011: 16), encouraged the media to also ignore and violate laws. In the midst of the crisis in January 2008, for instance, they ignored the fact that the media can set agenda that injure a country's interests (Ogola 2009) and promote genocide as happened with Radio Mille Collines in Rwanda (Chege 2007).

United States Ambassador Michael Rannenberger appeared particularly eager to violate local rules. He did it when the government instructed FM radio stations to delay 'live' broadcasts in order to avoid incitement, at the height of mass killings and evictions in January 2008. Rannenberger, noted diplomatic scholar Makumi Mwagiru, 'broke the rules of diplomacy by violating a rule of law in the receiving state, and doing so deliberately' (Mwagiru 2008: 79). He asserted, 'I am very happy that ... I am violating the ban because I do not agree with it' (Bartoo 2008). That particular station, in which the ambassador made his defiant statement, was known for inciting violence using hate words and telling listeners to 'clear the weed', meaning targeted people (Mute 2008)

Eventually, the Western policy-makers and Africanists in the think tanks got their wish, through Kofi Annan's team. Besides brokering a power-sharing deal, just as Brown, Miliband, and the master states 'experts' had wanted, Annan recommended a commission to investigate the alleged theft of votes at the Kenyatta International Conference Centre (KICC). The job fell to Johan Kriegler, a South African judge who led an international team of commissioners from Argentina, Tanzania, and Kenyans from the opposing camps. While the commission found no evidence of vote theft at KICC, it recommended overhaul of Kenya's electoral system which it said was undemocratic. The recommendations were accepted and the electoral commission was disbanded (Munene 2008a; Namunane and Shiundu 2008). More importantly, the Kriegler Commission discredited and blamed the EU observer mission for issuing misleading statements, the media for incitement, and Kenya's flawed constituency structures. In the Kenyan election crisis, the Kriegler Commission concluded, some media houses 'did not observe ethics and standards ... As a consequence, they ended up not helping Kenyans but added fuel to the flames' (IREC, 2008: 99–100).

Both the 2005 referendum and the subsequent 2007 election were thus not about 'democracy' but about unsuccessful regime change schemes. Since the master states felt frustrated, this set the stage for confrontations in the 2013 elections involving contested democracy ideals between their wishes on who Kenyans should vote for and perceptions of resistance to imperial dictates in Africa. In between, the West roped in the International Criminal Court (ICC) as a political instrument for barring particular candidates from vying for president. The ICC, so argued British writer and critic John Laughland in 2000, 'was just another excuse for superpower bullying ... another example in the over-globalised world of an institution that lends legitimacy to the Great Power bullying of weaker nations' (quoted in Kargbo 2009: 18). Seemingly knowingly, the US refused to be part of the ICC because it could be used politically to victimize people (Bolton 2001: 167–80).

The ICC and the Uhuru Kenyatta election

That logic of political victimization was seemingly applied to Kenya. Without doing proper investigation, the ICC proceeded to indict targeted people with clear intent to stop Uhuru Kenyatta and William Ruto from running for office (Kagwanja 2015: 144–61; Wolf 2015: 162–97). Luis Moreno Ocampo made it clear that his mission was political. He was going to make Kenya an example and indict the most responsible in equal numbers of the political divide. He later admitted his failure to investigate properly and that he was under pressure to stop certain individuals from being candidates (Menya 2014). And he had assistance from extraneous forces (Munene 2016). 'Many ... Western governments and lobbies', commented *The Economist* of London, 'invested heavily' in the election and 'hoped Mr Odinga would win' (*The Economist* 2013a).

The master states, mainly the United States, United Kingdom and France were more brazen than ever before in effort to manipulate Kenya's 2013 election. To help Raila, Miguna Miguna wrote, 'certain powerful foreign forces pulled strings, influenced and coerced Kalonzo into forming an alliance with Odinga' (Miguna 2013: 209). There followed a flurry of high-powered visits to Nairobi by Western officials such as UK Foreign Secretary William Hague, Kofi Annan, US Secretary of State Hillary Clinton, and ICC Prosecutor Fatou Bensouda to tell Kenyans not to make bad electoral choices (Kagwanja 2015: 153). They issued warnings to Kenyans not to elect Uhuru and Ruto on the pain of suffering the consequences of their supposed bad choice and of losing or having 'limited' contacts with the West (Kabukuru 2013: 6–10). They even reportedly contemplated military intervention to frustrate an Uhuru victory (Miguna 2013: 213).

This Western scheme pleased their favourite Kenyan politician, Raila, who wanted obstacles removed from his route to the presidency. He told his advisor, Miguna Miguna, that he 'preferred … both Uhuru and Ruto … locked up at The Hague during their first appearance in the pre-trial stages of their cases' (Miguna 2013: 222) so as to clear the political path for his rise to power. In December 2016, Raila confirmed these sentiments by asserting that the ICC should have locked up Uhuru and Ruto at The Hague, and should not have allowed them to run for office (Mbaka 2016). Similarly, the ICC officials had reportedly made it clear 'that they weren't interested in "new evidence" that could implicate "new culprits"'. They said: 'We are only interested in evidence that can prove the two cases against the four individuals we currently have, evidence [to] help us establish their guilt at trial at the ICC' (Miguna 2013: 131). If that had happened, Raila would have become president.

The scheme backfired because, instead of caving in, Kenyans dared the West and voted for Uhuru and the master states were not amused. Disappointed in their effort to secure Raila's election, they launched campaigns to malign Kenyan institutions. *The Economist* of London accused the Kenyan media, in stressing 'peace over justice', of becoming 'supine after their owners agreed to avoid coverage that might incite ethnic passions' (*The Economist* 2013b). Africanist Barkan, reportedly Raila's 'personal friend', accused the Kenyan Supreme Court of being 'shallow', undermining itself, and being the ultimate loser because it upheld the Uhuru victory (Kelley 2013; Odinga 2014; Kabukuru 2013: 7). He was probably disappointed that his predicted repeat violence like that of 2007 (Barkan 2013) did not materialize. Barkan's disappointment and sentiments were similar to those of Michela Wrong who termed the Uhuru victory 'the most useless exercise in Kenya' as she praised 'Raila Odinga's grim-faced but graceful acceptance of defeat'. She then accused Chief Justice Willy Mutunga of securing 'Kenya's place as a shining international symbol of impunity' (Wrong 2013). And, in joking with US journalists, President Barack Obama lumped 'Syria and Kenya' as dangerous places for reporters (Cillizza 2013).

Surviving such hostility and threats, however, found encouragement in the African circles which turned Uhuru into a new *Pan-Africanist* hero. His image moved from that of a sinner to that of a saint (Wolf 2015: 161–97). 'Kenyans', Miguna observed, 'are extremely sensitive about their sovereignty. Any proven western influence on our elections would be counter-productive as the majority of voters would most likely support candidates that appear to antagonize the west' (Miguna 2013: 209). They did exactly that, dared the master states, and voted for Uhuru. This daring caused President Yoweri Kaguta Museveni of Uganda to comment, 'I want to salute the Kenyan voters on one issue – the rejection of the blackmail by the International Criminal Court (ICC) and those who seek to abuse this institution for their own agenda ... They are now using it to install leaders of their choice in Africa and eliminate the ones they do not like' (Vision Reporter 2013).

Western over zealousness to manipulate elections and install favourites does not always work, and at times backfires. Kenya is a good example of a victim of orchestrated regime change strategies that use 'democracy' as an ideological tool of control. The West, in the twenty-first century, deliberately manipulated and tried to subvert a sense of democracy by imposing their will on the Kenyans with terrible consequences. The regime change campaigns, between 2004 and 2008, culminated in the 2007 election chaos with the West being in the thick of it in terms of resources, logistics, propaganda and misleading statements, and self-righteous pronouncements on what should be done to Kenya. They could not answer the Zenawi question to Frazer on their selective victimizing of the victim.

Instead, they manipulated the ICC and turned it into an organ of propagating impunity because of its unwillingness to conduct proper investigations and willingness to be led by politically pre-determined conclusions rather than evidence. The ICC went out of its way to achieve political ends of derailing specified candidates but it failed while leaving behind bitterness, calls for reforms, and a sense of rejuvenated Pan-Africanism. This was because the rest of Africa could see the imperial hand in the violence and the ICC activities. By January 2014, therefore, questions about the viability of the allegations against the Kenyans at The Hague were many. The ICC had blundered by starting with conclusions and then went looking for 'evidence' that was hard to find. It had goofed (Munene 2014: 15) and it eventually withdrew the cases.

Conclusion

The concept and practice of democracy in Africa is highly contested at all levels. It is the subject of geo-political rivalry with the word 'democracy' misused as an ideological tool for regime change by the big powers. The slogan 'democracy' tends to be an ideological tool for whipping 'client states' into line with the wishes of the master states and is thus a powerful commodity to give to favourites or to deny to potential victims. As a result, master states tend to bully perceived 'client states' and turn 'democracy' into an instrument of ideological warfare in geo-political confrontations with which to overthrow unwanted governments or to try to discredit them in the public arena. In the process, the application tends to be selective, as determined by perceived national interests, and it is limited to targeted states.

As much as possible, therefore, African states should keep safe distance from the Western practice of 'democracy' which amounts, rather, to subversion of 'democracy'. Those that suffer Western interference should reduce the amount of Western advice and endorsements they receive. In attempting to chart their own paths, however, Africans should be ready for rough treatment from the master states for attempting to act independently. That readiness for roughness would be one alternative approach. This calls for willingness of various states to invest heavily in their own institutions rather than expect *aid* from the very forces that appear determined to subvert African interests. In the process, ideas like that of Mengisteab (2011) calling on Africans to reconcile institutional interests in designing governing structures need serious attention.

It is possible that without the gross intervention of the master states in violating Kenya's interests, the practice of democracy in Kenya would have made great strides, would have been less violent in the twenty-first century, and would have placed Kenya on a higher geo-political plane than it is. Kenya is thus a good example of a victim of Western-orchestrated regime change strategies that use 'democracy' as an ideological tool of control. The long-term effect was to under-develop Kenya in the name of that 'democracy'.

Bibliography

Abdullahi, Ahmednasir M. 2003, 'Review Team Requires a New Chairman'. *Daily Nation* on the Web, Tuesday 25 November.

Africa Confidential. 2005, 'Kenya: A Proxy Election', 21 October, 46(21).

Agina, Ben. 2003, '"No Way", Raila's Party Tells Kibaki Over Order'. *East African Standard*, 31 December.

Barkan, Joel. 2008a, 'Breaking the Stalemate in Kenya', 8 January, CSIS Africa Program, Center for Strategic and International Studies, Washington, DC.

Barkan, Joel. 2008b, 'Testimony Before the Senate', 7 February, Hearing Before the Subcommittee on African Affairs, www.foreign.senate.gov/imo/media/doc/BarkanTestimony080207, accessed 19 April 2019.

—— 2013, 'Electoral Violence in Kenya: Contingency Planning Memorandum No. 17'. 9 January, Council on Foreign Relations, New York.

Barth, Kodi. 2005, 'State House Needs Media Expert Advise, But Media is Courting Trouble'. *Sunday Standard*, 15 May.

BBC. 2005, 'Kenya Referendum Could be Farce'. *BBC News*, Tuesday 6 September, http://news.bbc.co.uk/1/hi/africa/4215266.stm, accessed 1 October 2019.

—— 2008, 'Milliband urges Kenya Cooperation'. *BBC News*, Friday 4 May.

Bennett, George. 1963, *Kenya: A Political History, The Colonial Period*. Nairobi: Oxford University Press.

Bennett, George and Rosberg, Carl G. 1961, *The Kenyatta Election: Kenya 1960–1961*. Nairobi: Oxford University Press.

Benson's World. 2005, 'Team Loves What They're Yet to Read'. *Sunday Standard*, 9 October.

Berman, Bruce. 1990, *Conflict and Crisis in Colonial Kenya: The Dialectic of Domination*. Nairobi: East African Educational Publishers.

Blair, David. 2008, 'Kibaki Must Give Back Kenya's Stolen Election'. *The Telegraph*, 30 January 2008, www.telegraph.co.uk/comment/ 3554334/Kibaki-must-give-back-Kenyas-stolen-elec, accessed 23 April 2011.

Blundell, Sir Michael. 1964, *So Rough a Wind: The Kenya Memoirs of Sir Michael Blundell*. London: Weidenfeld & Nicolson.

Bolton, John R. 2001, 'The Risks and Weaknesses of the International Criminal Court from America's Perspective'. *Law and Contemporary Problems* 64(1), 167–80.

Branch, Daniel. 2011, *Kenya: Between Hope and Despair, 1963–2011*. New Haven, CT: Yale University Press.

Branch, Daniel and Cheeseman, Nic. 2005, 'Briefing: Using Opinion Polls to Evaluate Kenyan Politics, March 2004–January 2005'. *African Affairs* April: 332–5.

Carson, Johnnie. 2003, 'Fighting Back: What We All Can Do to Fight and Defeat Terrorism'. *Sunday Nation*, 1 June.

Chege, Michael. 2007, 'Weighed Down by Old Ethnic Baggage, Kenya Races to Another Historic Election', Africa Policy Forum, 22 June 22, http://forums.csis.org/africa.

Cherry, David. 2008, 'A Slow-Motion British Coup in South Africa', Book Review, *Executive Intelligence Review, EIR* 37(27): 52–4.

Cillizza, Chris. 2013, 'Read President Obama's Remarks at the Gridiron Dinner'. *The Washington Post*, 10 March, www.washingtonpost. com/news/the-fix/wp/2013/03/10/read-president-obamas-remark s-at-the-gridiron-dinner, accessed 21 October 2019.

Clay, Edward. 2003, 'Interview with Nation TV's Louis Otieno'. *Sunday Nation*, 29 June 29.

Daily Nation. 2005, Friday, 11 November.

Diamond, Larry. 1995, 'Promoting Democracy in Africa: The United States and International Policies in Transition', in Macharia Munene,

Korwa Adar and Olewe Nyunya (eds), *The United States and Africa: From Independence to the End of the Cold War.* Nairobi: East African Educational Publishers.

—— 2008, 'The Democratic Rollback: The Resurgence of the Predatory State'. *Foreign Affairs*, March/April.

Dowden, Richard. 2011, 'Remaking Kenya', www.royalafricansociety. org/component/content/article/454.html, accessed 23 April 2011.

Editor's Word. 2005, 'Foreign Funding Claims a Threat to Our Sovereignty'. *The Leader*, 7–10 October.

Editorial. 2003, 'Americans are Free to Pack Up and Leave'. *Sunday Standard*, 22 June.

Editorial. 2005, 'Demos a Curse of Business'. *Daily Nation*, 27 July.

GADO. 2000, Cartoons as printed in *Daily Nation* 25 November, 1 December; *Sunday Nation* 17 December.

Gaitho, Macharia. 2005, 'Will Anything Ever Move Kibaki?' *Daily Nation*, 13 December.

—— 2011, 'My Confrontation with Mr Ambassador's Security Escort'. Sunday Review, *Sunday Nation*, 24 April: 16.

Ghai, Yash Pal. 2004, Interview with Dennis Onyango, 'Ghai: Why I Would Not Accept to Chair Review Again'. *Sunday Standard*, 28 March: 16–17.

—— 2005, Interview with Dennis Onyango, 'It's Kibaki's Legacy that's on Trial Here'. *The Standard*, 20 November.

'Glint'. 2005, *Leader*, 11–17 November.

Goldsworthy, David. 1982, *Tom Mboya: The Man Kenya Wanted to Forget.* Nairobi: Heinemann.

Havelock, Wilfred B. 1994, Letter to the Editor, 'Of Majimboism at Independence'. *Daily Nation*, Thursday 28 July: 7.

His Majesty's Stationery Office. 1931, *Colonial Reports – Annual, No. 1606: Kenya Colony and Protectorate, 1931.* London: His Majesty's Stationery Office.

Human Rights House Foundation. 2008, 'The World Reacts to Crisis in Kenya', 2 January, Oslo.

Hunt, Richard P. 1957, 'Kenya May Face Political Strife'. *The New York Times*, Sunday 17 March.

Iraki, Frederick K. 2006, 'Political Survival and the Economy'. *Daily Nation*, 5 January.

IREC. 2008, 'Report of the Independent Review Commission on the General Elections held in Kenya on 27 December 2007'. IREC, Nairobi: 99–100.

Jefferson, Thomas. 1968 [1776], 'Declaration of Independence', in Daniel Boorstin (ed.), *An American Primer.* Chicago: University of Chicago Press, 83–93.

Jones, Nigel. 2012, 'Cameron, Churchill, Race ... and a Historical Howler'. *Mailonline*, 14 March, www.dailymail.co.uk/debate/article-2114950/

Cameron-Churchill-Race--historical-howler.html, accessed 21 October 2019.

Joseph, Richard. 2008, 'Challenges of a "Frontier" Region'. *Journal of Democracy*, 19(2): 94–108.

Kabukuru, Wanjohi. 2005, 'Kenya: Sir Edward's Crusade Has Clay Feet'. *New African*, May: 32–4.

Kabukuru, Wanjohi. 2013, 'The Return of President Kenyatta'. *New African,* April: 6–10.

Kagwanja, Peter. 2015, 'The Geopolitics of International Justice: ICC and Kenya's 2013 Presidential Election', in Kimani Njogu and Peter Wafula Wekesa (eds), *Kenya's 2013 General Election: Stakes, Practice and Outcomes.* Nairobi: Twaweza Communications and Heinrich Boll Stiftung, 144–61.

Kamau, Jean. 2005, 'Let's Do Not as Donors Say, But as They Did in the Past'. *Sunday Standard*, 3 April.

Kamau, John. 2016, 'Why the British Feared Jomo Kenyatta Rule and Rise of Power Men'. *Saturday Nation*, 10 December.

Kamau, Kiruri. 2005a, 'Britain, Moi Strike Back by Funding the No Team'. *The Leader*, 7–13 October.

—— 2005b, Quick Read, *The Leader,* December 23–December 29

Kargbo, Martin. 2009, 'The case against the ICC'. *New African*, July: 18.

Kelley, Kevin J. 2013, 'Supreme Court was 'Loser' in Kenya Election, Forum Told,' *Daily Nation*, April 24

Kersten, Mark. 2017, 'Could Yahya Jammeh End Up at the International Criminal Court?' https://justiceinconflict.org/2017/01/23/could-yahya-jammeh-end-up-at-the-international-criminal-court,accessed 25 January 2017.

Kiano, Gikonyo. 1957, 'Victory for Democracy, Elections in Kenya'. *Africa Today* 4(3), May–June: 3–6.

Kibaki, Mwai. 2002, Inaugural Address, 30 December, www.statehousekenya.go.ke/speeches/kibaki

Kihuria, Njonjo. 2003, 'Is there a Plot to Topple Kibaki?' *East African Standard*, 31 December.

Kihuria, Njonjo and Onyango, Dennis. 2005, 'New Split Derailing Banana Campaign'. *Sunday Standard*, 2 October.

Kissinger, Henry. 2001, *Does America Need a Foreign Policy for the 21st Century?* New York: Simon & Schuster.

Kyle, Keith. 1999, *The Politics of the Independence of Kenya.* London: Palgrave.

Langworth, Richard M. 2009, 'Democracy is the Worst Form of Government…', 26 June, http://richardlangworth.com/worst-form-of-government, accessed November 6, 2016.

Lumumba, P. L. O. 2005, Interview with Njonjo Kihuria, 'Political Interests Robbed Us of a New Constitution'. *The Standard*, Saturday 31 December.

Majteny, Cathy. 2004, 'Controversy Continues to Rage Over New Kenyan Constitution'. *Voice of America* Broadcast, 22 March.

Makokha, Kwamchetsi. 2003, 'Goodbye, Sir and Good Riddance'. *Daily Nation*, 4 July.

Mandela, Nelson. 1965, 'The Rivonia Trial', in *No Easy Walk to Freedom*. Nairobi: Heinemann Educational Books, 178–89.

Mathiu, Mutuma. 2004, 'Many Confusing Signals From Donors'. *Sunday Standard*, 26 September.

Matthews, Glenn. 1997, 'Forests of the Night: The Moralized Topography of Mau Mau', in Phillip Darby (ed.), *At the Edge of International Relations: Postcolonialism, Gender and Dependency*. London: Pinter, 106–22.

Maxon, Robert M. 1993, *Struggle for Kenya: The Loss and Reassertion of Imperial Initiative, 1912–1923*. London: Associated University Presses.

Mbaka, James. 2016, 'Raila: Uhuru and Ruto should have been jailed by ICC'. *The Star*, 14 December.

Mbitiru, Chege. 2003, 'There and About, US Verbal War on Allies Blunder'. *Daily Nation*, 30 June.

McArthur, Meher. 2010, *Confucius*. London: Quercus.

Mengisteab, Kidane. 2011, 'African Perspective: Why Democracy-Building in Africa Might Require Reconciling Modern and Traditional Institutions of Governance', in IDEA, 'Customary Governance and Democracy Building: Exploring the Linkages' (Report of Addis Ababa Conference 15–16 September 2011, organized by United Nations Economic Commission for Africa). International Institute for Democracy and Electoral Assistance, Stockholm, Sweden: 12–14.

Menya, Walter. 2014, 'Ocampo: Envoys wanted Uhuru and Ruto Out of Polls'. *Daily Nation*, 7 February.

METRO 97M . 2008, 'PM Backs Moves to End Crisis'. *webukometro*, 1 January.

Miguna, Miguna. 2005, 'Kenyans Beware, Steadman Opinion Poll Neither Objective Nor Conclusive'. *The Standard*, 22 December.

—— 2013, *Kidney for the King: De-Forming the Status Quo in Kenya*. Ontario: Integrity Books.

Mudhai, Fred. 2005a, 'Donor Dance Gets Better'. *Sunday Standard*, 2 October.

—— 2005b, 'Where Negotiations Fail, "Public Diplomacy" Works'. *Sunday Standard*, 30 October.

Mugonyi, David. 2005, 'Uhuru, Raila Meet US Envoy in Bid to Block Wako Draft: Six Other Countries Joined Two Hour Talks With MPs'. *Daily Nation*, Friday 26 August.

Mugonyi, David and Barasa, Lucas. 2005, 'Elections Now, Orange Says: Victory Rally Rules Out Talks With Kibaki on New Cabinet'. *Sunday*

Nation, 27 November.

Munene, Macharia. n.d., Intermittent Discussions with Gikonyo Kiano and Munyua Waiyaki, Founder Members of KANU.

—— 2002, 'The Colonial Policies of Segregating the Kikuyu, 1920–1964'. *Chem Chemi: International Journal of the School of Social Sciences* II(1): 36–48.

—— 2003, 'The Manipulation of the Constitution in Kenya, 1963–1996: A Reflective Essay'. *HEKIMA: Journal of Humanities and Social Sciences* II(1) 41–56.

—— 2005, 'Africa and Shifting Global Power Relationships'. *The Fletcher Forum of World Affairs* 29(2): 117–24.

—— 2006a, 'Expectations and Disappointments in Africa-US Relations'. *The International Journal of African Studies* 5(2): 119–39.

—— 2006b, 'Winning By Losing: The Politics of the 2005 Referendum', in Jan Kameju and P. Godfrey Okoth (eds), *Power and Power Politics in Kenya: An Interdisciplinary Discourse*. Nairobi: Security Research and Information Centre, SRIC, 215–36.

—— 2008a, 'Implications of the Kriegler report'. *Business Daily*, 7 October.

—— 2008b, 'Kenyans must respect the Constitution'. *Business Daily*, 5 February.

—— 2010, 'Africa's Prospects in the Obama Presidency'. *The Journal of Language, Technology & Entrepreneurship in Africa* 2(1): 277–91.

—— 2014, 'Stop this Charade: Bensouda Should Admit ICC Goofed and End Cases Against Kenyan Leaders'. *Daily Nation*, Wednesday 22 January: 15.

—— 2016, 'Comments on Peter Kagwanja's and Tom Wolf's Chapters', Heinrich Boll Foundation, University of Nairobi, and Twaweza Communications Symposium on the launch of Kimani Njogu and Peter Wafula Wekesa (eds), *Kenya's 2013 Election: Stakes, Practices and Outcome*, on 21 January, at the University of Nairobi.

—— 2018, 'Kenya and the End of the Cold War, 1981–1991', in Kipyego Cheluget (ed.), *Kenya's 50 Years of Diplomatic Engagement, From Kenyatta to Kenyatta*. Nairobi: Moran, 111–26.

Munene, Mugumo. 2005, 'NCCK Urges End to Campaign Violence'. *Daily Nation*, 10 October.

Musila, David. 2005, 'US Must Stop Piling Pressure on Kenya'. *Daily Nation*, opinion page, 11 May.

Mute, Lawrence M. 2008, 'Kenya: Legislation, Hate Speech, and Freedom of Expression'. *Pambazuka News*, 22 October, www.pambazuka.org/governance/legislation-hate-speech-and-freedom-expression-kenya, accessed 2 October 2019.

Mutua, Makau. 2005, 'The Orange Alliance is fraught With Landmines'. *Sunday Standard*, 20 November.

Mwagiru, Makumi. 2008, *The Water's Edge: Mediation of Violent Elec-*

toral Conflict in Kenya. Nairobi: IDIS Publications on International Studies 3. Institute of Diplomacy and International Studies, Nairobi,

Mwaura, Peter. 2005, 'Military Coups no Longer Tenable'. *Saturday Nation*, 5 November.

Namunane, Bernard and Shiundu, Alphose. 2008, 'Finally the Disgraced Kenya's ECK is Disbanded'. *Africa News Online*, 16 December. http://africanewsonline.blogspot.com/2008/12/finally-disgraced-kenya-eck-is.html, accessed 23 April 2011.

Njeru, Mugo. 2005, 'EU Offers to Donate sh 80m for Poll Agents'. *Daily Nation*, Thursday 27 October.

Nzengu, Musembi and Kamau, Clement. 2005, 'Musyoka: Draft Aims to Block Me'. *Kenya Times*, 7 October.

Nzioka, Patrick. 2005, 'Envoy Warns of Loss of Donor Support Over State Resources'. *Sunday Nation*, 9 October.

Obonyo, Oscar. 2005, 'One Man's Obsession With Street Protests'. *Sunday Nation*, 31 July.

Odinga, Oginga. 1967, *Not Yet Uhuru: An Autobiography*. Nairobi: Heinemann.

Odinga, Raila. 2014, 'A Tribute to Joel Barkan: A Friend of Kenya'. *Daily Nation*, 2 February.

Ogola, George. 2009, 'Media Has Abdicated Its Role to Politicians'. *Business Daily*, 26 March.

Okeya, Nicholas. 2005, 'Envoy Calls for Snap Polls'. *Daily Nation*, 12 December.

Oluoch, Fred. 2005, 'Will Kenyan MPs Bow to US Pressure or People's Will?' *The East African*, 4–10 July.

Onyango, Dennis. 2005, 'Yash Pal Ghai: The Enigma of Arrival'. *The East African Standard*, 11 December.

Opanga, Kwendo. 2000, 'Bush Win Exposes Flaws in the US Supreme Court'. *Sunday Standard*, 17 December.

'Palaver'. 2005, *The Standard*, 27 August.

Quinault, Roland. 2004, 'Churchill and Democracy', in David Cannadine and Roland Quinault (eds), *Winston Churchill in the 21st Century*. Cambridge, UK: Cambridge University Press.

Roelker, Jack R. 1976, *Mathu of Kenya: A Political Study*. Stanford, CA: Hoover Institution Press.

Sunday Nation. 2005a, 'Raila: Govt Should Quit if No Wins', 25 September.

—— 2005b, 'Uhuru Threatens Journalists: Media Paraded and Accused of Bias Against "No" Campaign Team', 25 September.

—— 2006, 8 January.

The Economist. 2013a, 'Kenya's New President: Will the New Centre Hold?' 6 April, www.economist.com/middle-east-and-africa/2013/04/06/will-the-new-centre-hold, accessed 2 October 2019.

—— 2013b, 'Kenya's Presidential Election: A Kenyatta is Back In Charge',

16 March, www.economist.com/middle-east-and-africa/2013/03/
16/a-kenyatta-is-back-in-charge, accessed 2 October 2019.

The Leade.r 2005a, 'Did Kibaki Sabotage the "Yes" Campaign?' 2–8
December.

—— 2005b, 'The Con Game that was Steadman Opinion Poll', 28 October
– 3 November.

The Standard. 2005a, 'Campaign Violence is Likely to Scare Investors,
Says Envoy', 20 September.

—— 2005b, 'Kibaki Accepts Ballot Outcome', 23 November.

—— 2006, 'Support My Bid For Presidency, Says Raila', Monday 9
January.

Sunday Standard. 2005, 'Kibaki's Nightmare as Kilimo Joins Raila', 9
October.

Vincent Bartoo. 2008, 'Envoy Defies Broadcast Ban'. *The East African
Standard*, 24 January.

Vision Reporter. 2013, 'Museveni's Speech at Uhuru's Inauguration'. *New Vision*, 10 April, www.newvision.co.ug/news_vision/
news/1317104/musevenis-speech-uhurus-inauguration, accessed
22 October 2019.

Voice of Kenya. 1955, 'Statement: Kenya Government Policy – Official
Analysis of Action taken by the Kenya Government on the Parliamen-
tary Delegation's Report (1954)'. *East Africa & Rhodesia*, 17 March.
Copy found in the African Studies Library, Boston University, Boston,
MA.

Wanjiku, Joy. 2005, 'How Mungiki Brought Down the Wako Draft:
Group Played Key Role in the Nairobi and R. Valley Vote'. *The Leader*,
9–15 December.

Warigi, Gitau. 2000, 'Uncle Sam Should Avoid Banana Republicanism'.
Sunday Nation, 12 November.

—— 2005a, 'Mwenje's Ambition After Confinement'. *Sunday Nation*, 9
October.

—— 2005b, 'Western Envoys are on Ego Trips'. *Sunday Nation*, 6
November.

WikiLeaks Releases. 2007, 'Meles Zenawi's Thoughts on Kenya's
2007 Elections', Nairobi Cable No. 51, http://Kenyastockholm.
com/2011/03/22/wikileaks-releases-nairobi-cable-no-51-meles-
zene, accessed 21 April 2011.

Wolf, Tom P. 2015, 'From Sinners to Saints? The ICC and Jubilee's
Triumph in Kenya's 2013 Election', in Kimani Njogu and Peter Wafula
Wekesa (eds), *Kenya's 2013 General Election: Stakes, Practices and
Outcomes*. Nairobi: Twaweza Communications and Heinrich Boll
Stiftung, 162–97.

Wrong, Michela. 2013, 'The Most Useless Exercise in Kenya'. *NYTimes.com*,
2 April, http://latitude.blogs.nytimes.com/2013/04/02/kenyattas-
victory-is-a-defeat-for-kenya-and-justice, accessed 3 April 2013.

9

Understanding the Three Paradoxical Trajectories: Democracy, Clan and Islam in the State-Building Process of Somaliland

MOHAMED A. MOHAMOUD (BARAWANI)

Introduction

Somaliland's particular form of bottom-up state formation has attracted the attention of domestic, regional and international observers. The Republic of Somaliland reinstated its sovereignty on 18 May 1991, when clan elders and the leadership of the Somali National Movement (SNM) declared the end of Somaliland's union with Somalia and the return of the country to its pre-union independence, which was attained from British colonial rule in 1960. Understandably, there was much euphoria, patriotism, healing and enthusiasm at the time of the declaration of restoration of sovereignty, as it represented the end of the era of the dictatorship of Mohamed Siad Barre (1969–91) following a decade-long bitter armed struggle (1981–91).

The restoration of sovereignty inaugurated a period of reconstruction, reconciliation, and rebuilding of state institutions. During the early years of restoration of independence, Somaliland faced enormous challenges in erecting institutions of a modern state in an environment where the involvement of clans was dominant in the country's political arena. The role of clans was facilitated by the traditional approach to politics, which was inclusive and participatory. The initial process of state formation was, thus, inclusive of representatives of all clans, traditional elders, religious leaders, business people, politicians and diaspora communities. At the same time, because of the atmosphere in which a return to war was a worrying possibility, the various actors were amenable to reaching political compromises.

The intermingling of state and non-state actors worked reasonably well, at least during the early years of restored independence. Regular engagement by the state with the traditional and religious leaders has been substantial and indispensable in keeping law and order. Over time, however, major incompatibilities of perspectives began to surface and pose challenges to the new state, although the country's political stability has remained largely intact, due to the close relationship between the leadership of SNM and clan authorities, and due to the consensus-building approach to decision-making that was in place. Yet the inclusive and consensus-based approach has come to hinder the introduction of needed reforms of state institutions and has led to growing challenges in harmonizing the various perspectives, particularly those of the state, the clan leaders and religious authorities. This divergence of perspectives of the major political actors in the country raises important questions. One is how traditional leaders and religious authorities have continued to be able to wield significant power in the political and state-building processes in the country. Another question is how this political system, which is often referred to as a 'hybrid' political order, has affected the development of a modern democratic state.

This chapter examines the trajectories of the interactions between the modern state, clan leadership and traditional authorities, and religious leaders, with the aim of explaining the interplay between these three authority systems. Another important issue, which has not been sufficiently analysed by much of the literature on the hybrid political order, is how the interplay among the three authority systems impinges on the development of a modern democratic state: in other words, how does the influence of clan elders and religious authorities impact the development of the institutions of the state? This chapter examines both the short- and long-term impacts of the hybrid system. It focuses not only on the positive contributions of the interplay of the three centres of power in the hybrid system but also the challenges the system has created. Further, it analyses the determinants of power in the country's political, social, economic and legal systems within the context of the interaction among the three key forces.

The *Guurti* and the 'hybrid' political order

During the period from 1991 to 1997, clans were prominent actors in peace-making, political reconciliations and state-formation processes. They exercised considerable influence on the political agenda in restoring peace, building of the institutions of the state, and unifying the population, which was divided during the war against the Siad Barre regime. Indeed, Somaliland's model of peace-making and state-building was largely based on the embedded authority of elders and was, by necessity and culture, inclusive.

The role of traditional leaders played in the state-formation stage led to institutionalization of the '*Guurti*', which has two meanings in Somaliland's political and social context. At the present time, the *Guurti* is the name of the upper house (the House of Elders) of Somaliland's bicameral parliament. The *Guurti* is selected by clans, while the lower house, House of Representatives, is popularly elected. But

'*Guurti*' also represents the social context in which prominent elders dedicate themselves to resolve any clan disputes that may arise. Since its institution in 1993 at the Borama Grand Conference, the *Guurti* has embodied several functions. It not only serves as the upper house in parliament, but it also leads the processes of political reconciliation and conflict resolution throughout the country, and additionally serves as a guardian of culture.

The creation of the modern *Guurti*, selected by clans, represented political inclusivity, where all clans inhabiting the territory of Somaliland are able to participate in state formation and political rebuilding. Inclusivity and decision-making by consensus, *Guurti*'s modus operandi, have been indispensable approaches in ensuring the stability of the country, especially in the early years of independence, when the institutions of the state were fragile. During this period traditional leadership proved to be an effective tool in sustaining peace and recovering from conflict. However, the role that traditional leaders played also represented a perpetuation of the clan system, which, over time, has raised a number of questions and concerns, including whether or not the *Guurti* is a sustainable institution in a situation where economic development needs to take place, state institutions of governance are to be developed, the state security system becomes more complex and where people expect their leaders to be elected. The general public, the intellectual class in particular, have also raised questions over the functionality of the state organs under the situation of prominence of the clan system and whether the role of clans hampers the development of state institutions. Since the *Guurti* is not an elected body, the power it commands without any direct accountability to the people is another concern.

As noted already, given the role of the *Guurti*, Somaliland's political system is often viewed as a hybrid political system that reconciles the traditional governance and authority system with the modern state system. Whether the two systems are reconcilable and how the fusion of the two systems impacts the development of democratic state institutions are major questions, however. What is clear is that the Somaliland state stands between two major paradigms. On the one side is the Western model of statehood, along with some institutions of a type of democratic system in which the constitution has some provisions for a political system based on multiple political parties, and checks and balances between state branches. On the other side is the system of clan and traditional authorities, which often is effective in conflict resolution but also uses traditional and religious justifications to block measures towards building a modern democratic political system, which are seen, especially by religious authorities, as Western agenda not suitable for local customs and lifestyles. For instance, the advocacy by traditional authorities for the customary system to be the only one used in the country in matters of conflict resolution among clans, families, and judicial and political disputes, undermines the rule of law and the work of the judiciary and law-making bodies. In addition, the traditional authorities impose on society edicts that contradict the modern democratic political system and rule of law. Additionally, religious leaders challenge the concept of women's political participation and the opening of conventional (non-Islamic) banks in Somaliland, succeeding in completely prohibiting the adoption in the country of conventional bank financial transactions, due to the interest rate factor.

From the sermons of religious leaders, it is obvious that the religious perspective takes a clear position that society is not allowed to be influenced by other cultures and civilizations, especially those of Westerners and non-Muslims. Most elements of the modern state are often called into question and face great challenges, as religious campaigns seek to drive a wedge between sharia and the framework of the modern state. In their capacity as guardians of culture, the traditional leaders are also heavily influenced by the sharia perspective.

As Richards (2009: 5) notes: 'With domestic pressure for modernization of government institutions, tensions between the traditional Somali style of governance and the new democratic government in the territory are becoming more apparent and problematic'. The tension between Islamic sharia and democracy signifies not so much an inherent incompatibility between the two systems, but a situation of confusion in which no single authoritative voice prevails. The state has an inconsistent and incomplete influence on religious actors. The Ministry of Religious Affairs represents the government on religious matters but has little ability to coordinate religious actors over the issues of political and social affairs. As a result, the orders and decrees of religious leaders are often independent and have little relation to those of the state.

Given the conflicting perspectives between the state and the traditional and religious authority systems, why the traditional and religious authorities occupy prominent roles within the political system is an important question. One answer as Richards notes is that, 'without the inclusion of this traditional element from the beginning of the state-formation process, the territory would not exhibit the level of peace and stability that exists today' (2009: 10). Like Richards, many others argue that the utilization of traditional forms of governance in Somaliland was reasonable, timely and essential since the state's governance structure was destroyed, the clans were armed, and many militias were mobilized by clans outside of SNM political and military structures.

Considerable literature underscores that the success in peace-building and state-building in Somaliland is rooted in the contribution and participation of traditional authorities and customary institutions more generally. Scholars such as Bradbury (2008), Richards (2009), Balthasar (2012), Renders (2012) and Walls (2014) have contended that Somaliland's current political existence materialized due to a mixture of inclusive governance and the clans' active participation in state affairs.

Marleen Renders' book *Consider Somaliland* (2012) also affirms the role of traditional and customary practices in the restoration of political stability and the rebuilding of state institutions in the country. According to her, 'Somaliland's political reconstruction was driven by indigenous initiative, indigenous capital reconstruction and indigenous political leaders' (2012: 3). Renders further argues that Somaliland's state-formation journey has involved multiple actors, as the concept of hybrid political order encourages stronger bottom-up civic participation in the political affairs of the country, based on the belief that such inclusivity contributed to political survival in the short and medium terms. In Renders' words, 'Somaliland statehood is the product of evolving negotiations between a wide range of local actors, including politicians, military men, businessmen, clan elders and mixed versions of these categories of actors' (2012: 224). In his book *Becoming Somaliland* (2008) Bradbury also provides a detailed historical account of how Somaliland's state-building and peace-building processes were concurrently maintained and how the leadership of the indigenous institutions played a profound role in both reinstating state structures and sustaining peace under circumstances of statelessness and post-conflict dynamics.

Many other scholars have participated in the debate surrounding the hybrid political order and the importance of the roles of traditional leaders. Walls (2014) and Renders (2012) have both emphasized the fundamental contribution of the hybrid political arrangement to the installation of a participatory and inclusive form of politics, with the inclusion of clan elders providing a crucial link between political systems and the grassroots. According to Walls, 'Somalilanders have succeeded in establishing a degree of stability and a functional state precisely by incorporating elements of clan structure and tradition' (2014: 27).

Renders (2012) has also claimed that Somaliland has been successful in managing its internal political and social reconciliation domestically and without assistance from the international community. Agreeing with this point of view, many other researchers have claimed that the Somaliland model of state-building has been a locally engineered, locally driven and locally financed project (e.g. Boege et al. 2008; Bradbury 2008; Richards 2009; Balthasar 2012; Walls 2014).

The credit many scholars attribute to the *Guurti* for leading a peaceful state-building process is hard to dispute. The *Guurti* certainly registered a pivotal achievement in state formation and the restoration of peace, in collaboration with other non-state actors, such as religious leaders, the private sector, civil society organizations, and the diaspora. However, the highly positive analysis of the hybrid political order neglects two critical issues. One is that it underestimates (and in some cases ignores) the participation and oversight on the political process by religious leaders whose intention has been to ensure compliance with sharia. Richards, for example, claims: 'The government being formed is a product of reconciliation between old traditional structures and the new "democratic structures and practices", thereby creating a central government inclusive of and dependent upon both' (2009: 9). However, this overlooks the penetration and influence of religious leaders on the SNM, which fought the dictatorship of Siad Barre between 1981 and 1991. During the state-formation stages and post-conflict reconstruction period also, the traditional authorities, representing various clans, aligned themselves with religious leaders and had significant influence on the process of state formation by using Islamic sharia as a point of reference to shape decisions by the political leadership and law-making institutions. Furthermore, the influence of religious leaders affected the drafting of the national constitution, which attests not only supremacy of sharia law, but also that nothing in contravention of sharia is allowed. Somaliland, in fact, is the second country in the Muslim world to have the *Tawhiid* (i.e. the name of Allah) written on its flag. Much of the analysis of the hybrid thesis either neglects the influence of religion or conflates the influences of religion and tradition.

The scholars that view the Somaliland state as a 'hybrid state' or 'hybrid political order', restrict the systems that are fused to the traditional institutions and the modern state structures. However, we must look beyond these two elements in the context of Somaliland, because religious institutions and actors, the private sector, diaspora, youth, women, civil society, media and scholars have all played a vital role in the state-making and state-building process in the country. The same forces cooperated to sustain the peace and political stability domestically. For example, in an environment where the Somaliland state is not recognized internationally, and thus receives little external development funding or foreign direct investment, the local private sector has played an unusually large role in building the state through paying taxes and allowing the government to borrow money from private companies with Somaliland, and this has strengthened the state-building process. In terms of power, the main players include not only the state and traditional leaders but also religious authorities.

Contestation of indigenous and modern state actors in Somaliland

As already noted, with the restoration of sovereignty, traditional institutions – namely elders guided by customary law – were inserted into the political process with significant formal and informal powers. The reasons for their insertion in a position of significant power are many. One reason was that the traditional institutions were still operational in the country, despite the colonial experience. Thus, when a political vacuum emerged in 1991, with the collapse of the Somali state and Somaliland's declaration to restore its sovereignty, the traditional leaders were in the best position to fill some of the vacuum by availing their institutions of conflict resolution and reconciliation and taking a leading role in moving the country from failed statehood to a more promising future statehood by utilizing their social capital in reconciling conflicts, filling the void with traditional structures. The traditional leaders were also the most legitimate authority able to stand above the fray and facilitate dialogue among the various other actors in the political process.

Another important reason for the inclusion of clan and the traditional leaders into the formal political structures is, as Richards (2009) notes, because of the relations the traditional leaders had established with the SNM during the struggle against the Siad Barre regime. 'Throughout the campaign of the SNM, the Somaliland clans were integral to the success of the liberation struggle as well as post-conflict reconciliation and state formation' (Richards, 2009:. 166). 'Given the positive role which the councils of elders played in peacebuilding, they were also entrusted with important roles in the successive process of building political order, and today they are constitutionally embedded in the political system of Somaliland' (Boege et al. 2008: 13). The new political system that emerged is largely founded on clan-based power sharing and inclusive representation (known as the *beel* system). It is also often described as a hybrid between traditional governance and the Western state system. This hybrid political order is 'the outcome of negotiated statehood. In Somaliland, the negotiation involved a wide range of actors: politicians, elders, the military, businesses, civil society, NGOs, and the international community' (Rift Valley Institute 2012: 1).

There is little disagreement that the hybrid political order has made a huge contribution in steering the country's peaceful transition. Somaliland stands out as a rare example of how political negotiation can succeed when led by social and political actors who are honest brokers. The Borama Conference of 1993, in which Somaliland's clans were active participants, installed a new leadership and a new system of government. As Renders and Terlinden (2010: 731) note, the Borama conference was arguably the most important event in the history of Somaliland's state-building process. What came out of it was the national charter, which addressed key issues, including the drafting and development of the national constitution, in order to conclude the transitional period.

With growing development of the institutions of the state, however, a number of challenging issues surrounding the hybrid political order have emerged. One of the challenges relates to its sustainability. In other words, as the state's management of security strengthens, might the role of the traditional leadership diminish or even disappear from formal government? In other words is the hybrid system a temporary transitional arrangement or is it a permanent political fixture of the country and, if it is a transitional arrangement, when is the appropriate time to reduce or abolish the formal role of the traditional system? These are difficult questions that divide opinions.

Another contentious issue is whether the legislative role of the unelected *Guurti* is consistent with the constitution or whether it impinges on the process of building a democratic state. Seth Kaplan (2008: 256), for example, argues that the hybrid system places significant limits on the development of fully representative and effective democracy. By contrast the *Guurti*, which is selected by clans, may be viewed as a safety net for the equitable representation of all clans and rural communities in the political process, which a fully electoral process may not be able to ensure.

Yet another challenge is whether or not the *Guurti*, which is a guardian of culture and religion, is too-conservative a force, to allow the development of a secular democratic state. This issue is discussed in detail in the next section. These debates about the relations between the role of the *Guurti* and the process of developing a modern democratic state are likely to continue to rage for some time.

There are also questions raised about specific interventions undertaken by the *Guurti*. One good example is the delaying of elections, likely contributing to failure in consolidating the electoral system. The House of Elders, the *Guurti*, has the authority to extend the term of elected bodies at different levels, including the presidency. In delaying elections, the *Guurti* is said to go against one of the key democratic principles – regular elections. The *Guurti*'s influence over elections is viewed as a challenge to the very foundations of democracy. Traditional leaders, however, view elections as a concept pushed by Western countries to undermine local culture, tradition and religion.

In this respect, Walls states that the House of *Guurti*'s reputation has been undermined by successive term extensions, which are legally debatable and paradoxical. 'The Guurti has already lost much of its status through serial extensions of elections, almost all of them controversial, and it is now crucial to the maintenance of the hybrid system that a form of legitimate election is devised' (Walls 2014: 309). As Walls contends, the *Guurti*'s integrity has diminished due to its controversial extensions of terms of elected government officials, including the tenures of the president, vice president and members of the lower house of parliament. The extensions have occurred on a number of occasions, resulting in the postponement of elections. For example the presidential elections were postponed from 2008 to 2010 and 2015 to 2017; the House of Representatives elections were postponed from 2010 to 2015 and 2016 to 2019; and local council elections were postponed from 2017 to 2019. Elections to the *Guurti* have never been held since their formation by selection at the Borama Grand Conference in 1993.

In some cases, however, the *Guurti*'s interventions in postponing elections have not been without merit. With its intervention when the electoral and political systems are in disarray, such as when there are major disputes between parties, postponing elections may be part and parcel of the *Guurti* taking responsibility for conflict prevention. However, in addition to its political role, the *Guurti* is also in charge of defending culture, and this duality of responsibilities seems to portray it as an institution often ridden by contradictions and conflicts of interest.

The fact that the *Guurti* does not have a mechanism for succession of its members is another controversy. The members of the *Guurti* have essentially stayed in power without having to undergo a new cycle of selections since the establishment of the body at the Borama Grand Conference in 1993. Bradbury contends that '[t]he role of the customary institutions has evolved and, in the view of some, they have become corrupted as they have been incorporated into government' (2008: 246).

As the institutions of the state develop, the hybrid system also creates confusion over spheres of responsibility between those of the state and those of traditional authority. Some political, economic and national decisions, which are expected to be undertaken by the elected authorities, are instead taken by traditional authorities.

The country continues to operate under three authority systems, the state, tradition, and Islam. Integration of all three authority systems in the country's political system was effective when the institutions of the state had limited capacity. As the state expanded its capacity, however, there emerged duplication of roles between the different authorities resulting in turf conflicts, especially when there was divergence of perspectives and policies. Women's rights issues, for example, are an area of conflicting views. In Somaliland, women are the majority when it comes to voting during the elections, as they have a higher turnout ratio than men. However, the customary and Islamic systems give more consideration and privilege to men, as women cannot become either elders or *Guurti* members. Women also are rarely fielded as candidates or elected as members of parliament or even local councils.

In addition, Islamic sharia is very restrictive against women in terms of politics and decision-making, because most religious leaders contend that women are not permitted to lead Muslims. Islamic sharia also does not endorse women being given a role in speaking in the public sphere or to expose part of their bodies in public. Taken together, these religious and traditional restrictions put Somaliland women in an under-privileged position. The ongoing manipulation of the clan and religious arguments against female participation has left the political system of the country in a male-dominated situation, despite the fact that constitutional provisions clearly highlight equal rights for all citizens.

The hybrid political system of power sharing is also regarded as lowering the required levels of ability or formal qualifications of the people in charge and therefore the quality of service to the public. At the present moment, many people in Somaliland believe that the state institutions are not capable of providing quality service or adequate representation because elections (if they take place) and appointments of the government officials come through clan-based power sharing with little concern for the competencies and levels of knowledge of the officials or representatives. As the criteria for appointments of officials is guided by the objectives of integrating traditional authorities and clan power sharing, the quality and professionalism of people in places of authority is compromised. With their association with the government, the traditional leaders also face conflicts of interest and lose the neutrality and non-partisan characteristics that have in the past made them successful as mediators of conflicts.

Given the identified challenges that the hybrid order has engendered, some have expressed the sentiment that the country must re-think the hybrid political order. Many Somalilanders now view the *Guurti* as a peril to democratic institutions, and as a hindrance to the development of state institutions and the entire political system of the country. The outstanding question for those disillusioned with the hybrid system is, thus, how the informal actors (traditional leaders) can relinquish their power to formal actors so that professional technocrats handle the political affairs of the country. Despite the many challenges associated with the hybrid system, the *Guurti* and the hybrid system cannot be easily discarded since the people of Somaliland, and Somalis in general, live under the religious and customary system. The clan protects the interests of society because the nomadic lifestyle does not easily fall under the control of the state and so any working state system will have to incorporate and contend with the clan and its traditional leaders.

The customary system still has many governance roles that complement the functions of the formal institutions of the state. The formal law and court systems, for example, have limited capacity to operate in the nomadic socio-economic system. As a result, customary law (*xeer*), which is not written formally but is mostly based on precedence and sharia legal principles, complements the role of the state in governing the rural communities. Customary law works throughout the social system as an instrument of conflict resolution and peace-building. Given the limited reach of the modern state's administrative system, the traditional system complements the state system. Moreover, the traditional system is, in many respects, more compatible than the state system with the way of life of the rural communities. As such, the traditional authority system remains essential in the context of pastoral communities.

Islam and democracy in Somaliland

As already noted, religion and religious authorities constitute the third constituent of the power structure in Somaliland's hybrid political system. However, the role and influence of Islam is largely neglected by analysts of Somaliland's hybrid political system. The impact of religion on the political order is not fixed, however, as interpretations of Islam tend to vary among adherents of different sects of Islam. This section of the chapter does not aim to examine in detail the relations between Islam and democracy in general. Its focus is on analysing the growing influence of Islam in the country's political system and how Islamic ideology and the legal structures of sharia impact the agenda of building a democratic state in Somaliland.

The relations between Islam and democracy and whether Islam is incompatible with democracy are contested terrains. Islam, without doubt, aims to transform societies by embedding Islamic norms and ways of living within their fabric. In contrast, democracy is an ideology that most of the world's nations recognize as a universal and ideal type of governance and political development, in one form or another. Going against this democratizing trend, Muslim Sunni countries have largely adopted monarchies, such as Saudi Arabia, the United Arab Emirates and Qatar; or dictatorships, such as Sudan (until April 2019) and Egypt. Yet, some Islamic countries have also embraced democracy, such as Indonesia and Turkey, although this is arguably a result of these countries' embrace of the West and adoption of at least some aspects of its culture.

A 2002 paper by the U.S. Institute of Peace notes that 'many Muslim activists, using broad and sometimes crude notions of secularism and sovereignty, consider democracy to be the rule of humans as opposed to Islam, which is rule of God'. The paper, however, contends that explanation of 'why so many Muslim countries are not democratic has more to do with historical, political, cultural, and economic factors than with religious ones' (2002: 1). The paper adds that many Muslim scholars contend that *shura* (consultative decision-making) is a model of Islamic democracy in which Muslims are expected to discuss matters and take decisions collectively. However, Muqtedar Khan noted in the paper: 'While there is considerable truth in this claim, one must also recognize the differences between *shura* and democracy before one can advance an Islamic conception of democracy based on *shura*' (*ibid.*: 4).

> The shura principle in Islam is predicated on three basic precepts. First, that all persons in any given society are equal in human and civil rights. Second, that public issues are best decided by the majority view. And third, that the three other principles of justice, equality, and human dignity, which constitute Islam's moral core ... are best realized, in personal as well as public life, under shura governance. (Qutb 1973: 83–5, quoted in Mubarak 2016: 12)

From this point of view, there is no doubt that Islam is often devoted to protecting justice and equality within society. At the same time, and in contrast to parliamentary democracy, the *shura* decision is taken based on what the majority of those involved in the *shura* agree, and in that sense cannot be seen as akin to a popular vote or a public decision, as the participants are a limited group.

Nader Hashemi's (2009) *Islam, Secularism, and Liberal Democracy* discusses the linkages between Islam and (liberal) democracy. He outlines in detail the contests and unresolved challenges encountered between Islam and liberal democracy, especially at the ideological level. He puts forward the argument that Western societies and Muslim societies are far away from one another in their views of and relation to liberal democracy.

> In the modern period, at first glance, the relationship between religion and democracy seems inherently contradictory and conflictual. Both concepts speak to different aspects of the human condition. Religion is a system of beliefs and rituals that are related to the divine and the sacred. (Hashemi 2009: 34).

As Hashemi indicates 'religion is a system' and as the only system made by Allah for humans, in the eyes of many religious leaders, it must be adopted unconditionally across all of society.

In addition, Islam is a universal religion, and the Qur'anic verses paint a picture in which the Muslim political and social identity rises above all other identities – in other words, all Muslims are brothers and sisters regardless of their colour, sex, language, ethnicity, clan, politics, class and geographical location. Generally, within Somaliland, loyalty and adherence to Islamic values and sharia principles have reached their peak, to the extent that Islamic sharia, the Qur'an and the Hadith have had more of an influence on Somaliland communities and the Somali ethnic group as a whole than ever before.

Islam has both metaphysical dimensions as well as more practical prescriptions for political and public life. As such, it has been difficult to arrive at a neutral ground between Islam and liberal democracy or democratic governance, because the two systems compete over the same territory (authority, law, etc.). Furthermore, Islam is very suspicious of newer global phenomena such as modernization, globalization, liberalism and other concepts of civilization that are backed by Western societies. 'The process of the rapid modernization of traditional societies sometimes produces a radical interpretation of religion as a response to social dislocation and political uncertainty. Islamic fundamentalism is a much more complicated social phenomenon than is generally appreciated' (Hashemi 2009: 55).

The contestation of the relations between Islam and democracy described above is relevant to Somaliland. On the one hand, the state has its formal laws, such as the penal code, which is secular. There is also the generally recognized goal of building a modern democratic state in the country. On the other hand, parliament cannot pass a law contrary to Islamic sharia, a principle enshrined as Article 5(2) of the constitution: 'The laws of the nation shall be grounded on and shall not be contrary to Islamic Sharia' (Somaliland Constitution 2000: 8). Therefore, the ratification and domestication of all national laws and international laws must comply with Islamic sharia otherwise they are considered null and void.

The country has also witnessed a growing religious influence from Saudi Arabia, which has become the main source of religious teaching and ideological orientation. Many mosques in Somaliland are funded by Saudi Arabia and have become powerful channels to advance the religious teachings and the spread of a particular brand of religion across society. The most prominent and well-known sheikhs in the country generally believe that religion and rule over the people cannot be separated within Muslim societies and that Islamic religion represents a universal and mandatory set of practices and laws to be followed without any competing authority.

Within this perspective, many people in Somaliland, most notably the older generation and religious leaders, oppose rapid socio-economic transformation and campaign against it on regular basis. Using mosques as a platform, they attempt to educate society on the perceived ills of modernization, in order to denounce and halt the process. Such practices seem to fit under what Hashemi viewed as 'radical interpretation', but it, in fact, may be more pervasive than Hashemi suggests, as there are some core issues of contention that Islam and liberal democracy categorically cannot ignore when it comes to trying to cohabit.

Islam is very assertive in delivering a message that is all encompassing, as it seeks to offer itself as the sole answer to matters of culture, religion and governance. As such, one cannot attempt to cordon off the religion from matters of politics, culture, social values, customs and norms, as these issues must all inherit their basis and justification from Islam itself. Ultimately, Somaliland faces the dilemma of confronting these competing political cultures, and it can be argued that its future success hinges on the fragile balance of reconciling its religion and culture on the one hand, and its desired modern democratic political system on the other. The goals of building and maintaining such a delicate balance are not unattainable. Democratization in Somaliland has, in fact, reached a level far beyond what one would expect to see in a context where Islamic foundations, Islamic civilization, and religious vigilance remain so prominent.

Conclusions

Somaliland's state-formation and state-building approaches are referred to as a hybrid political system that fuses the institutions of the modern state with the country's age-old traditional institutions. Although often neglected, religious institutions and religious leaders have constituted a third leg of the hybrid system. The performance of the fused system is generally lauded by observers because it was able to bring together a wide range of actors to participate in the political process. To the degree possible, it has also been able to, base decisions on consensus rather than on decisions by majorities, dominant identities or interest groups, or individual autocrats.

On the basis of this approach, the young country registered some impressive progress in bringing peace and reconciliation to a society torn apart by conflict during the last decade of the rule of Siad Barre. Progress in the area of economic development has also been notable, even though Somaliland has yet to obtain international recognition as an independent country. Lack of recognition continues to limit its engagement in the global system. Despite several postponements of elections, Somaliland is said to have conducted among the cleanest elections in the region.

Contrasting with these significant accomplishments, the hybrid system has come to face some important challenges. Differences of perspectives, objectives and policies between the three principal actors within the hybrid political system – the fledgling state, the traditional authorities (the *Guurti*), and religious leaders – pose some difficult challenges that can hinder the attainment of the goal of building a modern democratic state. The discrepancies among the three major actors are many. While the general agenda of the state seems to be the building of a modern democratic secular state, the principal objectives of the traditional leaders are to preserve culture and the clan system. The power-sharing arrangement between traditional institutions and the state is, thus, likely to preserve the clan system. Obviously, there are incompatibilities between the goals of the two actors. The main objective of religious leaders, which entails establishing the supremacy of sharia laws within the political system, also contravenes the goal of building a secular democratic state. In contrast to the state, the religious and traditional leaders also share a view that the institutions of democracy are foreign influences on the country. The lack of serious commitment by religious and traditional leaders to women's equality and rights of participation in the country's socio-economic life is another conflict with the goal of democracy building.

Opponents of the hybrid system note the identified challenges in their criticism of the system. Additionally, they question lack of legal definition regarding the interplay among the partners in the hybrid system. There are also questions about the significant role the traditional and religious leaders play on a daily basis in national affairs, when they often contest and run in parallel to the positions and policies of the elected state bodies.

Despite the concerns of the critics and the discrepancies among the perspectives, goals and policies of the three main partners in the hybrid system, the prevailing hybrid political order is not likely to be transformed in the near future. Islam is likely to remain influential in the country's political economy, although adherence to strict sharia law may possibly be relaxed in time, although this is not likely to happen in the current global environment. The religious leaders are more active now and have more doubts about the importation of Western civilization into Somaliland. They are also able to emphasize to the population their doubts about Western civilization and democracy by exploiting economic and political vulnerabilities. This indoctrination goes against multi-culturalism, diversity and internationalization, which would be aspects of democratization. The calling by religious leaders on young people to abstain from using technology in ways that might transform their religion and culture also complicates the state's ability to govern and regulate society.

The role of traditional institutions is also likely to prevail so long as the traditional pastoral economic system is not transformed. The clan system, which caters to the nomadic rural communities, is likely to endure also. The traditional institutions are generally preferred over the institutions of the state by rural communities because they are more compatible to their way of life.

To its credit, Somaliland has not allowed the discrepancies within the objectives and interests of the partners in the hybrid system to go out of hand and lead to conflicts. The hybrid order's ability to transform conflicts through compromises and reconciliation seems to be effective in this respect. The effectiveness of a political system is not measured in terms of ability to eliminate conflicts of perspectives and interests but rather to ensure that the competition of such interests takes place peacefully within the legal system. Somaliland seems to have managed to do this so far.

Bibliography

Abdullahi, A. 2017, *Making Sense of Somali History*, vol. 1. London: Adonis & Abbey.

Balthasar, Dominik. 2012, *State-Making in Somalia and Somaliland: Understanding War, Nationalism and State Trajectories as Processes of Institutional and Socio-Cognitive Standardization*. PhD thesis, London School of Economics.

Boege, V., Brown, A., Clements, K. and Nolan, A. 2008, 'On Hybrid Political Orders and Emerging States: State Formation in the Context of "Fragility"', http://edoc.vifapol.de/opus/volltexte/2011/2595/pdf/boege_etal_handbook.pdf, accessed 22 May 2018.

Bradbury, M. 2008, *Becoming Somaliland* (UK ed.). London, Oxford, Bloomington IN, Johannesburg, Kampala, Nairobi: James Currey.

Hashemi, N. 2009, *Islam, Secularism, and Liberal Democracy: Toward a Democratic Theory for Muslim Societies*. Oxford Scholarship online, www.oxfordscholarship.com/view/10.1093/acprof:oso/9780195321241.001.0001/acprof-9780195321241, accessed 13 January 2010.

Held, David. 1989, Political Theory and the Modern State: Essays on State, Power and Democracy. Cambridge, UK: Polity Press.

Huntington, S. P. 1997, *The Clash of Civilizations and the Remaking of World Order*. New Delhi: Penguin Books India.

Kaplan, Seth. 2008, 'The Remarkable Story of Somaliland'. *Journal of Democracy* 19(3), www.sethkaplan.org/doc/JOD,%20Democratization%20in%20Africa%20chapter%203.10.pdf, accessed 31 December 2018.

Laskar, M. 2017, 'Summary of Social Contract Theory by Hobbes, Locke, and Rousseau', SSRN Scholarly Paper 2410525, https://papers.ssrn.com/abstract=2410525, accessed 16 January 2019.

Mouritz, Thomas. 2010, 'Comparing the Social Contracts of Hobbes and Locke'. *The Western Australian Jurist* 1: 123–7, www.murdoch.edu.au/School-of-Law/_document/WA-jurist-documents/WAJ_Vol1_2010_Tom-Mouritz---Hobbes-%26-Locke.pdf, accessed 9 January 2019.

Mubarak, A. 2016, 'Democracy from Islamic Law Perspective'. *Kom: Casopis Za Religijske Nauke* 5(3): 1–18, https://doi.org/10.5937/kom1603001M, accessed 8 August 2018.

Qutb, Sayyid. 1973, *Tafsir Surat al-Shura*. Beirut: American University of Beirut.

—— 1992, *Ma'alim fi at-Tariq*. Beirut: American University of Beirut.

Renders, M. 2012, *Consider Somaliland*. Leiden and Boston, MA: Brill.

Renders, M. and Terlinden, U. 2010, 'Negotiating statehood in a Hybrid Political Order: The Case of Somaliland'. *Development and Change*

41(4): 723–46, http://hdl.handle.net/1854/LU-1231349, accessed 31 December 2018.

Richards, R. 2009, *Challenging the Ideal: Traditional Governance and the Modern State in Somaliland*, PhD dissertation, University of Bristol, www.academia.edu/1234919/Challenging_the_Ideal_Traditional_ Governance_and_the_Modern_State_in_Somaliland, accessed 16 February 2018.

Rift Valley Institute. 2012, 'Rethinking State-building in Somalia: Negotiated Statehood and the Realities of Hybrid Governance', Rift Valley Institute Meeting Report, Nairobi Forum, 6 December, http:// riftvalley.net/publication/rethinking-state-building-somalia, accessed 31 December 2018.

Sen, Amartya. 1999, 'Democracy as a Universal Value'. *Journal of Democracy* 10(3): 3–17.

Somaliland Constitution. 2000, *The Constitution of the Republic of Somaliland*, translated with extended annotations and explanatory notes by Ibrahim Hashi Jama, www.somalilandlaw.com/body_ somaliland_constitution.htm, accessed 6 May 2018.

U.S. Institute of Peace. 2002, 'Islam and Democracy', United States Institute of Peace, Special Report 93, September, www.usip.org/2002/09/ islam-and-democracy, accessed 7 August 2018.

Walls, M. 2014, *A Somali Nation-State: History, Culture and Somaliland's Political Transition*. Hargeysa: Redsea Cultural Foundation; Pisa: Ponte Invisible.

10

Developing an Alternative Approach to Democratization in the Transitional Societies of the Greater Horn

KIDANE MENGISTEAB

Introduction

As indicated at the outset, this manuscript has identified two principal objectives. One was to examine the key structural and institutional factors that impede the democratization process in the countries of the Greater Horn of Africa (GHA). The second objective was to explore alternative approaches to democratization that may be more effective in addressing the critical bottlenecks to the process of democratization in the region. The country cases examined in the different chapters have identified a number of structural, institutional, political, cultural and religious factors that have obstructed the democratization process and have proposed a number of changes and policy measures that would contribute in revitalizing the democratization process. This chapter attempts to draw together the underlying bottlenecks of democratization in the region and to consolidate the changes suggested in the various chapters into a coherent proposal of an alternative approach to democratization. The chapter is organized into three parts. The first explains how weak structural and institutional foundations impede democratization in transitional societies, such as those of the GHA. The second part proposes an alternative approach that aims to promote democratization while building the structural and institutional requisites that sustain the process. The third and concluding part summarizes the potential contributions of the contextualized comprehensive approach (CCA) to policy and theory on democratization.

Critical structural bottlenecks

Among the most important, but least recognized, factors that have undermined the democratization process in the GHA is the fragmentation of economic and institutional systems. As, observed in Chapter 1, African economies range from modestly developed capitalist economies with modern banks, and in many cases equity markets, to the traditional subsistence peasant and pastoral economic systems. These economic systems, along with their corresponding institutional systems exist side by side in the countries of the region. The populations of the region are not only fragmented along identity lines but they are also divided along economic systems that shape their institutions as well as their cultural values.

The parallel socio-economic spaces are highly unequal with the traditional sector marginalized not only in terms of access to resources and public services but also in terms of representation in the political process. Marginalization within the political system of the populations in the traditional economic systems, constituting roughly 70 per cent of the total population in the GHA, hinders the development of democratic systems with equal representation of all segments of society. The communities in the traditional systems are unable to master adequate representation in policy-making, due to their institutional detachment from the state, their poverty, and their lack of education and access to information. Lack of representation in policy-making perpetuates their marginalization in access to public services and other resources, which, in turn, preserves their lack of representation. It is hard to envisage a flourishing democratization process under conditions where the overwhelming majority of the population is marginalized in in the political process.

Deformity in the structures of the state, which concentrates power in the executive branch of government, is another major obstacle to democratization. Concentration of power in the hands of the executive denies the other constituent organizations of the state the ability to ensure accountability of the executive branch. It also frees leaders to become unaccountable autocrats, who are able to suppress opposition parties through various means in order to establish dominant parties, eliminate presidential term limits, rig elections and engage in corrupt practices. Under such deformed structures of the state, political arrangements put in place to decentralize power, such as federal arrangements, become hollow and largely symbolic. Human rights and respect of civil liberties also become untenable. Beyond the national level, building an effective regional integration scheme, which the countries of the GHA attempt to do, also becomes highly unlikely to succeed, as the autocratic leaders are unwilling to cede any power to the regional organization to enable it to coordinate regional policy or to promote regional security arrangements (Mengisteab 2012).

Poor management of diversity and crises of nation building are other critical factors that impede the democratization process in the region. In addition to the poor management of diversity along socio-economic systems (marginalization of communities in the traditional economic sector), the countries of the GHA face critical problems of mismanagement of diversity along the lines of ethnic and religious identities. The countries of the region are generally characterized by a glaring absence of effective institutions of governance that manage diversity by granting equitable citizenship rights and by accommodating the most important interests and values of the various identities within the citizenry. As a result, various ethnic, religious and social groups, facing economic, political or cultural marginalization, engage in protests, riots and armed rebellion against the state. As indicated in Chapter 1, most of the countries of the region have faced decades of devastations by countless armed rebellions and civil wars. Sustainable solutions to such conflicts require involvement of the aggrieved identities in designing new political arrangements that address their concerns and involve them in the political process through some level of decentralization of power. Such measures, however, hardly materialize under the autocratic nature of the political elite, who fortify their position through dominant parties and politicize identity by their failure to promote equitable access of participation for all identity groups. Without a change in approach, identity-based conflicts are likely to continue to ravage the region and stymie its democratization process.

Why an alternative approach to democratization?

Given the impacts of the institutional obstacles of democratization in transitional societies, such as those of the GHA, a sustainable democratization approach would need to incorporate mechanisms that tackle the identified underlying bottlenecks. As discussed in Chapter 1, and borne out in subsequent chapters, the prevailing election-centred approach lacks such mechanisms. Elections, no doubt, are critical components of the democratization process; however, they do not address the underlying structural obstacles to a sustainable democratization process. Elections, in themselves, do not erect the requisite structural foundations of democratization, such as reconciling the dichotomous economic and institutional systems, nor do they rectify the marginalization of certain ethnic and social groups, which engenders chronic conflicts that stymie democratization. Often, conducting elections has been seen as a major indicator that a country is democratizing. Most of the regimes in the GHA region have conducted several rounds of elections, even though many of these elections have been shrouded with various irregularities. Yet the structural obstacles of democratization remain largely intact.

Given the prevailing societal divisions, institutional fragmentation, and deformities of state structures, elections often are decided on the basis of identity affiliations and various other forms of manipulations rather than on the basis of policy choices. Additionally, the election-centred approach, as practised in the countries of the GHA, attempts to operate within the context of the neo-liberal ideological perspective. It operates on the ideological basis of limiting state involvement in the economy in favour of a less regulated market system, even though in transitional societies the populations in the traditional socio-economic space largely operate on the fringes of the market system, in large part due to the subsistence nature of their economic system.

Views on market-state relations under liberal democracy vary widely along a continuum. Some view the relationship to be flexible. Robert Dahl (1993), for example, argues that democratic countries have mixed economies, where the state and the market form a partnership in allocating resources. Many others, however, view the market system as a foundation for democracy and democracy as instrumental in advancing the market mechanism (Hayek 1960; Friedman 1962). In the post-Cold War era, the neo-liberal perspective has gravitated notably towards restricting the role of the state in economic activity, reflecting the surge in the power of capital in the global economic system. In line with this ideological shift, liberal democracy has become increasingly indifferent to 'persistent and systemic inequalities in both the distribution of benefits and the representation of interests', as Schmitter (1995) notes.[1] As a result, addressing the unrelenting marginalization faced by some identity groups as well as by the populations in the traditional economic sectors has, by and large, become external to the ideology of liberal democracy and its process of democratization. The liberal economic doctrine, which restricts the role of the state in economic activity, largely undermines the democratization process, especially in transitional societies, as marginalization and exclusion of the populations in the traditional systems, and of various ethnic and religious identities, is unlikely to be corrected by market forces alone. Unfortunately, they are also less likely to be corrected by the prevailing deformed state, which lacks mechanisms of accountability.

With respect to the structures of the state, separation of powers for checks and balances within the constituent organizations of the state is a critical aspect of the liberal approach to democratization (Beetham 1992; Held 2006). However, political leaders of the post-colonial states of the GHA, like those in much of the rest of Africa, flagrantly ignore this aspect of the democracy building process, as it restrains their power. They have successfully managed to practise electoral politics without establishing the structures of accountability. Hence, they have created

---

[1] A credible argument can be made that the market system would be preferable to a bad government. However, democracy implies good governance, and good governance can hardly leave it to the market to tackle problems of poverty and marginalization of large groups of citizens.

what are known as 'anocracies', a hybrid between democracy and autocracy (Kuhnhardt 2014: 85). It is also unlikely that strong mechanisms of checks and balances can be developed within the organizations of the state while the marginalization of various identity groups and the institutional delinkages of the traditional economic sectors remain in place.

Moreover, it is hardly feasible to build a vigorous system of accountability within the organizations of the state under conditions where marginalization of various identity groups is pervasive. A system of accountability would allow divergences among the organizations of the state with respect to how to deal with identity groups with grievances. The executive body is unlikely to allow the different components of the state to entertain divergent positions. The state is also unlikely to be accountable to the citizenry under parallel socio-economic systems, where the population in the traditional systems largely operates outside of the institutions of the state. In such societies it is highly unlikely that parliaments, for example, would legislate in a manner that reflects the interests of the population in the traditional systems, with which they can hardly identify. The judiciary is also unlikely to consider customary law and customary property rights in their deliberations and rulings when the customary property rights of land, for example, are not unequivocally enshrined in the constitution and are rarely recognized by the legal system. Under such conditions, the state can hardly be accountable to the population in the traditional sector even if the formal structures of accountability were in place.

Despite a few attempts, the literature on democratization in developing transitional societies has remained largely silent on developing a democratization approach that tackles directly the identified structural obstacles, especially the problem of fragmentation of economic and institutional systems. Over twenty-five years ago Claude Ake (1993) initiated an inquiry into democratization in the context of fragmented economic systems in Africa and suggested recognition of the traditional institutional systems. Unfortunately, his inquiry was not developed fully, perhaps due to his premature death in 1996.

The consociational model of democracy, proposed by scholars such as Lijphart (1969, 1977), represents another effort. This model attempts to adjust the liberal approach of democratization to make it workable in divided societies, where nation building has yet to be developed. The key elements of the consociational model include inter-ethnic power sharing through grand coalitions, decentralized governance to give self-rule (autonomy) for ethnic groups, proportional representation, and the power of veto for minority identity groups on ethnically sensitive issues. The consociational model represents a significant adjustment of liberal democracy so that it facilitates the process of nation building. The model has critics, who, among other things, express valid concerns that the rewards of power sharing may encourage elites to perpetuate ethnic fragmentation (Horowitz 2014). However, in conflict situations the model can play a critical role. It can avert or stop violent conflict giving the conflicting parties the opportunity to build political arrangements that address the root causes of the conflict. If the peace holds, it is also possible that the peace dividend would facilitate economic diversification, in the longer run. Economic diversification, in turn, can promote social ties across ethnic lines and reduce the salience of ethnicity. Regardless of its long-term implications, the model seems to offer promising results in the short term. South Africa's relatively peaceful transition from the apartheid system seems to have benefited from the application of some aspects of the model, such as power sharing. Kenya also was able to avert a potential civil war by applying a short-term power-sharing arrangement to resolve its post-election conflict in 2007.

The consociational model has other notable shortcomings, however. It neither addresses the conditions of fragmented economic and institutional systems nor does it tackle the deformities in the structures of the state. While it attempts to reconcile the elite from rival identity groups through a system of power sharing, it does little to correct the problems of uneven development and poverty, which are major factors in diversity-related conflicts. For example, neither South Africa nor Kenya has addressed adequately the problems of uneven development among their diverse identities, despite applying aspects of the power-sharing arrangement among their rival elites. The inter-elite power-sharing accords they instituted were also temporary arrangements.

What kind of alternative approach to democratization?

A four-pronged contextualized comprehensive approach to democratization was proposed in the introductory chapter as an alternative approach for the countries of the GHA, as well as to most other African countries. This section of the chapter addresses first the essential characteristics of the CCA, second why it would be more likely to promote a more sustainable process of democratization in the GHA (as well as much of the rest of Africa), compared to the prevailing election-centred approach, and third, feasibility of its implementation in the countries of the GHA.

Before delving into the discussion on its essential characteristics, it is important to point out that the CCA is not intended to discount the relevance of elections. Rather it aims to build the structural and institutional foundations that would make elections effective and the democratization process sustainable. The CCA also aims to tackle the structural impediments to democratization as an integral part of the democratization process rather than as exogenous policy measures.[2]

One of the four key components of the CCA is reconciling the dichotomous economic and institutional systems in order to establish a coherent system of institutions of governance, which would institutionally connect with the state the presently delinked populations in the vast traditional socio-economic systems. Reconciling the parallel institutions can facilitate integration of the fragmented economic systems and merge the dichotomous socio-economic spaces that characterize the countries of the GHA. Moreover, reconciling the parallel institutional systems can create conditions for adjusting the procedural practices of democracy to become relevant to all segments of society. In other words, reconciling the parallel institutional systems would facilitate the participation in the political process of the segments of the population that largely operate outside the formal institutional system, and thereby create conditions that foster an inclusive and sustainable democratization process. The peasant and pastoral communities constitute the largest voting bloc in the countries of the GHA, except Djibouti. Under reconciled institutions that allow this voting bloc to participate and be fully represented in the political process, policies are likely to be very different in the region.

The reconciliation process is likely to be rather challenging and it is also likely to vary from one country to another. Nevertheless, a number of measures are likely to facilitate its attainment. One critical measure would be constitutional recognition of the customary property rights laws, especially the customary ownership of land by rural communities. Such a measure would be a critical step in enhancing the empowerment of rural communities.[3] With recognition of customary property rights, land-takings by states would cease or would take place through negotiated compensatory arrangements, which may entail land rent, royalties, or possibly ownership of shares by customary land holders in the firms investing on mining, large-scale commercial farming, etc. on the acquisitioned land.[4] Such policy measures would make rural

---

[2] The proposed approach is referred to as contextualized because it aims to address the socio-economic context in places where it is applied. It is also comprehensive in the sense that it aims to address the key structural impediments to democratization simultaneously so that failure in some aspects does not undermine progress in others.

[3] The taking of lands by the state with little or no compensation to customary holders in order to make land available for large-scale commercial farmers and firms in extractive industries reflects lack of recognition of customary land ownership systems.

[4] Governments in the region, like those in most other African countries, own all underground resources. Several of them, including Ethiopia, Eritrea and Sudan, also do not fully recognize customary ownership of land.

communities participants and beneficiaries of the extractive industries and commercial farming rather than mere victims of evictions.

Establishing administrative structures that allow the participation of traditional leaders of rural communities in local governance and development is another critical measure. Traditional rural leaders would use such an arrangement as a springboard for influencing national policies, including those pertaining to allocation of land and underground resources as well as the distribution of public services. With participation in local governance and development, rural communities can form active rural civil society organizations capable of promoting their interests. Participation in local governance and development may also facilitate the grooming of rural leaders to represent their communities in parliament as well as in other organizations of the state, and enhance representation and participation of rural communities in the national political process. Under such conditions, participation of rural communities in national elections would be meaningful as they would have access to influencing policy. Such political empowerment of rural communities would also facilitate transformation of the subsistence sector of the economy. It is conceivable that their influence on policy would enhance their access to productivity-raising investments, extension services, transportation and marketing facilities, as well as health and educational services. In this respect there is a strong link between democratization and transformation of the traditional economic systems. Transforming the subsistence sector into an exchange economy helps integrate the fragmented systems not only economically but also institutionally, politically and culturally. It also creates conditions for a more inclusive participatory democratization process.

Adopting some of the conflict-resolution practices of the traditional systems by applying the consensus-based system of decision-making on key issues, can also bridge the gap between the parallel systems and is likely to prove useful in the prevention and resolution of state-identity conflicts. Political parties, which are often ethnic-based or ethnic influenced, can also reduce inter-party tensions and post-election conflicts by applying aspects of such an approach instead of relying on the widely practised 'winner-takes-all' approach. Somaliland's experience with the hybrid political order, discussed in Chapter 9, perhaps points to what is possible in institutional reconciliation.

Recognizing and reforming the traditional judicial systems, which presently adjudicate large proportions of disputes, as shown in Table 1.3 of Chapter 1, is another critical step in reconciling the fragmented institutional systems. Safeguarding women's rights and enhancing their participation in public deliberations and decision-making are among the areas where reforms are needed. Some of the major weaknesses of the traditional institutional systems are in the area of safeguarding women's rights and ensuring their participation in decision-making (see Table 10.1). Lack of access to inheritance rights, early marriages of girls, and unequal access to education between boys and girls are among the many factors that suppress women's participation in both public and private (at the family level) decision-making fora. Legislative reforms, along with participation of rural leaders, can help remove such barriers.[5] Training and logistical support of traditional conflict adjudicators can also enhance the effectiveness of the traditional judicial practice. All such changes, however, are not likely to take place without the understanding and commitment by the functionaries of the state and democracy activists to the importance of reconciling the parallel institutions.

A second component of the CCA entails addressing the problems of mismanagement of diversity and the persistent uneven development, which characterize the region, in order to arrest the crises of nation building and identity-related violent conflicts. As the empirical chapters have shown, most of the countries of the GHA suffer from serious challenges of nation building, as evident from the large number of chronic state-identity conflicts that ravage their economies and stymie the democratization effort. Transforming these conflicts and advancing a peaceful process of nation building is an indispensable requisite for successful democratization. A divided country, where state-identity conflict is active or where certain identities have no loyalty to the institutions of the state, is unlikely to have equitable representation or inclusive deliberation, essential attributes of a democratic system. Innovative political arrangements that advance proper management of diversity by alleviating the problems of marginalization, and by creating equitable opportunities for all identities to advance their political and economic interests and cultural values, need to be part of the agenda of the democratization process.

Building appropriate institutions of diversity management, like reconciling the parallel institutional systems, is a rather complex process. Underprivileged groups struggle to ensure access to political, economic and cultural privileges. Privileged groups, on the other hand often stand in defence of the status quo. Political entrepreneurs also stock the state-identity and inter-identity cleavages as a means of enhancing their own interests, thus complicating the nation-building process. Some of the countries of the region have instituted federal arrangements as a strategy of nation building. The federal system, however, remains largely hollow under autocratic rule and centralizing dominant parties. It is highly likely that peaceful management

---

[5] Despite the disadvantages women face in a traditional system, their support of the system tends to be little different from that of men (see Mengisteab 2017).

Table 10.1 Participation of Women in Selected Activities under Traditional Systems

	Ethiopia		Kenya		Somaliland	
Participation of women	*Yes %*	*No %*	*Yes %*	*No %*	*Yes %*	*No %*
As leaders	24.0	76.0	84.8	13.2	–	–
As elders	67.0	33.0	69.6	28.8	18.2	–
In meetings	92.5	7.5	97.2	1.2	51.5	7.1
In obtaining land	54.7	42.0	55.2	43.2	56.1	40.8
In inheriting property from parents	34.0	62.0	59.0	40.5	87.8	10.2
In inheriting property from husbands	71.3	21.3	94.0	6.0	90.8	7.1
In child custody	20.3	–	20.0	–	63.3	–
In obtaining equitable share of property if divorced	51.3	44.8	28.0	70.8	5.1	90.1

Source Mengisteab and Hagg 2017; data based on survey results in three areas in each of three countries, Ethiopia, Kenya and Somaliland

of diversity would entail representation of the complex web of diverse groups in establishing accommodative political arrangements to which all can consent. It also requires adherence to the rule of law in order to safeguard any consensus arrangements. Addressing the pervasive inequalities among identity groups in terms of access to resources and other opportunities is another requisite, which does not have a quick fix. Yet, without concrete state commitment and progress in such arrangements, multi-party systems and elections are likely to remain sterile. They may even exacerbate identity-related conflicts by attempting to legitimize the status quo or autocratic rule by the election victors.

A third component of the CCA involves rectifying the democracy-hindering structural deformities of the state. The process of democratization can hardly move forwards when state structures do not allow decentralization of power within the constituent organizations of the state so that they keep each other accountable in executing their responsibilities. The experiences of the countries in the GHA show that the absence of strong mechanisms of checks and balances within the organizations that constitute the state has led to concentration of power in the hands of the executive branch of government, paving the way for the rise of autocratic rule. Such concentration of power has also allowed the establishment of dominant parties and impeded the creation of political space, where opposition parties and civil society organizations could engage in the political process without harassment by autocratic regimes. Additionally, the concentration of power in the hands of autocratic leaders hinders the development of state structures with checks and balances as the elite in power thwart any changes that would restrain their power. Opposition parties and civil society organizations can play a critical role in breaking this vicious cycle by organizing a sustained struggle to transform the structures of the state. Unfortunately, autocratic regimes often suppress opposition parties. Opposition parties also have hardly distinguished themselves in advancing platforms that address the deformities in the structures of the state. Instead, they often merely concentrate on elections being free and fair.

A fourth component of the proposed CCA approach is strengthening accessibility of civil liberties, including freedom of speech, press and religion, the right to political organization, and a system of free and fair elections. Inclusive participation and equitable representation in the deliberations of a democratic system would not be possible without securing such rights. However, civil liberties are also unlikely to be fully guaranteed without securing the other three components of the CCA.

Figure 10.1 illustrates the four components (A through D) of the CCA for democratization in the context of the countries of the GHA. The figure consists of two boxes, with box 1 containing four compartments, each representing one of the four foundational requisites of the democratization process in transitional societies. Double-headed arrows linking the four compartments indicate that each of the components of the CCA reinforce each other. Success in reconciling the fragmented institutions, for example, would foster success in nation building and vice versa. By contrast, failure in establishing the conditions in any of the compartments would undermine all the others. Similarly, the double-headed arrow connecting boxes 1 and 2 indicates that, as the requisites of democracy develop, so does the substance of democracy – and vice versa.

The double-headed arrow connecting boxes 1 and 2 is to suggest the bidirectional relationship between establishing the four requisite conditions depicted in the four compartments within box 1 and the delivery of the expected emancipatory and developmental substances of democracy. Societal expectations of the substance of democracy are likely to be context specific and to vary from country to country and over time. However, given the similarities of the existing socio-economic conditions in the countries of the GHA, the expectations are likely to include the outcomes listed in box 2.

The contextualized comprehensive approach versus other approaches

As indicated in Chapter 1, with the post-Cold War democratization wave, there emerged considerable literature on democratization in Africa (Bratton and van de Walle 1997; Joseph 1997; Diamond 1999;

1

C Transforming state structures

Instituting checks and balances within the constituent organizations of the state in order to ensure horizontal accountability

D Nation building

Proper diversity management to build a community of citizens sharing common institutions

2

A selected list of substantive outcomes of democratic governance

- Human rights;
- Rule of law;
- Peaceful resolution of conflicts;
- Respect of customary property rights;
- Accountable and corruption-free governance;
- Development with equitable political, economic and cultural rights;
- Poverty alleviation

B Building the institutions of democracy

- Civil liberties;
- Competitive multi-party systems;
- Equitable representation;
- Free and fair elections

A Reconciling the parallel institutions to establish a coherent system of institutions that would be relevant to all segments of the population

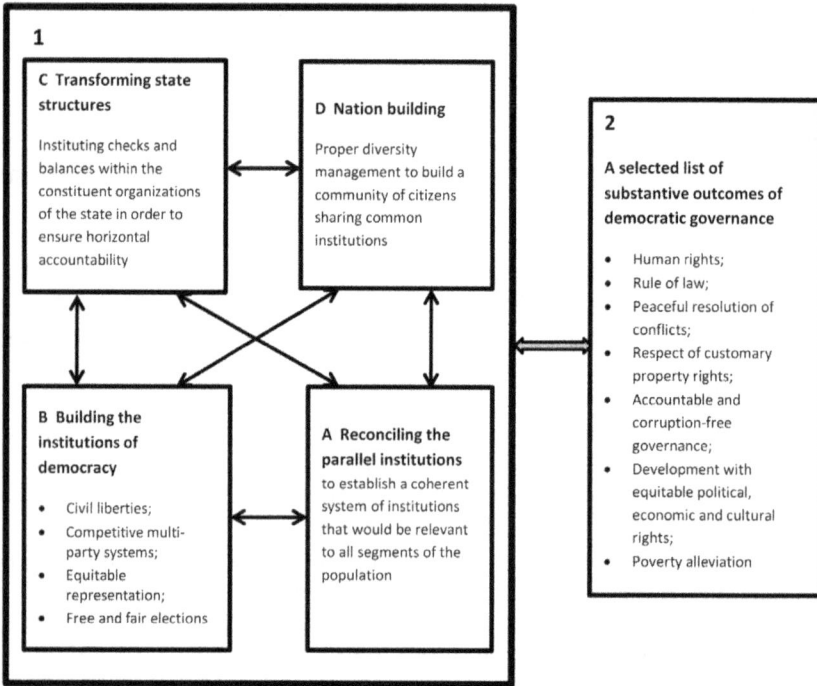

Figure 10.1 A Contextualized and Comprehensive Approach to Democratization

Gyimah-Boadi 2004; Lindberg 2009; Cheeseman 2015). Much of that literature deals with factors for the transition from single-party autocratic political systems to multi-party systems, along with civil liberties and competitive elections. The literature also identifies a number of conditions that facilitate or hinder transitions from autocratic regimes. The explanations essentially deal with the conditions that make regimes receptive or resistant to change during the struggle for transition. Cheeseman (2015), for instance, argues that incumbents are least likely to embark on reforms in countries with considerable natural resource wealth, weak institutions and a deeply divided society.

The existing literature recognizes that the transition from an autocratic single-party system to a multi-party system does not democracy make. However, it suggests that repeated rounds of elections, expected to engender peaceful competition among the contenders for power, have the potential to promote democratic values and democratic transition in Africa.

This literature, however, does not explain well how the absence or weakness of institutional and structural requisites impacts the democratization process. The impact of institutional fragmentation, in particular, is a serious omission. The optimistic view of the democratizing impact of elections has also essentially failed and the existing literature does not tell us much why the democratization process in many African countries that made the initial transition has stagnated. The CCA, thus, complements the existing literature by filling important gaps. It also contributes towards developing a theory of democratization in transitional societies where some of the foundational requisites of the democratization process are missing or are inadequate.

There is also ambiguity about when a country is said to have made the transition from the single-party autocracy to a multi-party system. A look at the transition process of the countries in the GHA manifests the ambiguity rather clearly. The regimes in four of the eight countries of the GHA (Uganda, Eritrea, Ethiopia and South Sudan) came to power through 'revolutionary liberation' fronts. While Uganda and Ethiopia have registered some transition from single-party rule (rule by liberation fronts) to rule by dominant parties with weak opposition parties around them, Eritrea and South Sudan continue to be ruled by naked autocracy. Two other countries in the region, Sudan and Somalia, were ruled for a long period of time by dictators that came to power through military coups. The Somali state collapsed in the process of armed struggle to rid the country of Siad Barre's dictatorship, while Sudan, which was under a dominant ruling party with elections and weak opposition parties, seems to have recently made a promising change largely through popular protests. These two countries have yet to make serious transition to a real multi-party political order with competitive parties. Djibouti is also still ruled by a dominant party. Kenya is, thus, the only country that may be considered to have made a transition from a single-party rule to a relatively competitive multi-party system. Yet, Kenya's political parties and elections remain heavily influenced by ethnic rivalries. The peasant and pastoral communities also remain largely marginalized in the country's political process.

Considering that the multi-party system is far less autocratic than the single-person or single-party regimes, it is hard to deny the relevance of the existing literature that deals with transitions from autocracies to a multi-party order, even though there is lack of clarity on when the transition is said to have occurred. Yet, the CCA is grounded on a premise that is highly sceptical of the multi-party system, through the dynamics of competitive elections, leading to mature and sustainable democracies in cases where there is a glaring deficit of the foundational requisites of a sustainable democratization process.

Feasibility of the contextualized comprehensive approach
The CCA has not yet been adopted fully in any country in Africa. Its impacts, thus, cannot be assessed empirically. However, the absence of real cases of the approach does not mean that reasonable solutions for prevailing problems cannot be proposed. Moreover, some African countries have registered modest progress in adopting aspects of the

CCA, giving some empirical indications of its potential. A few countries have undertaken measures that reduce the deformity of the state by distributing power among the constituent organizations of the state and thereby strengthening the checks and balances within the state. Botswana, South Africa and Somaliland are among the better performers in this regard. More advanced democracies are also characterized by more developed mechanisms of checks and balances, more coherent institutional systems and more advanced nation-building processes. In Africa, few countries have so far registered notable progress in diversity management and reconciliation of the parallel institutional systems. Somaliland, Botswana and South Africa are among the few countries that have put some effort in reconciling their institutional systems, and each of these three countries has espoused different approaches of reconciling the parallel institutional systems.

Somaliland has charted a distinct approach aimed at fusing the traditional community-based consensual system of decision-making with the modern liberal institutions of democracy. In this model, the House of Elders (the *Guurti*), a body selected by the clans of the self-proclaimed country, reviews the laws passed by the House of Representatives, which is elected through a competitive multi-party electoral system. The *Guurti* has the power to veto any bills. It also acts as a constraint on the powers of the executive. The *Guurti*'s role restrains the executive branch from using the legislative body as a rubber stamp. In addition, the *Guurti* has a broad mandate to settle inter-clan or political conflicts as well as to preserve religion and culture.[6] The *Guurti* applies traditional mechanisms in carrying out its responsibilities in conflict resolution and has already registered notable success in making the country peaceful relative to most of the countries of the region. The formal judicial system and the traditional court of clan (*tol*) elders also complement each other. The *Guurti* is organizationally rather weak at the present time and its effectiveness in the longer run remains to be seen. One of its major weaknesses relates to its failure to devise laws with respect to succession within its ranks and the term of service of its members. Despite the *Guurti*'s limitations, however, Somaliland's hybrid system has given a clear indication about what is possible in reconciling the dichotomous institutional systems and in diversity management. It has extended representation to rural communities as well as to all clan identities. Somaliland has also been able to conduct elections that are arguably among the cleanest in the region, although elections have been postponed on several occasions.

Botswana is perhaps the only African country that has espoused institutional reconciliation, especially in the areas of judicial process

---

[6] There is little evidence so far that the government or the *Guurti* have addressed the land issue, which seems to be in a flux.

and conflict-resolution mechanisms, since its independence. Both the formal and traditional systems operate in the country's judicial system and conflict-resolution mechanisms. Recognition of the traditional judicial process has allowed the country to reform the traditional system and to make the integrated institutional system relevant to the population in the traditional sector. The consultative approach of the *kgotla* (local community meeting and court) system, which incorporates the reconciliation aspect of the traditional system into the formal judicial system, also reconciles customary law and statutory law. Moreover, for the most part, the country's government has refrained from forcible confiscation of community land in favour of negotiated acquisition. More importantly, the legal system in the country allows communities to challenge in the court of law state acquisition of land to which they did not consent. While inequality remains very high in the country, respect for civil liberties places some restraint on the power of the executive branch.

South Africa's approach to institutional reconciliation revolves around integrating traditional authorities in regional and local governance. It also recognizes customary law, if it does not contradict the constitution. Compared to the other two cases, the authority granted to the traditional leadership is more limited in South Africa. Large-scale land appropriation and gross income inequality left behind by the apartheid regime, and slow progress in addressing these problems by the post-apartheid government, limit the impact of the country's approach to institutional reconciliation. They also limit progress in diversity management and nation building. Nevertheless, post-apartheid South Africa has given legitimacy to the traditional institutions, both the leadership and customary law. Its protection of civil liberties also acts as a check on the power of the executive.

The approaches to reconciling the parallel institutional systems by South Africa and Botswana extend representation to the marginalized rural inhabitants. Somaliland's approach, by contrast, enables the leaders of the adherents of the traditional institutional systems to become major players in the country's system of governance. Despite the differences in approach, institutional reconciliation charted by these three countries is likely to contribute to democratization of the process of nation building by promoting representation of and dialogue among various segments of society, including the rural segment of the population. By enhancing representation, institutional reconciliation also has the potential to weaken the structures of the state that hinder accountability. The jury is still out on the democratic performance of the three countries. Yet, indications are that these countries are more peaceful, and their institutions are more coherent, relative to their neighbouring countries. As a result, the prospects of their democratization are better. They also give indications that the CCA can be a promising approach to democratization in Africa's realities.

Application of the contextualized comprehensive approach

The protest leaders in both Sudan and Ethiopia were able to mobilize large groups of people from all walks of life to topple regimes through peaceful protests. Both cases show us that the forces of democratization have emerged in the countries of the GHA. However, democracy activists, whether they are scholars, civil society groups, political parties, opposition leaders, students or workers, often fall into the trap of prioritizing elections over the difficult legwork of building the foundational requisites of democratization. Sudan's recently agreed three-year transition period is said to be largely to give political parties time to organize and prepare for an election. It is not yet clear whether the transitional government, consisting of military and civilian leaders, will be able to address the difficult problems of ethnic conflicts and the fragmentation of the economic and institutional systems.

Ethiopia with Prime Minister Abiy Ahmed's agenda for change perhaps has the best prospects for making progress in democratizing, provided the prime minister is serious with his agenda for change. However, the country also faces daunting challenges of centrifugal forces within the various ethnic-based regional states. Several of the regional states have also serious boundary and territorial conflicts. There is also the problem of some sub-regions demanding to form their own regional states. In other words, the federal system that has kept the country together over the last two and half decades is facing tremendous challenges. Under the circumstances, the government's primary goal would seem to be conducting serious analysis of the federal arrangement in order to identify its shortcomings and bring together a wide array of identity leaders and other relevant actors to find solutions to these by forging common ground among the different regional states. While the country is facing these acute threats to its unity, the government has scheduled a general election for August 2020. Unfortunately, the ethnic problems that the country faces will still be there the day after the elections, regardless of which parties emerge victorious. The election results may, in fact end up angering already aggrieved groups. There is also the risk that election victors may feel they have a mandate to govern without addressing the grievances of different groups, especially if the needed solutions would restrain their power. This volume is intended to alert the activists that lead the forces of democracy that elections, while important, do not constitute shortcuts to democratization. Such awareness among the forces of democratization perhaps will strengthen the cause of a sustainable democratization process.

Conclusion

Democracy, as a system of governance that creates mechanisms by which the general population is represented in advancing its interests in the process of decision-making, is perhaps recognized as a universal value. The arrangements or type of institutions by which the general population advances its interests are, however dependent on the existing socio-economic systems and cultural values of specific societies. The fragmentation of institutional systems, divided societies, and deformed state structure that exist in the countries of the GHA and in most other African countries is not universal. Thus, the democratization approach in these countries has to be contextualized in order to address the impediments to inclusive participation in the political process that prevail in specific contexts.

The major structural and institutional obstacles to democratization, such as fragmented economic and institutional systems, crisis of nation building, and deformed state structures, also need to be addressed simultaneously in a comprehensive manner. Progress in addressing one or two of such bottlenecks can easily be undermined by lack of progress in the other bottlenecks. Progress in addressing state deformity and crisis of nation building, for example, is unlikely to lead to inclusive and sustainable democratization without addressing the fragmented socio-economic spaces. They are also unlikely to be implemented fully, much less succeed, under conditions where civil liberties are restricted.

An election-centred multi-party system with civil liberties represents progress over the single-party system or single-person autocracy that gripped the African continent for roughly three decades until the early 1990s. With the multi-party system, the ballot box has, largely, replaced violent coups as the pathway for acquiring political power. Unfortunately, after about two and half decades the election-centred approach has proved to be inadequate for engendering a sustainable process of democratization. It has mostly produced elected autocrats with little interest in addressing the structural impediments of democratization. It has even failed to bring change of leaders and ruling parties in the GHA countries, except in Kenya and Somaliland. The peaceful competition for power among political rivals was expected to engender democratic transition. Contrary to that expectation, the competition among rivals for power has produced the craft of establishing dominant parties, suppressing the opposition, rigging elections, and manipulating voters through various means, including bribes and ethnic mobilization, instead of competing on platforms that enhance the well-being of citizens.

Under the circumstances, the democratization process in the GHA, as in much of the rest of Africa, needs to be re-energized with new approaches. An approach built around reconciliation of the fragmented institutional systems and political arrangements for proper management of diversity is likely to be more successful in transforming the largest group of voters (peasant farmers, pastoralists and marginalized ethnic groups) from passive voters, who are unable to influence policy, to more active participants in the political process. Programmes that address the deformed structures of the state are also essential in order to overcome the concentration of power in the executive body of government. Such changes can spur new dynamism in the democratization process.

Bibliography

Ake, Claude. 1993, 'The Unique Case of African Democracy'. *International Affairs*, 69(2): 239–44.

Beetham, David. 1992, 'Liberal Democracy and the Limits of Democratization'. *Political Studies* 40 (Special Issue): 40–53.

Bratton, M. 2007, 'Formal versus Informal Institutions in Africa'. *Journal of Democracy* 18(3): 96–110.

Bratton, M. and van de Walle, N. 1997, *Democratic Experiments in Africa: Regime Transitions in Comparative Perspective*. New York: Cambridge University Press.

Cheeseman, Nic. 2015, *Democracy in Africa: Successes, Failures, and the Struggle for Political Reform*, www.researchgate.net/publication/290275977_Democracy_in_Africa_successes_failures_and_the_struggle_for_political_reform, accessed 28 November 2018.

Dahl, Robert. 1993, 'Why All Democratic Countries Have Mixed Economies', in John W. Chapman and Ian Shairo (eds), *Democratic Community*. New York: New York University Press, 259–82.

Diamond, L. 1999, *Developing Democracy: Toward Consolidation*. Baltimore, MD: Johns Hopkins University Press.

Friedman, Milton. 1962, *Capitalism and Freedom*. Chicago, IL: Chicago University Press.

Gyimah-Boadi, E. 2004, *Democratic Reform in Africa: The Quality of Progress*. Boulder, CO: Lynne Rienner.

Hayek, F. A. 1960, *The Constitution of Liberty*. London and Henley: Routledge & Kegan Paul.

Held, David. 2006, *Models of Democracy*. Stanford, CA: Stanford University Press.

Horowitz, Donald. 2014, *Ethnic Groups in Conflict*. Berkley, Los Angeles, London: University of California Press.

Joseph, Richard. 1997, 'Democratization in Africa after 1989: Comparative and Theoretical Perspectives'. *Comparative Politics* 29(3): 363–82.

Kuhnhardt, Ludger. 2014, *Africa Consensus: New Interests, Initiatives, and Partners*. Washington, DC: Woodrow Wilson Center Press; Baltimore, MD: Johns Hopkins University Press.

Lijphart, Arend. 1969, 'Consociational Democracy'. *World Politics* 21(2): 207–25.

—— 1977, *Democracy in Plural Societies: A Comparative Exploration*. New Haven, CT: Yale University Press.

Lindberg, Stephen. 2009, 'A Theory of Elections as a Mode of Transition', in Stephen Lindberg (ed.), *Democratization by Elections: A New Mode of Transition*. Baltimore, MD: The Johns Hopkins University Press: 314–41.

Mengisteab, Kidane. 2017, 'Leadership Structures and Adherence levels of Traditional Institutions', in Mengisteab and Hagg 2017, 16–30.

Mengisteab, Kidane and Hagg, Gerard (eds). 2017, *Traditional Institutions in Contemporary African Governance*. London and New York: Routledge.

Mengisteab, Kidane. 2012, 'Relevance of Regional Integration in the Greater Horn Region', in Kidane Mengisteab and Redie Bereketeab (eds), *Regional Integration, Identity & Citizenship in the Greater Horn of Africa*, Woodbridge: James Currey, in association with the Greater Horn Horizon Forum.

Schmitter, Philippe. 1995, 'Democracy's Future: More Liberal, Preliberal, or Postliberal'. *Journal of Democracy* 6(1): 15–22.

11

Conclusion

KIDANE MENGISTEAB

Summary of the factors leading to the crisis of democratization

Most of the countries of the Greater Horn of Africa (GHA) participated in the post-Cold War democratization wave by broadening access to some aspects of civil liberties to their populace, liberalizing the press, establishing multi-party systems, and conducting elections. However, the democratization process in the region has not advanced much beyond these initial steps. Over two and half decades after the initial changes, democratization in the region remains stagnant with widespread human rights violations, dominant parties controlling the political process, and elections that hardly bring about changes in ruling parties or leadership. Widespread violations of customary land rights by the state, marginalization and poverty of various identity groups, rampant state-identity conflicts, corruption, persistent inequality of women, and disproportionate unemployment and alienation of the youth are other manifestations of the stagnation of the democratization process. Under such conditions, it is safe to say that political power in the region continues to serve the interests of the elite in power rather than the interests of the public.

Given the conspicuous crisis of the democratization process in the countries of the GHA, one principal objective of this volume has been to explain the key factors that engender the crisis. A second objective was to explore an alternative approach that would transform the structural and institutional factors that have choked the democratization process.

As pointed out in many of the chapters, the factors that impede democratization are many, although they vary in importance. The primary group of factors are the underlying structural and institutional conditions. One such underlying factor relates to the problems of diversity management and crisis of nation building, which foster numerous conflicts that stifle the democratization process. Another underlying factor is the institutional fragmentation that delinks large segments of the population from the institutions of the state and hinders their effective participation in the political process. A third factor is deformed state structures that concentrate power in the hands of the executive body of the state (often autocratic men) and hinder the establishment of strong mechanisms of horizontal accountability within the different organizations of the state as well as vertical accountability to citizens at large. The book has argued that sustainable democratization is highly unlikely without simultaneously transforming these primary groups of structural and institutional hindrances to the democratization process.

A related group of secondary factors that contribute to the stagnation of the democratization process relates to problems of leadership and a balance of power among social classes that is tilted in favour of the political elite. It is possible that a leadership that is committed to democratization can address the above-identified underlying barriers and advance the cause of democracy. However, such leaders have been scarce in the region. More importantly, it is not likely that a top-down democratization that transforms the structural obstacles would be sustainable without active participation in the political process of civil society groups and the general populace. Leaders, even those who have shown promise early in their leadership role have shown the tendency to gravitate over time towards becoming self-serving and autocratic. Sustainable democratization requires the agency of social forces that are knowledgeable and organized enough to ensure accountability of the political elite. There are indications that such forces are emerging in some of the countries of the GHA but they have not yet been strong enough to decisively tilt the balance of power in favour of democratization.

The absence of strong opposition parties and civil society groups that can mobilize the population with political platforms that articulate appropriate approaches of advancing democratization, is another factor that undermines democratization. Problems, such as limited economic diversification, low levels of urbanization, and high levels of illiteracy and poverty, in conjunction with societal fragmentation along primordial lines, also limit interdependence and networking among populations across identity lines, and weaken the forces of democratization.

Another obstacle to democratization, which has received little attention, is the lack of proper understanding by the forces of democratization of the underlying bottlenecks to meaningfully achieving it, together with the absence of a vision of contextualized approaches to democratization that address the fundamental bottlenecks. This problem has led to over reliance on imported ideologies and institutions that often are incompatible with the cultural values and economic systems of transitional societies. The ideological basis of liberal democracy and political interferences by external actors, who perceive that liberal economic policies are essential requisites of democratization, have complicated the democratization process in African countries with large subsistence sectors, in a number of ways. External interferences, motivated by self-interest or ideological conviction, weaken the democratization process by taking away ownership of vision formation and policy-making from domestic forces and by imposing an ideology, which does not have a strong socio-economic basis on the ground. Such external interferences were particularly rampant during the post-Cold War economic regime of Structural Adjustment programmes. However, external interferences still remain significant problems. Imported ideologies also affect democratization adversely by crowding out the search for alternative approaches that may be more reflective of African realities and values. From this perspective, a successful democratization process would take time to develop as it requires establishing the fundamental structural and institutional requisites. Establishing these requisites, in turn, entails contextualization of the approach so that the process of democratization and the forms of democracy are compatible with the economic and institutional systems and cultural values of society.

Recapping the essence of the contextualized comprehensive approach

As noted in Chapter 1, the political competition involved in elections was expected to be instrumental in driving the democratization process. However, it is evident from the experience of the last two decades that the existing election-centred approach to democratization has been ineffective in promoting a sustainable democratization process in the transitional societies of the GHA. The political elite have developed various mechanisms that enable them to conduct elections without much risk of losing them. They often divide the electorate along identity lines or employ tactics to bribe segments of the electorate. They also employ various tactics to render opposition parties uncompetitive. In the few cases that elections were genuinely competitive, they were marred by rigging followed by post-election conflicts, as witnessed in the 2005 Ethiopian general election and Kenya's 2007 elections. In the rare event that the ruling elite lose, as in the 2002 elections in Kenya, they transfer power to another elite group that introduces little change to promote the cause of democracy by building the mechanisms of state accountability. More fundamentally, the election-centred approach, in itself, does not have mechanisms that are effective in addressing the institutional and structural barriers, such as institutional fragmentation, crisis of nation building, and deformed state structures. Elections, even when deemed fair, would hardly settle diversity-related state-identity conflicts in divided societies. Rather they become a means of legitimizing the policy of the winners while the conflicts continue to fester.

Elections also hardly address the institutional fragmentation that marginalizes segments of society in the traditional economic sectors. It is not even clear that political parties fully realize the adverse socio-economic impacts of fragmented institutional systems. This brings us to the second principal objective of the volume, i.e. exploring an alternative approach to democratization that would address the underlying structural and institutional obstacles and establish conditions to foster a sustainable democratization process.

The proposed 'contextualized comprehensive approach' (CCA) to democratization does not discount the relevance of elections and the other key components of the liberal approach to democratization, including civil liberties and separation of powers. Rather it contextualizes the democratization approach by expanding its scope to address, as integral components, the key requisites including managing diversity and nation building, reconciling the fragmented institutions, and rectifying the deformed structures of the state, which concentrate power in the executive body subordinating all the other components of the state.

In transitional countries, such as those of the GHA, the structural and institutional conditions that are necessary for sustainable democratization are underdeveloped. The democratization process, thus, needs to build these requisites for its own development and sustainability. To this end, the CCA advances the building of political arrangements that would foster peaceful nation building by bringing into the political process marginalized identity groups, and managing diversity in a manner in which the state extends equitable citizenship rights to all identities and thereby arrests the numerous state-identity and inter-identity conflicts. The CCA also aims to bring the largely marginalized peasant and pastoral communities into the political and economic processes by reconciling their traditional institutions with those of the state. Furthermore, it aims to develop the state's structures of checks and balances so that the executive body is accountable to the other organizations of the state and to the populace, including those in the traditional sector, who are on the fringes of the state's institutional orbit.

By building the structural and institutional foundations for sustainable democratization, the CCA has the potential to contribute in changing the balance of power between the political elite, who generally use power to advance their own interests, and the general population, who want power to be used in advancing broad public interests, in favour of the latter. The CCA, through institutional reconciliation, has the capacity to empower the populations in the traditional socio-economic space and to enable them to participate more actively in the political process and to have greater influence on policy than they do in their current marginalized state. By enhancing diversity management and nation building, the CCA also reduces societal fragmentation along identity lines and creates conditions that foster cooperation and organization of civil society across ethnic and other lines in demanding democratic rights and in influencing policy. In other words, by bringing into the political process the populations in the traditional socio-economic space and those in the marginalized identity groups, the CCA can broaden the participation and equalize representation of citizens in the political process. In other words, the CCA aims to bring about inclusiveness in the political process by ending the marginalization of political forces, including marginalized identity groups, marginalized rural communities, and organizations of the state marginalized by the executive branch of government or the autocratic leadership.

Prospects of success of the contextualized comprehensive approach

Despite its apparent failure in advancing the democratization process, the election-centred approach to democratization is rather pervasive in the GHA, as well as in much of the rest of Africa. Conducting elections has come to be viewed as a barometer of a country's democratic credentials. For this reason, even autocratic regimes with little appetite for building a democratic system have been conducting elections to disguise their autocratic rule. The elections in the GHA countries have been carefully managed or rigged and they rarely produce leadership changes. However, there are growing indications that the general population in the region has begun to reject the facade of democracy and to push for a substantive democratization process. Recent developments in Ethiopia and Sudan provide good indications.

After facing recurrent popular protests for about three years, Ethiopia's coalition ruling party, the Ethiopian Peoples' Revolutionary Democratic Front, relented to the pressure. The party shed its domination by the Tigray-based Tigray People's Liberation Front (TPLF) and elected a new prime minister in March 2018 from another member of the EPRDF coalition, the Oromo People's Democratic Party, now renamed the Oromo Democratic Party (ODP).[1] Although the same coalition party, the EPRDF, remained in power until 1 December 2019, the appointment of Abiy Ahmed as the new prime minister seemed like a regime change. Under

---

[1] The TPLF was dominant within the four-party coalition of the EPRDF because it was the Front that militarily dislodged the military dictatorship, the *Derg*, from power. It was also responsible for establishing the EPRDF. However, in terms of population Tigray is the smallest state among the states of the other three parties in the coalition.

Prime Minister Abiy Ahmed, the EPRDF has introduced several changes. Among them are the lifting of the State of Emergency that was enacted to control popular protests, releasing political prisoners, and broadening the political space by allowing formerly excluded or restricted actors and social groups to participate in the political process. Armed rebel groups were also invited to abandon their armed struggle and pursue their political objectives through peaceful and legal means. The Prime Minister also ended the twenty-year-old state of war with Eritrea by signing a Peace and Cooperation agreement with Eritrea in September 2018. These changes, in themselves, do not necessarily represent advancement of the democratization process. However, they create favourable environment for building the foundational requisites of democratization and have generated a great deal of optimism in the country and throughout the region.

The successive Ethiopian-Eritrean conflicts, along with the numerous civil wars in Ethiopia, Somalia and Sudan, have been major factors in rendering the entire Horn of Africa a zone of conflict and dire human insecurity for roughly six decades. The Peace and Cooperation agreement between Eritrea and Ethiopia has, thus, the potential to spur significant changes in the region's security and economic development.[2] Soon after the signing of the Peace and Cooperation agreement, Ethiopia was able to make peace with many of its rebel groups. The long-disrupted diplomatic relations between Eritrea and Somalia were restored. With Ethiopia's and Somalia's mediation, Eritrea and Djibouti have also restored ties, although their border dispute remains unsettled. It is also likely that the peace agreement will pave the way for improving relations between Eritrea and the other countries of the region as well as between Eritrea and the Intergovernmental Authority on Development (IGAD), since Eritrea's strained relations with the countries of the region were largely related to the Ethiopian-Eritrean conflict.

With improving relations among them, the states of the region could now have the flexibility to address domestic conflicts more effectively. The region's governments are likely to cease engaging in proxy wars against each other by supporting each other's rebel groups. Rebel groups are also likely to abandon armed struggle in favour of political struggle, as they are less likely to find neighbouring governments that would host and support them. As noted, Ethiopia's rebel groups, which were hosted by Eritrea, have already abandoned their armed struggle. Among such groups are the Patriotic May 7 Movement, the Oromo Liberation Front (OLF), the Amhara Democratic Forces Movement (ADFM), the Tigray

---

[2] It is important to recall that Ethiopia and Eritrea signed a Friendship and Cooperation agreement in July 1993 following Eritrea's *de jure* independence. Despite its early promise, that agreement collapsed after about five years. The Peace and Cooperation agreement also faces formidable challenges and it remains to be seen if it will be successful and sustainable.

People's Democratic Movement (TPDM), the Ogaden National Liberation Front (ONLF), the Afar Liberation Movement (ALM), and the Gambela People's Liberation Movement (GPLM). They all have signed agreements with the government to pursue their political objectives through peaceful means. With these agreements Ethiopia has made remarkable progress in reducing armed rebellion, although it continues to face widespread sporadic inter-ethnic violence. Deepening divisions within the coalition ruling party have also led to its replacement by the Prosperity Party, a development likely to put a strain on the federal arrangement, since the TPLF has declined to join the new party.

Sudan is another country in the region where popular protests have led to the toppling of an autocratic regime. After months of protests, in April 2019, the country's military removed from power President al-Bashir, who ruled the country for thirty years. The fall of Bashir was followed by a period of uncertainty with wrangling about the nature and leadership of the transition among different social forces, including the different components of the military and security forces, supporters of the deposed regime, armed rebel groups, opposition parties, the protesters and civic organizations. The uncertainty of the country's transition now seems mitigated as a three-year power-sharing agreement has been reached between the military and the leaders of the protests with mediation by Ethiopia's Prime Minister, Abiy Ahmed and the African Union. However, the transition is likely to continue to face threats as the supporters of the previous regime are likely to attempt to undermine the transition. Some foreign powers, such as the Kingdom of Saudi Arabia and the United Emirates, are also said to have attempted to influence the transition in various ways (Lynch, and Gramer 2019). Despite risks from spoilers, Sudan seems poised to make notable progress towards democratization, provided that the protesters, who encompass a wide range of the country's identity groups and social classes, remain vigilant. It is, however, too early to tell how the transitional government will deal with the various internal conflicts that have devastated the country.

With the two largest countries in the region undergoing changes, Eritrea is perhaps the next country to undergo change. The hot-and-cold wars with Ethiopia were the justification the autocratic regime in Eritrea gave for not implementing constitutional governance over the last two decades since the border war broke out. Given the end of the war and the signing of the Peace and Cooperation agreement with Ethiopia in September 2018, the Eritrean regime is unlikely to be able to continue to rule for long without a constitution and without allowing the formation of independent civil society organizations and opposition political parties, or without liberalizing the press. The regime is also unlikely to be able to maintain the open-ended national service, which, as noted already is often equated with slave labour. The regime is facing growing popular pressure, although it has, so far, shown little indication that it is prepared to introduce change.

In any case, the GHA is presently at a crossroads. Autocratic regimes in the region are presently under growing pressure due to general dissatisfaction of and protests by their populations. Mismanagement of diversity, mismanagement of the economy, lack of accountable governance, neglect and marginalization of the populations in the traditional economic systems, and unemployment and poverty of the youth are among the many factors for the general dissatisfaction. Recent changes in Ethiopia, including its bilateral peace agreements with neighbouring countries and the peace deals it has struck with internal rebel groups, are steps in the right direction that are likely to have spill-over effects on other countries of the region. Sudan's protests also seem to have set the country on a path to positive changes. Whether the changes in these two countries continue to progress and if the other countries in the region follow suit, however, remains to be seen.

There are also important lessons from the protesters in both Ethiopia and Sudan. The protesters in both cases expressed a number of demands that suggest some level of understanding of the relations between a democratization process and proper diversity management. In Sudan the protests, which brought together a cross-section of the population both from rural and urban areas and from different ethnic identities, raised issues of mismanagement of diversity and widespread poverty. The Ethiopian protests, which mostly took place in the two largest states, Oromia and Amhara, also raised issues of diversity management and widespread poverty, in addition to their demands for democratization. The protesters in both countries articulated demands for equitable citizenship rights to end domination of some groups by others. They also expressed grievances against land-takings by the state as well as against widespread poverty. These demands do not clearly articulate the need for a new approach to democratization, along the lines the CCA proposes. However, they suggest that there is some level of understanding that democratization is closely intertwined with diversity management and nation building, and that one cannot be attained without the other.

Neither the Sudanese protests nor the protests in Oromia and Amhara states in Ethiopia articulated demands for reconciliation of fragmented institutions. However, by raising concerns over land rights and poverty of rural communities, they signalled that nation building and democratization also require addressing the marginalization of the populations in the traditional subsistent sector of the economy. The demands of protesters in both Ethiopia and Sudan, thus, give indications that the approach to democratization in the region would need to go beyond elections in order to establish the institutional and structural requisites for sustainable democratization.

In conclusion, this volume makes notable contributions in two areas. First, it broadens our understanding of why the election-centred approach to democratization has not been successful in transitional societies, such as those in the Horn of Africa. That fragmented institutional systems impede democratization is, for example, an area that has attained little attention in the literature on the challenges of democratization in transitional societies.

Second, the book proposes an approach that might be more effective in fostering a sustainable democratization process by addressing the underlying obstacles that undermine the process. In both regards the book makes theoretical and policy contributions. At the theoretical level, the book contributes in explaining why the election-centred approach to the democratization process stagnates in transitional societies. The proposed approach to democratization is also likely to contribute to generating debate on how a sustainable democratization process might be promoted in transitional societies. At the level of policy, it alerts the forces of democracy in transitional societies, such as those in the GHA, to the complex nature of their democratic struggle, and suggests a new approach for them to consider.

Bibliography

Lynch, Justin and Gramer, Robbie. 2019, 'Arab States Foment Sudan Chaos While U.S. Stands By'. *Foreign Policy*, 5 June, https://foreignpolicy. com/2019/06/05/arab-states-foment-sudan-chaos-while-u-s-stands-by-sudan-khartoum-protests-violent-crackdown-saudi-arabia-united-arab-emirates-egypt-democracy-push, accessed 19 October 2019.

Index

EASTERN AFRICAN STUDIES

These titles published in the United States and Canada by Ohio University Press

www.ingramcontent.com/pod-product-compliance
Lightning Source LLC
Chambersburg PA
CBHW080643270326
41928CB00017B/3177